# KIDEX for

# Twos

## Practicing Competent
## Child Care for Two-Year-Olds

### R. Adrienne Boyd, R.N., B.S.N.

THOMSON

DELMAR LEARNING

Australia Canada Mexico Singapore Spain United Kingdom United States

**THOMSON**

**DELMAR LEARNING**

KIDEX for Twos: Practicing Competent Child Care for Two-Year-Olds
R. Adrienne Boyd, R.N., B.S.N.

**Vice President, Career Education SBU:**
Dawn Gerrain

**Director of Editorial:**
Sherry Gomoll

**Acquisitions Editor:**
Erin O'Connor

**Developmental Editor:**
Patricia Osborn

**Associate Editor:**
Chris Shortt

**Director of Production:**
Wendy A. Troeger

**Production Manager:**
J.P. Henkel

**Production Editor:**
Amber Leith

**Technology Project Manager:**
Sandy Charette

**Editorial Assistant:**
Stephanie Kelly

**Director of Marketing:**
Wendy E. Mapstone

**Channel Manager:**
Kristin McNary

**Cover Design:**
Joseph Villanova

**Composition:**
Pre-Press Company, Inc.

Library of Congress Cataloging-in-Publication Data

Boyd, R. Adrienne.
  Kidex for twos : practicing competent child care for two-year-olds / R. Adrienne Boyd.
       p. cm.
  Includes bibliographical references and index.
  ISBN-10 1-4180-1272-6 (alk. paper)
  ISBN-13 978-1-4180-1272-4
  1.  Day care centers—Administration. 2.  Toddlers—Care. I. Title.
  HQ778.5.B693 2006
  362.71'2—dc22

                                        2005023605

**NOTICE TO THE READER**

# Contents

# Preface

## INTRODUCTION

*KIDEX for Twos* is a proven management tool and essential resource for all child care personnel. It is one of a five-part series which includes KIDEX for infants, one-year-olds, three-year-olds, and four-year-old children. To assist in providing competent infant care, *KIDEX for Twos* provides helpful information for start-up and existing programs. To accommodate all the demands of creating a well-planned environment while ensuring children are receiving the best possible care, time-saving suggestions are extremely important. This book provides easily accessible tools to help you arrange, plan, and organize your program. It provides a format with examples, detailed information, and suggestions to assist you in delivering competent child care. *KIDEX for Twos* provides communication tools that assist communication between current and new staff members. In addition, KIDEX provides forms and templates for keeping active files for each child and serving as a documentation record and filing system for important information. Essentially, *KIDEX for Twos* will help you, the child care professional, fulfill your role in the daily care of the children you are charged with.

## HOW TO USE THIS BOOK

There are eight chapters, three perforated appendices, and a CD-Rom in the back of the book. Many chapters include examples of appropriate forms and/or templates necessary for rendering infant care. The Forms and Templates Appendix offers blank duplicates of the examples for you to photocopy, and the CD-Rom gives you the capability to customize the forms according to your state's specific standards and your center's requirements. The chapter examples (also indicated as figures) are there to guide you in completing your own forms when you are ready to use them.

    *KIDEX for Twos* begins with suggestions on how to create an environment suitable and equipped to render care, and moves on to provide guidance and class management tools to help in providing physical care for the children. Where readers begin will depend on the degree of guidance they are seeking. For instance, a brand-new program would best start at the beginning and work through to the end. An already-existing program searching to strengthen only certain aspects might choose to skip around the various chapters.

- Chapter 1, *Typical Two-Year-Old Behavior*, profiles patterns and characteristics one can expect for two-year-old children and offers suggestions for establishing activities of daily living suitable for the child that is 24–27 months, 28–30 months, 31–33 months, and 34–36 months of age.

- Chapter 2, *Creating and Organizing a Two-Year-Olds' Room*, provides guidance for creating environments that take into account their specific needs and how to best arrange the room to accommodate a two-year-old groups' natural tendencies. This chapter explores room arrangements and organization, equipment needs, how to establish learning centers and play spaces, outdoor play, selecting appropriate learning materials, choosing equipment for expanding vocabulary, choosing learning materials with cultural diversity in mind, varied learning styles, creating accessible environments for children with special needs, establishing a diapering area, setting up a napping area, room appearances, housekeeping checklists, music, and lighting.

■ Chapter 3, *Establishing an Excellent Path for Communication*, provides classroom management tools to maximize communication between the children's families and all other personnel who interface with your program on a daily basis. It also provides the tools for developing written plans, beginning with detailed examples and instructions, for assembling a KIDEX Class Book. A KIDEX Class Book is similar to an operating manual for your individual group. Use the examples and templates to write an organized plan for the two-year-old group, detailed daily schedules, individual profiles pertinent to their specific needs, lesson plans, etc.

■ Chapter 4, *Hygiene, Cleaning, and Disinfecting*, will help you establish such hygienic practices as diapering procedures, hand washing consideration, and sanitation procedures.

■ Chapter 5, *Health*, provides guidance with regard to medications, measuring body temperatures, individual illness recording, establishing practices to track illness trends, and other health tips.

■ Chapter 6, *Safety*, addresses accident and incident reporting, establishing practices to track accident or incident trends, and how to conduct emergency evacuation drills. This chapter also provides tools for recording drills, first-aid objectives and instructions, and other general safety practices.

■ Chapter 7, *Facilitating Two-Year-Olds and Their Families*, provides suggestions for providing daily two-year-old care, and ways to include the family, assisting both child and family from the moment the child is received in the center to daily departure. Some examples of forms you will find in this chapter include receiving sheets, an introduction form for the families to provide information about their two-year-old, individual child profiles for teachers to keep a written record of each individual two-year-old's activities and progress, and developmental milestone guidelines.

■ Chapter 8, *Educational Articles for Families and Staff*, provides short articles relevant to the care and understanding of two-year-olds. You can post these articles on the current events bulletin boards, print program newsletters, or use them as a basis for a parenting and/or education classes for families and staff. Store copies of these prepared articles, and other information you collect for the KIDEX Class Book, for future reference.

## FEATURES

■ Over 40 forms are available to assist child care professional care for infants including:

■ Nutrition schedules, observation sheets, diaper changing procedures, and daily medication sheets.

■ An icon identifying Best Practices is used throughout the book to highlight best practices.

■ Best Practices identified in the book are in alignment with Child Development Associate credential requirements.

## BACK OF THE BOOK CD-ROM

The CD-ROM at the back of the book provides

■ customizable forms.

■ state contact information to search for specific state rules and regulations

■ a list of organizations and their contact information for further research

■ additional resources for teachers and families

## EACH STATE IS DIFFERENT

A listing of all state licensing agencies is available online at the National Resource Center for Child Care Health and Safety Web site at http://nrs.uchsc.edu. This resource will be referred to at the beginning of each chapter in the form of this icon:

To find your specific State's Licensing, Rules and Regulations go to:

http://nrc.uchsc.edu

It is extremely important to research the laws relevant to your own state licensing standards for compliance, as well as those of your specific child care center and/or facility. Although you must follow state rules and regulations, most states require minimum standards. It is debatable whether or not state requirements reflect the highest level of care, also known as best practices. The term "best practices" comes from 981 standards identified by a panel of experts in the early 1990s. These standards were extracted from a compilation entitled *Caring for Our Children* provided by three organizations: the American Academy of Pediatrics (AAP), the American Public Health Association (APHA), and the National Resource Center for Health and Safety. Best practices standards were identified as having the greatest impact on reducing frequent or severe disease, disability, and death (morbidity and mortality) in early education and child care settings. *KIDEX for Twos* incorporates these standards and an icon highlighting best practices is within the margins to help you identify what is considered best practices.

## KIDEX AND THE CDA CREDENTIAL

KIDEX for Twos incorporates essential information that aligns with many of the CDA competencies. There is a growing trend to raise the bar for child care practices in the United States. Many professional organizations manage accreditation systems for early care and teaching programs, such as the National Association of Educating Young Children (NAEYC), National Association of Child Care Professionals (NACCP), and National Association of Childcare (NAC). Accreditation is a voluntary process designed to improve the quality of child care programs by establishing benchmarks for quality. Caregivers who desire to be recognized for demonstrating competence in the early care and education field can pursue a Child Development Associate (CDA) credential. Candidates for the CDA credential are assessed based upon the CDA competency standards. The guidelines for the national CDA credential through the Council for Early Childhood Recognition can be found at http://www.cdacouncil.org.

## ABOUT THE AUTHOR

Adrienne Boyd, R.N., B.S.N., has dedicated the majority of her professional life to the early care and education field. With over 22 years experience in the field, Adrienne previously was Executive Director and co-owner of Somersett Heights Center for Child Care, Inc. in Indianapolis. During that time she was active in the community, serving on the Governor's Task Force for Juvenile Justice, Indiana Task Force for Step Ahead Program, the advisory board for the local high school child care vocational school, and the Child Development Training Committee Workgroup on early care.

Adrienne served on the National Association of Child Care Professionals (NACCP) Board, as a validator for the National Accreditation Commission for Early Child Care and Education Programs (NAC), and continues to serve the Editorial Advisory Board for *Early Childhood News,* a national publication for child care professionals.

In 1995, Adrienne and her husband Bob launched Child Development Services, Inc. Through this venue they publish manuals, books, and child care training videos. Adrienne has received many Directors' Choice Awards for her work. She has contributed and published several articles for *Early Childhood News* and *Professional Connections,* the trade publication for National Association of Child Care Professionals.

She is a mother of two grown sons, John and Alexander, and resides with her husband in Lebanon, Indiana.

## ACKNOWLEDGMENTS

Through the process of writing this material there were many individuals who supported, encouraged and shared their expertise along the way. I wish is to extend my deepest gratitude to all of you.

To my husband Bob and two sons, John and Alexander, for accompanying me on my journey as owner and Director of Somersett Heights Center for Child Care, Inc.

To Annette Wilson, who so patiently transcribed my writing. To Patricia Osborn, who provided editorial assistance during the revisions of this text. And to the Thomson Delmar Learning staff who caught my vision and helped to birth this project.

To my colleagues Melissa Gaddo, Lois Struck, Julie Butz, and Courtney Callowas for your supportive research, feedback, and suggestions.

To my sister Lois, who so eloquently captures the imagination of the children I have had the privilege of working with throughout my early care and education profession.

To my sister Nancy, for her great love of children and how it is a source of inspiration to me. And finally, love and appreciation to my mother, Helen Struck, my very first teacher.

## REVIEWERS

I would like to thank and acknowledge the following highly respected professionals in the child care field who provided invaluable suggestions, comments, and feedback on *KIDEX for Twos* to help make it the effective tool it is.

Patricia Capistron, BA
Lead Teacher
Rocking Unicorn Pre-School
West Chatham, MA

Vicki Folds, Ed.D.
Director of Curriculum
Development
Children of America, Inc.
Parkland, FL

Sally Harris
NACCP State Liaison and
Validator
NAEYC Validator
Circle C Ranch Academy
Tampa, FL

Marsha Hutchinson, M.Ed., M. Divinity
Executive Director
Polly Panda Preschool
Indianapolis, IN

Bonnie Malakie
Head Start Director
Orleans Community Action
Committee
Albion, NY

Lynnette McCarty, M.A.
President of NACCP
Executive Director
Serendipity Children's Center
Tumwater, WA

Wendy McEarchern, M.A.,
Early Childhood Education
Executive Director
Gulf Regional Childcare
Management Agency
Mobile, AL

Nancy Picart, M.S.
Head Start Teacher
Bright Beginnings, Adventureland
Child Care Center
Woodside, NY

Michelle Rupiper, Ph.D.
Ruth Staples CDL-UNL
Lincoln, NE

# CHAPTER 1

# Two-Year-Old Behavior

Early care and education professionals who demonstrate a thorough knowledge of children's normal growth and developmental traits have a solid foundation for running a program well. A comprehensive understanding of two-year-old nature and behavior is imperative to create an environment that provides realistic expectations based on the children's growing needs. Just as we would not consider forcing children to grow an inch taller, we would not push them to accomplish more than they are capable of before they are ready. Your understanding of their natural growth and development patterns will help you discern what to ignore as a passing phase and what might be a red flag, something to pay closer attention to. During the course of this next year, these two-year-olds will require a healthy, loving, patient, and enriching environment to achieve their potential as they gradually leave behind the vestiges of their babyhood and approach their third birthdays.

## RHYTHMS OF GROWTH

Around the time the little ones reach their second birthdays, the upheavals of their emerging independence during the last six months most often calm down for a short while. The children begin to demonstrate a bit more confidence in their newly-acquired life skills. Their bodies are becoming more agile and capable as they pursue an intense desire to explore everything. Their little minds, bodies, and spirited selves follow an accelerated path of growth. Experience teaches us that growth seldom occurs in a smooth sequence. Much like a tree that drops its leaves and is recharged during dormancy before the emergence of spring, a rapidly-growing child often finds the calm periods necessary to practice and assimilate new skills to be followed by awkward and less skillful periods—also vital for new growth and expanding development. Drs. Louise Bates Ames and Frances Ilg of the renowned Gesell Institute of Human Development contend that children naturally travel through periods of growth "Alternate[ing between] ages of Equilibrium and Disequilibrium . . . noting that the good, solid equilibrium of any early age seems to need to break up into disequilibrium before the child can reach a higher or more mature stage of equilibrium." These observations and findings demonstrate that it is normal for a child—such as a two-year-old—to experience greater periods of calm at the beginning of a birth year. Their findings also show that normal children experience more turmoil and upheaval in behavior as their growth accelerates, often in the second half of their birthday year. The time spent in a *calm period* provides the necessary space to practice and assimilate newly acquired skills before nature again calls them forward. It is a joyful experience during the moments when their sunny little dispositions and sweetness shine. By the same token, a period of disruptive and tumultuous behavior, often termed "the terrible twos," is also as natural as rainfall and as necessary to bring about change and growth for the two-year-old to become fully who he or she is.

## "THE TERRIBLE TWOS," TEMPER TANTRUMS, AND PLAY HABITS

"The terrible twos" is a common term used to describe two-year-old children in our society. Actually, "terrible twos" behavior begins to intensify in the second half of age one, marked by temper tantrums, periods of oppositional behavior, crying, and a fondness for the word "no." Defiant behavior and use of the word "no" surfaces as children begin testing and practicing their newfound independence. Temper tantrums are intense emotions that often result from frustration, fear, and inability to solve a problem. When life becomes too overwhelming for little children they experience the *mini meltdowns* that most adults refer to as temper tantrums. Frequently, the children are as surprised by the emotional outburst as the observers.

It is common for two-year-old children to pass through a period of oppositional behavior. One frustrated mother shared that she was certain her son would become an expert debater, since he seemed to want the opposite of everything she attempted to offer him! Little children also have a natural tendency to dawdle (adopting slow movements in an attempt to control a situation), which requires a great deal of patience and understanding from the adult in charge. Remember that this is a period of intense and rapid growth for a very inexperienced little person just beginning to negotiate life's path as an individual. Children's behavior is now often influenced by a driving internal force to explore and understand how they influence others and the environment they inhabit. They are building on their newfound independence with very primitive skills when they make decisions. An athlete will spend hours, days, even years focusing on developing the skills necessary to achieve mastery. Two-year-olds have a similar drive, although their efforts are instinctively driven, rather than being premeditated. They don't awake in the morning and say to themselves, "I need to throw a big tantrum in line at the grocery store in order to show my mom I am tired, hungry, and no longer able to cope with the surroundings outside my house!" Patience and acceptance from you will help them achieve their goals and lay the groundwork for strong self-esteem.

Two-year-olds are naturally very self-centered. They have a big job to accomplish! This period of self-focus is necessary for them to accomplish their task of unfolding. They are very limited in their ability to think about others' needs and they have yet to master their own self-sufficiency. Their limited ability to practice self-control, coupled with rudimentary social skills, makes them appear very aggressive to their peers at times. Biting, hair-pulling, scratching, and knocking another child down can happen in a moment's notice. "Terrible twos" behavior often occurs as an outburst, a reaction to the child's overwhelming need to possess an object or dominate a space they feel belongs to her or him. Early care and teaching professionals understand the motives that drive the aggressive behavior expressed by two-year-olds, and they use their skills daily in an attempt to head off disputes before they occur, maintaining vigilant attention to the group at all times.

Many of children's quarrels are caused by their inability to express their thoughts quickly. In their attempt to communicate something they can become quite frustrated and physically lash out. They are not yet aware of the needs of others. They aren't purposely selfish and do not actually see their behavior as a problem. Continuing to describe the emotions they exhibit, and using the words "show me" are very useful to a two-year-old. They will require continuous practice to learn how their actions affect others, and patience from the adults who care for them as they develop the skills that lead to increased self-control. Learning and practicing, consistent socially acceptable behavior will continue to build over the next several years. These skills are not something a two-year-old can display consistently, all the time.

During the course of age two, the child will leave behind *solitary play* and predominantly engage in *parallel play,* where they enjoy other children's company but usually remain independently focused on their play. As they move closer to their third birthday, *cooperative play* (actively engaging in play with others) will begin to emerge.

## RITUALISTIC BEHAVIOR AND ROUTINES

Not all two-year-old behavior is defiant. Two-year-olds can be exuberant and exhilarated with their new abilities. Activities of daily living take on a new meaning for them as they practice manipulating their environment. They quite frequently enjoy opportunities to help. Provide small, wet washcloths to a group of two-year-olds and they will happily wash their tables, chairs, and dolls. Their possessions—such as clothing, shoes, hats and coats, even "my mommy" and "my daddy"—become very important to them. The words "me" and "my" are now part of their vocabulary. They often refer to their name in first person. A child might say "Hailey hungry now." They still do not possess enough skill to complete the task of dressing themselves without help, but are often quite adept at removing their clothing.

As the year progresses, it is common for two-year-olds to become more rigid in every area of their lives. Of course, their personality sets the tone for the varying degrees to which they exhibit this behavior. Their families often report their increasing rigid adherence to experiences and behaviors. They insist that the same story be read, exactly word for word, day in and day out. Or, they demand to wear the same shirt every day and throw themselves into a crying fit when it is removed for laundering. For a two-year-old, rigid routines and resisting change are their way of coping with all the changes they are experiencing and their lack of confidence. Resistance is their motivating internal force for practicing and assimilating their newly acquired skills. They are comforted in knowing what to expect next. The next time a new child in your group throws a fit when his or her family leaves, put yourself in the shoes of that child. Remember how you felt on the first day your new job began? You probably didn't know anyone or where to find the bathroom. This memory will give you a sense of how overwhelmed the child is feeling at that moment. When children grow more confident and build their abilities to understand how to attain their goals, their need for ritualistic tendencies will gradually fade.

## PHYSICAL ACTIVITY

Sometimes it seems that two-year-olds are in perpetual motion. They continuously use all their senses to explore the wonderful world they inhabit. They use their large muscles to climb, walk, run, and jump, just to name a few of their favorites. Their small muscle group allows more refined movement, thus improving their ability to manipulate such activities as using eating utensils, operating snaps on clothing, and working three- to four-piece puzzles. A two-year-old thrives on physical movement and needs plenty of opportunities to use his or her little body. A two-year-old cannot be expected to sit for long periods of time. It requires a great deal of focused energy for a young child to sit still.

Considering the amount of energy the two-year-old expends, it is not uncommon for them to reach a stage of over-fatigue. They have not developed enough self-restraint to set limits on their driving need to move. In a busy center setting they can easily become over-stimulated with too much activity. Unless their activities are modulated, they will often lose their ability to cope and acts of aggression—such as biting, hitting, and scratching—increase in the group. A wise early care educator will plan active sessions suitable to accommodate their attention span, such as circle games or riding toys, followed by a period of quiet activities such as story time or exploring with play dough. The ebb and flow of such planning creates a pace that's beneficial to the whole group.

## NUTRITION

Parents frequently express concerns about their two-year-old's eating habits. Sometimes parents worry because their child doesn't eat well at the center but displays a voracious appetite at the evening meal. Or they have a hearty appetite at the center and pick at their evening meal. With two-year-olds, appetite fluctuations are quite common. They might develop a desire to eat only certain foods and refuse all others. These eating jags quite commonly disappear in time. Offer them a balanced diet that includes protein, vegetables, fruits, and breads. Provide healthy snacks between the main meals of the day. Avoid snacks high in sugar content. As long as children are healthy and are not grazing endlessly on empty calories provided by so-called junk food, they will most naturally choose the types of foods in the proper amounts their bodies need. By 24 months they have become very skillful in feeding themselves. Sometimes, if they are especially hungry, they might skip the use of their utensils and revert to the use of their hands. Gentle encouragement will guide them to continue mastering proper food handling skills.

## MINI NAPS AND SLEEPING

Most two-year-olds are very good "nappers." They have given up their need for two naps a day. In a busy center setting, consider providing a small 10–15 minute rest after snack. This is a perfect time to help them regenerate from their early morning start, and the constant stimulation a group of children naturally create. Play soft music, nursery rhymes, or read them a story. Let them hold their special blankets or comfort items as they rest. They often roll around on the floor, kicking their feet and arms about. Occasionally, one or two will drift off asleep and awaken quickly when the group begins to move to the next activity. This *tiny rest* helps them regroup and finish their morning activities refreshed.

Two-year-olds will often sleep 1½–2 hours after lunch. Occasionally a child will exhibit signs of restlessness and seem tired, but struggle to fall asleep. Quite often they are comforted and able to relax if their backs are rubbed or gently patted until they drift asleep. Play soft music for the children during nap time. Music can be very soothing and may help lull them into a gentle sleep.

## THEIR GROWING LANGUAGE

Their language skills are a marvel to observe as the year progresses. They commonly begin the year with an average vocabulary of about 50 words, with 2 and 3 simple-word sentences exploding to an average of 1000 words in their repertoire, using more complex sentence structures. A child immersed in an environment rich with spoken words will experience a better opportunity to build language skills. Talking, speaking, and verbalizing with the children cannot be overemphasized. It is a joy to observe their growing command of the language!

Not all of their words will be clearly understood. Teaching and using sign language symbols with babies, toddlers, and two-year-olds is a rapidly-growing trend in this country. Research has proven that children who learn basic sign symbols are less frustrated and that their use of verbal language accelerates at a quicker pace. Recommended resources for this practice are located in Chapter 7, "Facilitating Two-Year-Olds and Their Families."

As their vocabulary expands, children will mispronounce words. Avoid interrupting their conversation with you if they incorrectly pronounce words. It is more beneficial to repeat their thoughts back, parroting what they said, using the proper pronunciations. As long as there is not a hearing problem, it is safe to assume they will eventually assimilate the correct usage. For an online hearing test check http://www.hss.gov.yk.ca and enter "hearing test" in the search field or call 1-800-661-0408.

Two-year-olds love to verbalize, and often speak to themselves. They especially enjoy hearing and listening to books that relate to their everyday activities and reflect cultural pictures they can identify with. Expose them to a variety of songs, nursery rhymes, and finger plays every day. Their sense of humor continues to increase, and some of them will enjoy different variations on how the story ends or inserting their name instead of the story character's. As they move closer to age three, they adopt the use of "I" in their vocabulary.

Provide two-year-olds with plenty of opportunities to discover sensory experiences such as water play, sand play, and exploring the outdoors. Sensory activities provide a multitude of teachable moments and opportunities to discuss and share observations with the children. If you don't provide sand play indoors, consider using dry oatmeal or corn meal in the water/sand table as a substitute.

The two-year-old child's attention span progressively expands each month, and he or she demonstrates abilities to focus longer on activities. Independent toileting is also another area in which they might verbally demonstrate an interest during this year, and many of them are quite successful accomplishing the task. Chapter 4, "Hygiene, Cleaning, and Disinfecting" covers this subject in detail.

## NURTURING THE NURTURERS

Working with two-year-olds is very physically demanding work that requires a great deal of understanding and patience. Some days, teachers wonder if they have the stamina necessary to weather the extreme mood swings a two-year-old group has the capacity to present. A wise teacher learns to recognize when it is time to take a break and replenish his or her energy reserves. It is amazing how a small break, planned on a regular basis to experience a peaceful moment and regroup, will help you maintain a fresh perspective. Continuing education, books, and workshops provide early care and teaching professionals with new information, different approaches for solving similar situations, and opportunities to share with other professionals in meaningful ways. Read humorous books on the subject, such as *Just Wait til You Have Children of Your Own!* by the beloved Erma Bombeck, or the informative and witty book *Outwitting Toddlers* by Bill Adler Jr. and Peggy Robin. Books such as these can help restore a waning sense of humor and serve as a reminder that you are not alone. You are very important to the early care and teaching community and the children you care for every day. A rested, well-informed teacher, dedicated to the whole child's being has the best opportunity to promote positive life-lasting results for the little ones entrusted to her or him.

### REFERENCES

Ames, L. B., & Ilg, F. L. (1976). *Your two-year-old.* New York: Dell Publishing.

### RECOMMENDED RESOURCES

Adler, B., & Robin, P. (2001). *Outwitting toddlers.* New York: Kensington Publishing.

Ames, L. B., Ilg, F. L., & Haber, C. C. (1982). *Your one-year-old.* New York: Dell Publishing.

Elkind, D. (1998). *Reinventing childhood.* Rosemont, NJ: Modern Learning Press.

Fisher, J. J. (1988). *From baby to toddler.* New York: The Berkley Publishing Group.

Healy, J. M. (1994). *Your child's growing mind* (Rev. ed.). New York: Dell Publishing.

Masi, W. S. (2001). *Toddler play.* Singapore: Weldon Owen Publishing.

**SUPPLY AND EQUIPMENT RESOURCES**

Early Childhood Manufacturers' Direct, 1-800-896-9951, http://www.ecmdstore.com

Educational Resources, 1-800-860-7004, http://www.edresources.com

To find your specific
State's Licensing, Rules
and Regulations go to:

http://nrc.uchsc.edu

# Creating and Organizing a Two-Year-Olds' Room

**CHAPTER 2**

The quality of a child's environment can have a significant impact on his or her emotional well-being. Healthy children require a safe physical environment in which to eat, sleep, and play in order to accommodate their growth and developmental needs. A well-thought-out room, properly equipped, clean, organized, and well-maintained, will provide the environment necessary to support their growing needs.

## SQUARE FOOTAGE CONSIDERATIONS

There is always a fine balance between meeting local government mandates and the cost of your finished square footage. The governing bodies who determine minimum suggested standards for licensure differ from state to state. Check your local governing body to determine the guidelines expected for programs in your area. Plan at least 35 square feet of useable indoor play space per child. The more square footage available, the more opportunities to create optimum play spaces. In a room that is oversized, arrange it in a manner that creates natural boundaries. Square footage costs vary in different regions and will be an important factor to consider when determining the size most financially feasible for a program.

## SUGGESTED ROOM LAYOUTS AND ARRANGEMENTS

Plan to arrange the room in a manner that discourages running and sprinting about. Two-year-olds are beginning to establish some restraint when the space is clearly defined. It is logical to assume that, if the space is wide open and without any clear definition of boundaries, two-year-old children will follow their natural instincts to run! Natural boundaries can be created during learning center and play space development. Learning centers and play spaces are discussed later in this chapter. Create areas that form natural boundaries by using low shelving that avoids obstructing the teacher's view. It's important to securely fasten all lateral pieces of equipment, such as cubbies and toy shelves, to the floor or wall to prevent dangerous tipping in the event an exuberant two-year-old attempts an un-planned climbing expedition. Figure 2–1 provides a suggested room layout, and how to arrange it with learning centers and play spaces.

## ESTABLISHING LEARNING CENTERS AND PLAY SPACES

Early care and teaching professionals create optimum environments for children through the deliberate development of learning centers and play spaces. A well-planned space will provide for their daily living activities and facilitate safe play spaces, both self-directed and supervised. A functional layout of the room will successfully accommodate large and

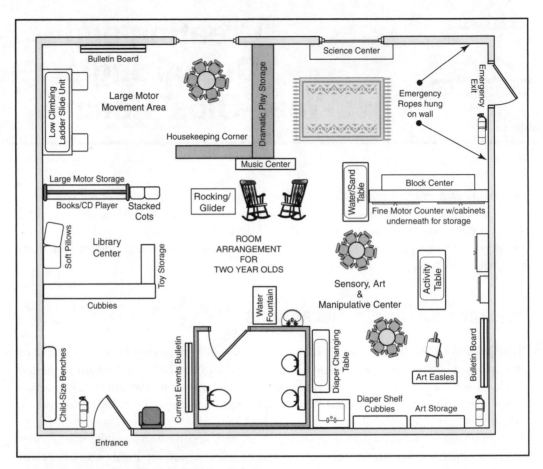

**FIGURE 2–1** Suggested Room Arrangement

small group activities. Large groups usually include the group as a whole and require adequate space for the children to comfortably assemble. For example, this space will accommodate active physical play for large muscle activities, such as circle games, riding, push and pull toys, large dump trucks, and quiet activities such as napping. Small group activities require suitable space for fewer children to meet and pursue a specialized activity such as small learning center activities found in block play, library centers, or fine muscle activities.

The nature of the activity level and the amount of noise the activity creates will determine how much space to devote to each learning center or play space, and where to locate it in the room. For instance, in an active play area where large muscle activities occur, devote a large amount of space. Two-year-old children are physically active and their skills flourish in an environment that offers plenty of practice to hone their growing skills. For best results, group activities that complement each other together. Keep active spaces and quiet spaces separate from each other. For instance, quiet library spaces do not work well near a dramatic play area. Placement of eating areas, art, small muscle manipulative activities, and sensory exploration require tables or sometimes require a source of water for cleanup. Create these centers with floor surfaces that are easy to clean, preferably without carpet. Provide a running source of water nearby for water and sand activities, art exploration, snack and mealtimes, and clean-up. Since two-year-old children are just beginning to learn about boundaries, it is not advisable to set up creative activities, such as building blocks, near movement activities because they will constantly experience crashing interruptions.

The learning center and play spaces are equipped to provide learning-enhanced activities related to each area, inviting young children to explore and play. The most common learning centers and play spaces include areas devoted to: art, manipulative, science and sensory, library, music, block center, dramatic play, and housekeeping.

Two-year-olds' imaginations are budding, and they love to practice and mimic common activities they observe or experience in their own lives. Create a housekeeping center with a play kitchen, beds for their dolls, and accessories to play house. Equip the dramatic play area with props, such as an old telephone or typewriter for office play. Choose simple dress-up clothing because their fine motor skills are limited.

With their high activity level, two-year-old children need a great deal of practice developing the use of their bodies. They require opportunities to pursue large muscle activities throughout the day that do not require teacher interaction. Such activities might include a low-level climbing center with activities especially designed for indoor play. A basket full of soft balls, or sock balls, and bean bags will provide hours of pitching and throwing practice. Place the music center adjacent to the large motor area to provide enough space for parades, active movement, and a suitable space to create loud joyful noises with their instruments!

## SCIENCE AND SENSORY CENTERS

The science and sensory area is best placed near the window in order to experiment and grow projects. If the budget permits, a fish aquarium is a delightful center for observation. Pet stores often lease fish aquariums and will provide the food for the fish and regular maintenance, all in the cost of the lease.

## BLOCK CENTERS

The block area is best suited to an area that provides plenty of space to spread out creations. Pick an area that will not have heavy foot traffic. Choose carpet that has a low pile so the surface does not interfere with the construction projects. Stock the block area with a variety of blocks in assorted colors, textures, weights, shapes, sizes, both hollow and solid. The children will use them in a variety of ways, such as building towers, lining them up, or using them for filling and dumping activities. Provide toy props such as people, cars, trees, and landscaping. Low shelving marked with pictures of the different-sized blocks will help the children learn how to return the blocks to their designated areas at clean-up.

## KEEP YOUR LEARNING AND PLAY CENTERS ORGANIZED

Organization is an essential component of all learning centers. Clean-up time will be facilitated by labeling all the toys, equipment, book shelves, and clothing hooks with photos that match where items are to be returned. Spending time to organize the center and teach the children how to return the materials before they leave the area will maintain an inviting learning center. Provide a place for all the materials in each center. Make the containers easily accessible for the children so they can retrieve and return the materials in an organized fashion. For best results, use clear containers so the contents inside are easily identified. Use photos of the object, covered in clear contact paper, to label every container and for the shelves, to indicate where the containers should be stowed. The pictures help the two-year-olds locate where the toys belong during clean-up. Generally, two-year-old children love to be included in housework. Some days they will cooperate better than others. In difficult moments they will require encouragement and assistance. It is a necessary part of their growth. Treating clean-up time as a fun activity often helps—for instance have them gather mail (blocks) to put in the mailbox (the block container you are holding) while you act as if you are the postmaster!

## ESTABLISH RULES

Establishing general rules for taking turns, sharing, and general care of the learning centers and play spaces are very important components for successful learning center activities.

Two-year-old children are just on the threshold of learning patience, and they will attempt only periodically to take turns and share with their peers. It is also important for the teaching staff to structure adequate time periods for children to pursue their imaginary play uninterrupted or thwarted by a rigid rotation schedule. Optimum play experiences require a concerted effort on behalf of the teacher to learn how to create play spaces and how to utilize methods necessary to facilitate them in the early care and teaching environment. Many talented authors have devoted whole books to this subject. Refer to the "Recommended Resources" at the end of the chapter for a list of books that explore the subject in detail. See Figure 2–2 for a list of materials and equipment suitable for preschool children. Refer to this list for suggested items to stock the learning centers.

## CREATING AN ACCESSIBLE PLAY SPACE FOR ALL CHILDREN

Plan your play spaces so they are accessible to children with special needs. Although some children with special needs require help in adapting the use of toys, most will not require specially designed toys to accommodate their play periods. *Children With Special Needs in Early Childhood Settings* (2004) by Carol Paasche, Lola Gorrill, and Bev Strom is a wonderful resource book to assist with identifying, intervening for, and including special needs children in your early care and education program.

### SELECTING APPROPRIATE TOYS

Toys are props used in play by all children. Play is valuable for all areas of growth and development. There are some basic facts to consider when choosing toys for children under the age of three. It is their nature to explore and research with all of their senses. Choose toys that are sturdy and capable of withstanding repeated washing and disinfecting. Safety is an important aspect to consider when selecting toys and creating a safe environment. Refer to Chapter 6, "Safety," for a more detailed discussion regarding toy safety. Two-year-olds continue their fascination with toys that produce cause-and-effect action. "If I do this, this occurs." Push and pull toys, pop-up toys, or toys that react to touch offer plenty of cause-and-effect practice. Toys that allow children to collect items and dump them are also a favorite activity. Large dumping trucks are a great source of fun. Choose sturdy models in case they decide to explore riding the toys themselves!

Open-ended toys are a better investment in the long run rather than the more sophisticated toys that often require batteries to operate. Blocks are a perfect example of an open-ended toy. One day they could be the tallest tower in the world, and another day they could be the longest road ever built. Open-ended toys offer the child many opportunities to explore and use their imagination and will hold their interest. Refer to Figure 2–2 for suggested selections of toys and equipment young children enjoy.

In a group of two-year-olds, there will always be favorite toys. Two-year-old children are just learning how to share with others. A prudent early care provider wisely provides several copies of favorite toys and books to help avoid potential skirmishes.

### VOCABULARY EXPANDING TOYS AND ACTIVITIES

Brain development research has provided sound evidence that reading to children for as little as 15–20 minutes per day from an early age contributes to a myriad of positive brain developments. Early care and education professionals are well aware that reading helps develop children's attention span, builds vocabularies, enhances self-esteem, increases the ability to visualize and imagine, and provides many opportunities to understand words and how they create spoken language.

Based on this evidence, an enriched environment for two-year-olds is filled with pictures and books that contain simple stories, rhymes, and finger plays. Place sturdy books,

## EQUIPMENT AND SUPPLIES FOR TWOS

**PERMANENT EQUIPMENT:**

Balance beam (6"–8" wide board)
Balls (6"–8")
Bean bag chairs
Bookcase
Broom
Carpet samples
CD player
Chest of drawers/costume box
Child-size sinks, stove, pots, pans, dishes & utensils
Connecting blocks
Dishpans
Dolls—variety of cultures and gender represented
Doll bed
Doll blankets
Doll carriage
Doll clothes
Dress-up clothes
Dust pan
Hollow blocks
Indoor climbing unit (stairsteps)
Inner tube
Lacing cards
Large wooden peg boards and pegs
Large wooden threading beads
Logs
Mirror—full size
Nesting blocks
Picture books
Pillows
Plastic hats
Play table and chairs
Play telephone
Pull apart large plastic beads
Puppets
Riding toys
Rocking boat (one that turns over to stairs is ideal)
Sand and water table
Shape sorting boxes
Simple puzzles
Small suitcase
Small jungle gym and slide
Small cars and planes—wheeled vehicles (designed for infants and toddlers)
Soft area for books (beanbag chairs, pillows, put soft things in a wading pool or a box with a cushion)

Soft toys to throw
Soft toys to hug
Stuffed animals
Unit blocks
Used food boxes—cleaned and covered with clear contact paper for durability
Washable, unbreakable dolls
Wooden family

**MUSICAL:**

Clacking sticks
Cymbals
Drums make-shift—metal tins, oatmeal containers, cans or other containers with plastic lids
Movement tapes & CDs to promote different types of music
Nursery rhyme tapes & CDs
Scraping instruments—blocks can be covered with sandpaper
Shakers (use film containers filled with rice, beans—with lids secured with glue)
Soothing recorded music
Tambourines (make by using plastic lid— punch holes, string ribbon or shoe lace with bells attached and double- knot the ribbon end)
Tape recorder/CD player
Variety of bells (designed for infants and toddlers only)
Xylophones with plastic mallets

**BOOKS AND PICTURES:**

Books with real photos of children from all cultures
Catalogues/magazines
Easy short story books
Nursery rhyme and finger play books
Pictures/books showing people in action
Pictures of many common items for vocabulary and matching picture- to-picture and picture-to-item
Simple picture books/board books
Simple story books
Touch and feel books

**ART SUPPLIES:**

Baggies—ziplock variety
Butcher paper
Cardboard

**FIGURE 2–2** Equipment and Supplies

Chalk (recipe for chunky chalk included)
Colored tape
Colorful fabric swatches
Contact paper
Cotton balls
Cotton swabs
Crayons
Dark construction paper
Glue/paste (recipe included)
Grocery paper bags
Index cards
Jumbo crayons
Multi-cultural crayons, paint & paper (full range of skin colors)
Masking tape
Newsprint (plain)
Newspaper
Non-toxic finger paints
Non-toxic color markers
Non-toxic color chart
Packing peanuts
Paint containers
Paint brushes—large, easy to hold
Paper towel rolls
Paper cups
Paper plates
Pellon
Pieces of netting material
Powder tempera
Sandpaper
Sand (gallon container)
Shaving cream*
Shelf paper
Sponges—different shapes & sizes
Straws
Styrofoam trays (large)
Toilet paper rolls
Tree leaves
Wax paper

### GENERAL SUPPLIES:

Balls all sizes—include cloth, crochet, nerf, yarn
Beach ball
Bean bags
Big tweezers

Boxes
Bristle blocks or Duplo blocks
Bubbles
Buckets
Camera & film
Cardboard boxes
Carpet squares
Cloth bag or pillow case
Coffee cans & plastic rings
Colored scarves
Egg cartons
Empty matchboxes
Felt/felt board
Flashlight
Low slide
Muffin tin
Plastic curlers (small)
Plastic blocks
Plastic salt & pepper shakers
Plastic bowls and lids
Puppets
Sandwich baggies w/re-sealable edges
Several plastic jars with lids
Several matching items (mittens, socks, flowers)
Several pine cones
Several 2–4 piece knob puzzles
Several shoe strings
Shoe boxes
Shower curtain or plastic to protect painting area
Silhouettes & matching tools
Small cars
Smocks
Stacking rings
String for "pretend animal leash" 12" or less
Tennis balls
Texture squares to feel
Variety of feathers
Variety of large sea shells
Variety of smooth & rough rocks—choke-proof size
Wind sock
Wooden clothespins with container
Zippers

*Some states do not allow the use of shaving cream—check your regulations

**FIGURE 2–2** Equipment and Supplies *(Continued)*

books with real photos of children from all cultures, pictures and books showing people in action, simple picture board books, touch and feel books, photo albums, and soft seating or mats in the library center away from active play. Board books are sturdy books specifically designed for very young children and have pages that are easy to turn. The board books generally have bright-colored pictures and simple stories, rhyming words and repetitive phrases that appeal to young children. The library center is an area where two-year-olds can experience solitary time. Create a quiet area for peaceful exploration or daydreaming, free from interruption by others. A space that provides natural boundaries, such as soft cushions and pillows, will provide the two-year-old a place to decompress and reduce interaction for a small time period before re-entering the group. Selections of appropriate books that appeal to two-year-old children are listed in Chapter 7, "Facilitating Two-Year-Olds and Their Families."

### CHOOSING TOYS WITH CULTURAL DIVERSITY IN MIND

Responsible early care and teaching programs strive to address diversity in the classroom. Special thought and planning is required to create a diverse environment that is considerate of different genders and racial and ethnic differences within our growing population. In order to integrate appropriate practices, choose toys that include all the diverse backgrounds and cultures represented in the population and of the individual children in your classroom. Make an effort to choose dolls with different-colored skins, representing various cultures. Display a diverse selection of pictures that represent a variety of all nationalities and represent the children in the group. Show different combinations of family groups such as a father and child, grandparents and grandchildren. Don't assume all families are Caucasian or that both parents live under the same roof. Seek information from the parents that will help your group explore other traditional interests such as food, spices, and words familiar to their culture. Explore the different types of music the children hear in their own family environments, or special activities they enjoy during the holidays they celebrate. Parents will appreciate your effort to include them in the process of integrating practices that recognize the various cultures their children represent.

Carol J. Fuhler, author of *Teaching Reading with Multicultural Books Kids Love,* is an excellent resource on diversity. She encourages many approaches for a teacher to integrate multi-cultural teachings relevant in today's diverse society. "[For children] to make a strong connection with a book, to elicit that all important affective response, every child should see his or her face reflected in some of the illustrations. His or her culture should be explored realistically within well-crafted stories." A teacher who continuously makes a deliberate effort to integrate and explore differences and likenesses between all people will provide an environment that communicates acceptance for all of the children she or he cares for.

### OUTDOOR PLAY SPACES

Give the two-year-olds daily opportunities, year-round, to play outdoors. For two-year-olds, it is important to provide a space for them to play separately from children older than they are. Two-year-old play habits are completely different, and they need more supervision. For instance, they could easily collide with an older child running at full force. They are not able to exercise good judgment yet, and are likely to sustain an injury if they are grouped with older children. Many state licensing agencies require separated playgrounds for infants, toddlers, and two-year-old children. Provide the two-year-olds play equipment and materials suitable for their level of development.

The playground is a place to explore nature. For example, creating small gardening areas during the growing season is just one way to observe with the children how nature unfolds. Choose projects that are simple and will require little maintenance. A small prepared plot of ground or an old tire filled with dirt is a perfect place to plant a garden. The children will love watching a package of sunflowers grow, or making a salad from the lettuce they grow. A tree planted nearby not only provides shade, but also offers the children many opportunities to observe the natural cycle of the seasons.

Gone are the days when a swing set, slide, and a plenitude of grass constituted a playground for children. A great deal of planning is necessary to design and construct a modern playground that is both equipped with safe materials and play equipment and accessible to children with special needs. Playgrounds today need to offer children opportunities to use their bodies and imagination. Vogel suggests "In the outdoor area children enjoy swinging, running, climbing, balancing, digging, pedaling, throwing, and catching" (p. 35). Create a soft fall zone under and around all climbing and play equipment. A hard surface area will provide opportunities for riding toys. Wearing proper safety helmets when using riding toys is recommended to protect children from dangerous head injuries. The National Program for Playground Safety (NPPS) is an excellent source for playground safety advice. The NPPS is a nonprofit organization that serves as a national resource for the latest education and research on playground safety. The NPPS Web site address is http://www.playgroundsafety.org. For the playground to meet the needs of children with disabilities, the play equipment and surfaces will need to conform to recommendations from the American with Disabilities Act (ADA). For guidance to build, equip, and inspect a playground that meets all suggested accessibility standards and safety requirements, refer to the recommended resources at the end of this chapter.

## MUSIC AND LIGHTING IN THE ROOM

Sunlight, bright lighting, peaceful music and sounds provide a sense of well-being in a room, and can encourage pleasant and cheerful feelings among those who occupy it. It is a well-documented fact that children require low stress environments to thrive.

Provide several sources of music and lighting to enhance the two-year-old room and promote a peaceful, home-like atmosphere. Soft lighting is soothing for resting and napping children. Wire the rooms to create soft lighting, equipped with dimming switches, in the resting and quiet areas. Table lamps are another alternative if wiring a more sophisticated lighting pattern is not feasible. Skylights also provide a gentle, natural lighting source. Check with your local licensing agents to determine the amount of lighting mandated during waking and sleeping times, since requirements vary from state to state.

Activities such as singing and playing and listening to music support positive change in the brain and increase intelligence. Current research tells us that reading and singing to children is a simple and effective way to promote brain development. Music serves many functions in the early care and teaching environment. Dr. Gordon Shaw, the co-founder and chairman of the M.I.N.D. Institute and author of *Keeping Mozart in Mind,* shows us how music can make us understand how the brain works and how music may enhance our thinking, reasoning, and ability to create. He contends that the use of music, particularly at certain stages of development, can promote children's abilities to reach high levels of their potential. Studies have demonstrated that Mozart's classical and Baroque music strengthens the pathways in the brain for future math development!

Children enjoy many different musical experiences. Expose children to a wide variety of music, from various cultures and classical lullabies to the exciting sounds of marching and parade music. A vast amount of literature is available on how the brain develops in the early years and suggestions for measures to facilitate growth. To find more information and studies related to measures that enhance optimum brain development for children, refer to the National Child Care Information Centers (NCCIC). It is a national clearinghouse and technical assistance center. Its mission is to link parents, providers, policymakers, researchers, and the public to early care and education information. Their Web site address is http://www.nccic.org.

## NAPPING AREA

Cots for sleeping are available in several varieties. Choose cots that can withstand regular sanitizing and will store easily and compactly, to save space. Pick a space large enough to create a pattern that allows adequate space between each cot. Set them 2–3 feet apart. Rest one child's head at the same end as the next child's feet, and so on. By laying the children's heads at different ends of the cots, you are adding an additional 2–3 feet between contact with another head. This is particularly important in the winter months, when many children have upper respiratory conditions. If the children do not have the same assigned cot every day, then disinfect the cot by following proper sanitation outlined in Chapter 4 "Hygiene, Cleaning, and Disinfecting."

Some two-year-olds enjoy rocking and cuddling prior to their napping periods, or if they aren't feeling well. Place several gliding rocking chairs in your two-year-old rooms. A gliding chair provides a rocking motion without the hazard of pinching a curious two-year-old's fingers. Glider rocking chairs are available in large baby superstores and can be found in Early Childhood Manufacturers' Direct at http://www.ECMDStore.com or 1-800-896-9951. Create a quiet play area equipped with books, puzzles, and table activities for the first few awakening two-year-olds so they can enjoy the last few moments of nap time before all of the children have awakened.

## BATHROOM AND DIAPER AREA

The majority of two-year-old children embark on serious toilet training at some point during this year. When they demonstrate the ability to control the sphincter muscles needed to perform the task and demonstrate the desire to try, it is the duty of the teacher and families to help them begin training. Embarking on a toilet training program with the two-year-old child is covered in detail in Chapter 4.

Equip the bathrooms with flushing toilets. Special child-size flushing toilets are available so children can sit on the toilet and touch the floor with their feet. There are many available alternatives for adapting larger toilets for two-year-old use. Many two-year-olds seem comfortable with portable potty–chairs because they are small and do not have a flush that some children find frightening. It is important to check with your licensing agency for specific guidelines on equipping two-year-olds' bathrooms. The rules tend to vary from state to state. For the most part, early care and learning environments opt to use items that are disposable—diapers, training pants, bibs, or wipes—in place of cloth, to promote the highest level of sanitary practice.

Sometimes children are allergic to the materials found in disposable diapers and require the use of cloth diapers. The flushing toilets will provide a handy and safe area to discard soiled soap; water and disinfecting solutions created by daily cleansing of soiled diaper and clothing containers. To insure their hygiene and safety, caregivers need to employ special handling when changing cloth diapers or using cloth diaper services when handling children conditions such as allergies. Diaper changing procedures are explored in greater detail in Chapter 4.

The diapering area will require a nonabsorbent changing surface with running water at an adult height, liquid soap with a pump or dispenser, disposable nonabsorbent gloves, nonabsorbent paper liner, disposable wipes, each child's personally labeled prescription, ointments, diapers, cotton balls, plastic bags, tissues, lidded hands-free plastic lined trash container, disinfectant, and paper towels. When changing cloth diapers, prepare a special receptacle to collect the soiled diapers. Prepare a washable container labeled "soiled cloth diapers." The container should be lined with plastic and kept tightly lidded. Soiled cloth diapers don't require separate bagging. However, any soiled diapers sent home are to be secured in a plastic bag, separately bagged from soiled clothing. Clean and disinfect receptacle daily and dispose wastewater in the toilet or floor drain only.

Several varieties of diaper changing tables are available on the market today. Some of the tables are equipped with pullout staircases. The children can walk up the steps, with assistance, to the changing mat. Considering the number of diapers changed on a given day in a two-year-old room and the weight of each child, providing steps is recommended. The steps help reduce injuries a teacher might experience from frequent lifting and straining. Safety support belts are useful to wear when performing repetitive tasks. They provide extra support for the back.

If you choose a diaper table that does not provide individual storage space for each child's personal supplies, then attach shelves above the changing area to store each child's supplies.

Instruct the plumber to install sinks—one at adult height and one at a child's height—next to the changing table, and a water fountain at a child's height in the changing area. All sources of hot water feeding into the room will require an anti-scald device. Devise a turn-off valve for available water sources, out of reach to little hands but convenient to yours, to avoid unnecessary water exploration.

## STORING PERSONAL BELONGINGS/CUBBIES

Avoid spreading germs and potential cross-contamination of each child's personal articles. It's best to store personal belongings such as coats, hats, and extra clothing separately, in cubbies. Consider creating a space near the entrance door or in an area that will handle heavy traffic in the busy arrival and departure hours. Commercial cubby or locker units are widely marketed in school catalogues such as: Discount School Supply, http://www.DiscountSchoolSupply.com or 800-627-2829 or KAPLAN Early Learning Company http://www.kaplanco.com or 800-334-2014.

## ROOM APPEARANCES

It doesn't take long for a busy two-year-old room to begin to clutter. To keep up the center's appearance and maintain a safe environment, always make an effort to reduce clutter and maintain cleanliness in your center. Without a consistent effort to maintain order, the room's appearance and safety elements will become compromised. A room haphazardly strewn with toys is not only unsightly, but creates potential tripping, risks for adults and children. Furthermore, an active group of two-year-olds in an area filled with too many toys strewn about can create an over-stimulating environment. A two-year-old often will aggressively lash out with behavior such as biting, scratching, or hair pulling when feeling stressed and overwhelmed. Reduce the frustration created by a chaotic environment.

Imagine how you prepare your home for a party, before guests arrive. You survey the house and stow all miscellaneous clutter in its proper place. The floors are vacuumed, dust removed, fingerprints washed away, leaving the room sparkling and clean. Fresh flowers, in a non-breakable vase, are always a nice touch. You are motivated to create a pleasant environment for the guest you are about to receive. Think about the environment you

## Cleaning Schedule

For the Week of <u>February 4th</u>

Classroom <u>Twos</u>

| # | Daily Cleaning Projects | Mon | Tue | Wed | Thr | Fri | Once-A-Week Projects | Initial | Date |
|---|---|---|---|---|---|---|---|---|---|
| 1. | Mop floors | C | C | C | C | C | Scrub brush & mop (corners) | CM | 2/4 |
| 2. | Clean all sinks (use cleanser) | C | C | C | C | C | Wipe down all bathroom walls | LS | 2/5 |
| 3. | Wipe walls (around sinks) | C | C | C | C | C | Scrub step stools | LS | 2/6 |
| 4. | Clean & disinfect toilets (with brush in & out) | C | C | C | C | C | Use toothbrush on fountain (mouth piece) | CM | 2/4 |
| 5. | Clean water fountains/wipe with disinfectant | C | C | C | C | C | Clean windows | AH | 2/7 |
| 6. | Clean inside of windows and seals | C | C | C | C | C | Wipe off door handles | AH | 2/8 |
| 7. | Clean inside & outside glass on doors | C | C | C | C | C | Organize shelves | CM | 2/5 |
| 8. | Clean & disinfect changing table & under the pad | C | C | C | C | C | Move furniture and sweep | CM | 2/4 |
| 9. | Run vacuum (carpet & rugs) | C | C | C | C | C | Wipe underneath tables & legs | LS | 2/7 |
| 10. | Dispose of trash (replace bag in receptacle) | C | C | C | C | C | Wipe the backs and legs | AH | 2/4 |
| 11. | Wipe outside of all cans & lids with disinfectant | C | C | C | C | C | Wipe off cubbies/shelves | LS | 2/7 |
| 12. | Repeat 10 & 11 for diaper pails | C | C | C | C | C | | | |
| 13. | Clean & disinfect tables/chairs | C | C | C | C | C | **Immediate Project** | | |
| 14. | Clean & disinfect cots | C | C | C | C | C | Disinfect any surface contaminated with body fluids such as blood, stool, mucus, vomit, or urine. | CM | 2/6 |
| 15. | Reduce clutter! (Organize!) | C | C | C | C | C | **Quarterly** | | |
| 16. | Wipe/sanitize toys | C | C | C | C | C | Clean carpets | | |
| 17. | | | | | | | | | |
| 18. | | | | | | | | | |

Lead Teacher: <u>Ms. Marshall</u>          C – Complete   N/A – Not Applicable

**FIGURE 2–3** Cleaning Schedule

create for the children in your care. Imagine that every day is grand opening day. Look around the room and see where a pile of clutter has begun to form. Are toys scattered about the room, creating a potential for tripping or falling? Are old magazines, used sippy cups, or used washcloths sitting around? A routine for handling soiled toys and soiled clothing is covered in detail in Chapter 4.

Two-year-old rooms require continuous of clearing off, cleaning up, and putting away. Establish regular housekeeping routines and post a cleaning schedule (see example Figure 2–3) for all to follow. Your efforts to create a pleasant environment will promote everyone's level of comfort and will provide the staff with an enjoyable atmosphere to work in. It truly does make a big difference.

### REFERENCES

Fuhler, C. J. (2000). *Teaching reading with multicultural books kids love.* Golden, CO: Fulcrum Resources.

Paasche, C. L., Gorrill, L., & Strom, B. (2004). *Children with special needs in early childhood settings.* Clifton Park, NY: Thomson Delmar Learning.

Shaw, G. L. (2000). *Keeping Mozart in mind.* San Diego, CA: Academic Press.

Vogel, N. (1997). *Getting started.* Ypsilanti, MI: High/Scope Press.

### RECOMMENDED RESOURCES

Bogen, B. N., & Sobut, M. A. (1991). *Complete early childhood curriculum resource.* West Nyack, NY: The Center for Applied Research in Education.

Bombeck, E. (1971). *Just wait till you have children of your own.* New York. Doubleday Books.

Brain Development Resources. (2002). *Health Start.* Retrieved December 21, 2004, from http://www.ed.gov./parents/earlychild/ready/healthystart/newborn.doc

Bredekamp, S., & Copple, C. (1997). *Developmentally appropriate practice* (Rev. ed.). Washington, DC: National Association for the Education of Young Children.

Clifford, R. M., Cryer, D., & Harms, T. (1990). *Infant/toddler environment rating scale.* New York: Teachers College Press.

Hall, N. S. (1999). *Creative resources for the anti-bias classroom.* Clifton Park, NY: Thomson Delmar Learning.

Healy, J. M. (1994). *Your child's growing mind* (Rev. ed.). New York: Doubleday.

Marhoefer, P., & Vadnais, L. (1988). *Caring for the developing child.* Clifton Park, NY: Thomson Delmar Learning.

McGovern, E. M., & Muller, H. D. (1994). *They're never too young for books.* Buffalo, NY: Prometheus Books.

### HELPFUL WEB SITES

ASTM International (formerly American Society for Testing and Materials). 1-610-832-9585, http://www.astm.org. Brain Wonders, http://www.zerotothree.org/

National Program for Playground Safety 1-800-554-7529, http://www.playgroundsafety.org

Talaris Research Institute, 1-206-529-6898, http://www.talaris.org

State Public Interest Research Groups (PIRGs). 1-202-546-9707, http://www.pirg.org

U.S. Consumer Product Safety Commission, 800-638-2772, http://www.cpsc.gov

### SUPPLY AND EQUIPMENT RESOURCES

*Constructive Playthings,* 13201 Arrington Road, Grandview, MO 64030, 1-800-448-1412 http://www.cptoys.com

*Kaplan Early Learning Company,* P.O. Box 609, Lewisville, NC 27023, 1-800-334-2014, http://www.kaplanco.com

*United Art and Education,* P.O. Box 9219, Fort Wayne, IN 46899, 1-800-322-3247, http://www.unitednow.com

To find your specific
State's Licensing, Rules
and Regulations go to:

http://nrc.uchsc.edu

# Establishing an Excellent Path for Communication

## CHAPTER 3

It requires a well managed atmosphere with an attention to detail to achieve an excellent path of communication between the center staff and the families they serve.

## KIDEX FOR TWOS CLASS BOOK

A KIDEX Class Book organizes, supports, and promotes consistent two-year-old care. As noted in the book instructions, a KIDEX Class Book is similar to an operating manual for each individual group. *KIDEX for TWOS* provides the examples and templates you will need to assemble your own KIDEX Class Book for your group of two-year-olds. The templates help the busy lead teacher and other program personnel to create, update, and maintain current written documentation with ease. They are designed for multiple uses and can be duplicated with a copy machine allowing you to adapt and personalize each individual program. Use the examples and templates to write an organized plan for the two-year-old group, detailed daily schedules, individual profiles pertinent to their specific needs, lesson plans, etc. Place the KIDEX Class Book in a visible location so that when you are absent or unavailable, the substitute teacher or program personnel can find it in a moment's notice.

The KIDEX Class Book can also serve as a valuable reference at program meetings. It is also a good idea to share your class book with a colleague in order to review your *Daily Outline* and *Daily Schedule Outline Details* to verify that written instructions reflect your intentions.

## HOW TO ASSEMBLE A KIDEX CLASS BOOK

Figure 3–1 provides a flowchart for creating the KIDEX Class Book. Purchase a 1–2" binder, preferably one that has a clear-view front and an index, to create about 16–17 sections in the book. Note that some sections on the flowchart refer to specific examples and blank templates (referred to as *Figures* in parentheses). Organize your KIDEX Class Book according to the sections indicated on the flowchart. Feel free to customize and add categories to the KIDEX Class Book that comply with your organization's regulations and goals. Figure 3–2 provides an example of a cover for the KIDEX Class Book. To customize a cover for your own KIDEX Class Book, use the blank template provided in the Forms and Templates Appendix and cheerful stationary or the center's logo paper.

## DAILY OUTLINE

The *Daily Outline Schedule,* located on Figure 3–3, is a brief summary of the groups' planned daily schedule. (It is designed in a simple format to provide a quick orientation

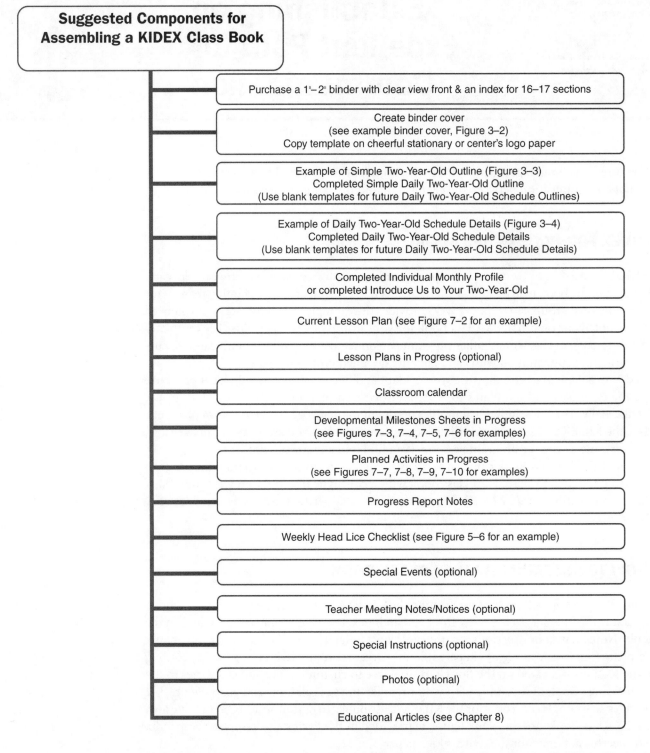

**Suggested Components for Assembling a KIDEX Class Book**

Purchase a 1"–2" binder with clear view front & an index for 16–17 sections

Create binder cover
(see example binder cover, Figure 3–2)
Copy template on cheerful stationary or center's logo paper

Example of Simple Two-Year-Old Outline (Figure 3–3)
Completed Simple Daily Two-Year-Old Outline
(Use blank templates for future Daily Two-Year-Old Schedule Outlines)

Example of Daily Two-Year-Old Schedule Details (Figure 3–4)
Completed Daily Two-Year-Old Schedule Details
(Use blank templates for future Daily Two-Year-Old Schedule Details)

Completed Individual Monthly Profile
or completed Introduce Us to Your Two-Year-Old

Current Lesson Plan (see Figure 7–2 for an example)

Lesson Plans in Progress (optional)

Classroom calendar

Developmental Milestones Sheets in Progress
(see Figures 7–3, 7–4, 7–5, 7–6 for examples)

Planned Activities in Progress
(see Figures 7–7, 7–8, 7–9, 7–10 for examples)

Progress Report Notes

Weekly Head Lice Checklist (see Figure 5–6 for an example)

Special Events (optional)

Teacher Meeting Notes/Notices (optional)

Special Instructions (optional)

Photos (optional)

Educational Articles (see Chapter 8)

*All blank forms can be obtained by copying from the Forms and Templates Appendix at the back of the book.

FIGURE 3–1 Suggested Components for a KIDEX Class Book

# KIDEX *for* TWOS
# Class Book

*The Bananas*
_____
**GROUP NAME**

**FIGURE 3–2** KIDEX Cover Example

# DAILY OUTLINE SCHEDULE

| | |
|---|---|
| Early Morning | Children arrive, hello, health assessment / breakfast / self-directed learning centers / clean up and diaper change, toileting, hand washing / KIDEX Activities |
| Mid Morning | Language activities, stories / flannel board, songs, finger plays or vocabulary<br>Snack, clean up, mini rest<br>Large motor activities (indoors or outdoors)<br>KIDEX Activities |
| Late Morning | Sensory / Creative Expression<br>Diaper changes, toileting, hand washing<br>Small motor activities<br>Lunch, clean up<br>Medications as needed<br>Prepare for nap time |
| Mid Day | Nap time begins |
| Early Afternoon | Nap time cleanup<br>Diaper changes, toileting, hand washing, grooming<br>Quiet time (books) and manipulative play<br>Snack time and clean up |
| Mid Afternoon | Outdoor play or large motor activities & hand washing<br>Small motor activities |
| Late Afternoon | Diaper changes, toileting, hand washing, face washing<br>Singing songs, playing music, self-directed play centers<br>Medications as needed<br>Gather items for departure |
| Early Evening | KIDEX Activities<br>Organized music and movement<br>Puppet stories, puzzles, table toys<br>Close room / Prepare for tomorrow |

FIGURE 3–3 Daily Outline example

for a substitute teacher and for steady visitors at the center such as parents who are seeking future care for their children. The information found on the *Daily Outline* will give them a *general idea* what a common day in the group looks like. It does not contain specific details that are outlined in the *Daily Schedule Details*. The *Daily Schedule Details* is a more in-depth look at the day, providing information about where to find things, why we do this and who has specific instructions for care. Blank templates for creating your own *Daily Outline* are located in the Forms and Templates Appendix and to create the *Daily Schedule Details* found in Chapter 7, "Facilitating Two-Year-Olds & Their Families." This schedule provides a method for substitute teachers and other program personnel to quickly orient themselves to your group before diving immediately into the details. Post a copy of the *Daily Outline* on the Current Events Bulletin Board for the parents to view, and in your centrally-located KIDEX Class Book for the substitute to view.

All early care and education providers know children thrive with a steady routine. Try to recreate your daily routines in this written *Daily Outline Schedule* form. A successful plan will assure a consistent day for the two-year-olds in your absence.

## DAILY SCHEDULE DETAILS

At first glance, the *Daily Schedule Details* might appear one-dimensional. Initially, the schedule may seem overwhelming and busy, and one might wonder how a teacher can accomplish all the outlined tasks. Yet, in reality, the child/staff ratios maintained in many outside-the-home programs include several adults, such as ratios of 1–6 or 1–7 two-year-olds per adult. The National Association for the Education of Young Children (NAEYC) recommends that the staffing ratio for the maximum-sized two-year-old group be 1–6 per group of 12 children ages 24–30 months, or 1–7 per group of 14 children ages 30–36 months. More detailed information is available on NAEYC's Web site, http://www.naeyc.org. A group always works more efficiently with at least two adults. Working in tandem, the schedule will develop into a multi-dimensional plan. For instance, while one teacher performs toileting routines, diaper changes, and sharing time, the other teacher can supervise activities such as fine motor manipulatives, flannel board stories, or nap time clean-up with the other children.

Observe the *Daily Schedule Details* examples (Figure 3–4) to gain insight into creating your own individualized group schedule. When you are ready to create your plan, duplicate the blank template provided in the Forms and Templates appendix and follow the instructions in Chapter 7 for completing it. Explain in detail where equipment or specific items are stored, such as art supplies and extra clothing. Paint a complete picture of every component listed on the *Daily Schedule Details*. After the substitute has reviewed the *Daily Outline*, he or she can refer to the *Daily Schedule Details* and recreate a similar routine that the children are familiar with, thus promoting the stable, secure feeling that two-year-olds need in order to thrive.

## INTRODUCE US TO YOUR TWO-YEAR-OLD

Upon enrolling a two-year-old in the center program, provide the parents/guardians with an *Introduce Us to Your Two-Year-Old* form (see Figure 3–5). This form provides the families a means for familiarizing the center staff with their two-year-old's needs and requirements. Because every two-year-old will change rapidly, it is advisable to update each one's personal information on a monthly basis. After the first month of attendance, replace the original *Introduce Us to Your Two-Year-Old* form with the KIDEX *Individual Monthly Profile* form provided in this chapter.

# DAILY SCHEDULE DETAILS

| | |
|---|---|
| Early Morning | Ms. Tonya arrives, opens the room, does a safety check of environment and sets up play activities chosen from KIDEX; see lesson plans in KIDEX class book. She welcomes each child as they arrive. Marlon is new and is still experiencing separation anxiety. He calms himself in the little yellow rocker with his blanket watching the other children awhile before joining them. The breakfast cart arrives by 7:00. Caden, Clara, Emily and Max are the breakfast eaters. All others ate before. See Caden's Individual Profile in the KIDEX class book to review his food allergies. I arrive around 7:45 while Ms. Tonya completes the breakfast schedule. I give any scheduled medications and supervise the play center activities. Around 8:45 we begin our clean up. Ms. Tonya begins toileting/diaper changes/sharing time and hand washing. While she is doing that, I supervise clean up and begin language activities outlined in the lesson plan. |
| Mid Morning | Snacks are served—only Timothy needs a cup with a lid. The children retrieve their blankets and nap toys for an informal short rest about 10-15 min. We do not use our cots, we lay on our blankets. Turn on soft music. Harriet and Carter will settle in if their backs are rubbed. Marlon takes a pacifier. Clara and Max sometimes fall asleep! After resting we help put away blankets and nap toys. Ms. Tonya conducts the Sensory or Art activities scheduled on the lesson plan with 4-5 children and I work with the other half exploring more Language activities - See our lesson plans (KIDEX book) |
| Late Morning | We clean up our art center and prepare for outdoor play (about 25-30 min). If the weather does not permit see alternative large muscle activities on lesson plans. Upon arrival back to our room encourage all the children to hang their outdoor coats and hats in their cubbies with assistance. Mr. Jared joins us and relieves Ms. Tonya for lunch. Mr. Jared begins the toileting routines and diaper changing, sharing time and hand washing. I disinfect the table, assist with hand washing and begin serving drinks, once we finish toileting and diaper changing. We begin serving our family style lunch. Since Max is in a wheelchair we push him to the end of the table so he can participate but his lunch is served on his special tray. |

**FIGURE 3–4** Daily Schedule Detailed Outline example

| | |
|---|---|
| Mid Day | The lunch cart arrives about 11:30, we serve lunch. While the lunch is in progress I sit and eat a small plate of food with the children and Mr. Jared prepares the room for nap and administers any scheduled medications. As each child finishes lunch we clean their hands and faces, they retrieve their blankets and soft nap toys. Remember Marlon's pacifier. Turn on soft music and rub Harriet and Carter's backs. The children will nap around 2 hours. Ms. Tonya joins Mr. Jared to help settle the nappers and I catch up charting, then I take my lunch while the children sleep. Once I return from lunch I have about 1 hour prep time to work on my bulletin boards, lesson plans and written communications. Ms. Tonya and Mr. Jared clean up the lunch area / perform toy cleansing and housekeeping responsibilities. |
| Early Afternoon | As the children begin to awaken around 1:45 I begin toileting routines, diaper changes, sharing time, hand washing and grooming. Mr. Jared disinfects the cots and assists the children to put their blankets and nap toys away. Note: we keep the soft music and lights low (shades are opened) to allow the children to waken with ease and join back into the group. Ms. Tonya goes home, we say goodbye. Once we are ready for snacks we turn the overhead lights on and turn off our nap music. |
| Mid Afternoon | As we complete the toileting routines, diaper changing, and hand washing we serve snacks to those ready. Once snacks are completed we go outdoors for about 30 min. |
| Late Afternoon | Once again indoors we put away outdoor coats, hats, wash our hands and begin our chosen KIDEX activities with half the group while Mr. Jared supervises play centers / self directed activities about 15 min then switch. Mr. Jared begins the final toileting routines and diaper changing, sharing time and hand washing. He changes clothing that is extremely soiled and grooms the children. Ms. Roberta, our floating assistant teacher, arrives about 15 min before I leave. She administers any scheduled medications then organizes table activities such as puzzles, peg boards, blocks etc. See lesson plan suggestions. We usually play the Jungle Book CD (or another choice they decide) while they are enjoying the table toys. Some of the children finish the CD with a dance while I review the final charting notes. |
| Early Evening | Ms. Roberta will stay with Mr. Jared until only 5 children remain. Mr. Jared reminds the parents to pick up their mail and assists with departures. He prepares the room for closing and tomorrow's activities for the children. |

**FIGURE 3–4** Daily Schedule Detailed Outline example *(Continued)*

# Introduce Us to Your Two-Year-Old
## (25–36 Months)

Date ___07/08___

Last Name: _(Enter last name)_  First Name: ___Sameer___  Middle: ___A___

Name your child is called at home: ___Sameer___

Siblings: Names & Ages: ___Shalamar - 5___

Favorite Play Materials: ___Bear___

Special Interests: ___dinosaurs___

Pets: ___Dog___

What opportunities does your child have to play with others the same age? ___Home and relatives house___

Eating Patterns:

    Are there any dietary concerns? ___Very picky eater___

    Does your child use a bottle/breast feed at home?  Yes ___✓___  No _____

    If yes, when? ___at night before bed___

    Does your child feed him/herself? ___Sometimes___

    Are there any food dislikes? ___No___

    Are there any food allergies? ___None Known___

    When eating, uses:  fingers ___✓___  spoon ___✓___  fork ___✓___  cup ___✓___

                    needs assistance ___✓___

Sleeping Patterns:

    What time is bedtime at home? ___8:00 pm___  Arise at? ___7:30 am___

    What time is nap time? ___12:15 pm___ How long? ___2 1/2 hours___

    Does your child have a special toy/blanket to nap with? ___Yes___

    How is your child prepared for rest (e.g., story time, quiet play, snack)
    ___Story Time___

Eliminating Patterns:

    Toilet trained yet?  Yes _____  No ___✓___

    If not, when do you anticipate introducing toilet training? ___Closer to age 3___

    Would you like more information? ___Yes___

    In training? ___No___  If trained, how long? _____

    Is independent—doesn't require help. ___No___

    Does your child need to be reminded? ___No___

    If yes, at what time intervals do you suggest? _____

**FIGURE 3–5** Introduce Us to Your Two-Year-Old

Does your child have certain words to indicate a need to eliminate? _Not yet_

Child wears:

Nap time diaper __✓__ Disposable training pants _____

Cloth underwear _____ Plastic pants over cloth underwear _____

Stress/Coping Patterns:

Does your child use a pacifier at home? Yes __✓__ No _____

If yes when _____ Brand _Baby Buddy_

Does your child have any fears: _____ Storms __✓__ Separation anxiety _____

Dark _____ Animals _____ Stranger anxiety _____

Being alone __✓__ Other _____

How do you soothe him or her? _Rocking and patting on back_

Personality Traits:       shy/reserved   outgoing/curious   (sensitive/frightens easily)
(Circle all that apply)   very verbal     active              restless
                          cuddly          demonstrative      (cautious)
                          (warms slowly to new people or situations)

Health Patterns:

List other allergy alerts: ___None Known_____

List any medications, intervals, and route (mouth, ears, eyes, etc):

_____

List any health issues or special needs: ___None Known_____

_____

How often each day do you assist your child with brushing their teeth? _2 x a day_

Activity Patterns:

When did your child begin: Creeping _6 mo_ Crawling _11 mo_ Walking _14 mo_

Is there any other information we should know in order to help us know your child better?
_Shameer tends to bond best with a smaller group of people_

_____

_____

_____Mr. Shibli_____

Parent / Guardian completing form

OFFICE USE ONLY
Start Date: _____ Full Time: _____ Part Time: S M T W T F S ½ a.m. p.m.
Group Assigned: a.m. _____ p.m. _____
Teacher(s): _____
Please keep an adjustment record yes _____ no _____ for _____ weeks.
Assign a cubby space: _____ Assign a diaper space: _____

**FIGURE 3–5** Introduce Us to Your Two-Year-Old *(Continued)*

## KIDEX INDIVIDUAL MONTHLY PROFILE

The KIDEX *Individual Monthly Profile* form (see Figure 3–6) is one of the most important documents for providing details of each child's individual preferences and needs. The KIDEX *Individual Monthly Profile* is an in-house document intended for internal communication among the rotating staff and shifts. Because two-year-olds have limited language skills, they are not yet able to communicate their needs effectively. Information such as a food allergy, or that they only wear a nap time diaper, could easily be overlooked with rotating personnel. The lead teacher spends the largest amount of time with each child and becomes quite familiar with their individual needs. (By creating and maintaining a current copy of the KIDEX *Individual Monthly Profile* for each child, he or she can assure that those important details are not overlooked.

Indicate any allergy alerts to avoid triggering serious health conditions. This is a very important notation. For the continued safety of all children with known allergies note the information here and on the Current Events Bulletin Board discussed later in the chapter. Next, mark the level of assistance needed with regard to *dietary patterns.* Note the child's ability to handle eating utensils and if continued assistance is required. If the child is using a spoon, fork, or cup without difficulty then indicate independent. Note any food dislikes. Young children have a very sensitive palate for taste. They often reject newly introduced flavors, yet grow to love them at a later time, so their food likes and dislikes may change on a regular basis. Gathering information concerning weaning, bottles, and breast feeding will help solve mysteries at the center. Sometimes two-year-old children continue to use a bottle, breast feed, or use a pacifier at home. Their parent might feel embarrassed that they have not weaned them yet. Or, they continue the practice due to the influence of their cultural beliefs. It is helpful to know if the child is still dependent on those forms of nutrition. The little one might experience difficulties napping or relaxing and often need help such as gentle back patting to reach a relaxed state. The parents might use the opportunity to seek guidance or suggestions to help extinguish their child's dependency.

Diaper changing and toileting habits are recorded next. If the child only wears a nap time diaper and uses the toilet during waking hours, record it here. It can be confusing to the little one who has just learned to use the toilet if their nap time diaper is not removed and replaced with underwear. Parents, family members, or guardians of the toilet training two-year-old also can become quite frustrated to find their child wearing a nap time diaper later in the evening because the changing shift was unaware of toileting/diaper instructions! Make a notation on the *Diaper Changing Schedule* to remove the nap time diaper, so that this important task is not overlooked.

Record *personality traits* you have observed and those communicated by their family from initial enrollment information. Circle all that apply.

List any *health concerns,* such as that a child with a leg brace might require it be removed for 30 minutes in the morning and afternoon. If the parents do not have any health concerns, then indicate "none known." *Daily medications* only requires a "no" or "yes." Circle the "see med sheet for details" reminder listed on this line.

It is not uncommon for some two-year-olds to be easily frightened by loud or unfamiliar noises, such as fire drill alarms, vacuum cleaners, and thunderstorms. Yet others never seem to notice. Indicate under *Stress/Coping Pattern* if the child does have these, and add any others you are aware of.

Two-year-olds thrive on ritual and will appreciate consistent nap time routines. Describe all details, such as "rests best with soft yellow duck and gentle patting." Include information of the child's current napping pattern, including average length of time.

# KIDEX for Twos
## Individual Monthly Profile

Month: _August_   Teacher: _Mrs. Morgan_   Teacher: _Mr. Hail_

Child's Name: _Olivia (Enter last name)_   Group: _Toddler 1_

Age: _18 mo_   Birth Date: _1/27/2004_   Allergy Alerts: _None Known_

Parent/Guardian's Names: _Mr. & Mrs. Burner_   Start Date: _6/6/2005_

When eating uses:   fingers _✓_  spoon _✓_  fork _✓_  cup _✓_   needs assistance _✓_

Weaned: Yes _✓_   No _____   Uses bottle/breast feeds at home: Yes _____ No _____

Food dislikes: _pears and beets_

Diapers: _✓_   Nap Time Diaper Only: _____   Toilet Trained: _____

Independent: _____   Needs reminding/assistance: _____ Toilet training: _____

Special Diapering Instructions (special ointments, etc): _Rx 402302 if redness develops_

Personality Traits:   (shy/reserved)  outgoing/curious   sensitive/frightens easily
(Circle all that apply)  very verbal   active   restless
  (cuddly)   demonstrative   (cautious)
  (warms slowly to new people or situations)

Health Concerns: _None Known_

Daily Medications:   yes _____   no _✓_   (see med sheet for details)

Special Needs Instructions: _____

Stress/Coping Pattern: fears _✓_   storms _____   loudness _✓_   strangers _____
  dark _____   animals ____   separation anxiety _____   others _____

Uses pacifier at home  Yes _✓_   No _____   Pacifier Type: _Nuk_

Special Blanket/Toy: _Pink_   Name: _"Pinkie"_

Average Nap Length: _12:30_ to _2:30_

Special Nap Instructions: _Likes to hold "Pinkie," her blanket cover is with the blue blanket_

Favorite Activities This month: _Feeding her doll "Pricilla"_

Days Attending:   Sun.  (Mon.)  (Tues.)  (Wed.)  (Thurs.)  (Fri.)   Sat.   1/2 days  Full days

Approximate Arrival Time _7:45 am_ Approximate Departure Time _5:15 pm_

Those authorized to pick up: _Grandmother Alice_
_Aunt Helen_

*Warning: If name is not listed, consult with office and obtain permission to release child.  If you are not familiar with this person, always request I.D.*

FIGURE 3–6 Individual Monthly Profile

*Favorite activities* will change from month to month, but are very important to two-year-olds as they practice skills over and over. Share all you are aware of in this section.

Finish the KIDEX *Individual Monthly Profile* form by marking the *days they are scheduled to attend, half days or full days, approximate arrival and departure time. Authorized pick up is extremely crucial to document and abide by.* See *Authorized Person Cards* later in this chapter for a more in-depth discussion of how to facilitate authorized pick up procedures. In this section of the KIDEX *Individual Monthly Profile,* provide a list of authorized people for the staff to refer to. Make it a solid policy that, if the person is not listed, consult with the administrative office and always I.D. any unfamiliar person.

## ENROLLMENT APPLICATION

Use the enrollment application to begin building an administrative file for each new child. Note that this document is different from *Introduce Us to Your Two-Year-Old.* The application is generally stored in the administrative offices with permanent health records and legal documents. Items to include on an application for collecting general information are

> child's name, address, home phone number, date of birth, gender, legal guardian
>
> mother's name, address, home phone number, employer's name, work phone number
>
> father's name, address, home phone number, employer's name, work phone number
>
> emergency contact's name, relationship, address, home and work phone numbers
>
> name of other people residing with the child, their relationship, age (if under 21)
>
> names of all people authorized to remove the child from the center, relationships
>
> days the child will attend, full or part time
>
> medical emergency information and authorization
>
> permission to leave with the child for neighborhood walks, bus ride to and from center, etc. (see Figure 3–7)
>
> Immunizations are discussed at greater length in Chapter 5, "Health."

## AUTHORIZED PERSON CARD

On the enrolling application template "authorization cards" (see Figure 3–8) are mentioned under "people authorized to remove the child from the center." Consider using authorization cards for those occasions when parents/guardians are unable to remove their child from the child care center due to some unforeseen circumstances. They might need to depend on a substitute, such as a co-worker, neighbor, or family member not listed on the "authorized list." Upon enrolling, provide the family with a couple of blank authorization cards. Instruct them to complete a card and give it to the person planning to pick up the child. The guardian will need to call the center to give verbal permission. Some states require a code number or word to accompany the authorized person. Check with your local licensing agency for specific password mandates. When the substitute person arrives, request a picture I.D. to verify that the name matches the one on the authorization card. Collect the card and return it to the parents on their next visit to the center.

# PROGRAM ENROLLING APPLICATION

Child's Full Name: _Jamae (Enter last name)_ Nickname: _Jamae, Bear_

Date of Birth: _10/30/08_ Sex: _M_ Home Phone: _XXX-XXX-XXXX_

Address: _(Enter street #/Apt. #)_ City: _(Enter city)_ Zip Code: _(Enter zip code)_

Legal Guardian: _Mrs. Rust_

Mother's Name: _Mrs. Rust_ Home Phone: _XXX-XXX-XXXX_

Cell Phone: _XXX-XXX-XXXX_ E-Mail: _RusN@sbcglobal.net_

Address: _(Enter street #/Apt. #)_ City: _(Enter city)_ Zip Code: _(Enter zip code)_

Employer: _St. Joseph's Hospital_ Work Phone: _XXX-XXX-XXXX_

Address: _(Enter street #/Apt. #)_ City: _(Enter city)_ Zip Code: _(Enter zip code)_

Father's Name: _Mr. Jackson_ Home Phone: _XXX-XXX-XXXX_

Cell Phone: _XXX-XXX-XXXX_ E-Mail: _JacksonH@aol.com_

Address: _(Enter street #/Apt. #)_ City: _(Enter city)_ Zip Code: _(Enter zip code)_

Employer: _John Deere & Associates_ Work Phone: _XXX-XXX-XXXX_

## IN THE EVENT YOU CANNOT BE REACHED IN AN EMERGENCY, CALL:

Name: _Ms. Rust_ Relationship: _Grandmother_ Phone: _XXX-XXX-XXXX_

Address: _(Enter street #/Apt. #)_ City: _(Enter city)_ Zip Code: _(Enter zip code)_

Name: _Mrs. Jackson_ Relationship: _Grandmother_ Phone: _XXX-XXX-XXXX_

Address: _(Enter street #/Apt. #)_ City: _(Enter city)_ Zip Code: _(Enter zip code)_

## OTHER PEOPLE RESIDING WITH CHILD

Name: _Rodney_ Relationship: _brother_ Age: _7_

Name: _Dwight_ Relationship: _brother_ Age: _6_

Name: _Sara_ Relationship: _sister_ Age: _3_

**FIGURE 3–7** Enrollment Application example

**PERSONS AUTHORIZED TO REMOVE CHILD FROM THE CENTER:**

Your child will not be allowed to go with anyone unless their name appears on this application, or you provide them with an "Authorization Card," or you make other arrangements with the Management.  Positive I.D. will be required.

Name: _Mrs. Rust_ Relationship: _Mother_

Name: _Mr. Jackson_ Relationship: _Father_

Name: _Ms. Rust_ Relationship: _Grandmother_

Baby Will Attend:  (Mon) - Tues - (Wed) - Thur - (Fri) - Sat - Sun

Baby Will Be:  (Full Time) or Part Time

Time Child Will Be Dropped Off (Normally): _8:00 am_

Time Child Will Be Picked Up (Normally): _4:30 pm_

### MEDICAL INFORMATION/AUTHORIZATION

Physician's Name: _Dr. Gillespie_ Phone: _XXX-XXX-XXXX_

Address: _(Enter street #/Apt. #)_ City: _(Enter city)_ Zip Code: _(Enter zip code)_

Dentist's Name: _Dr. Cooper_ Phone: _XXX-XXX-XXXX_

Address: _(Enter street #/Apt. #)_ City: _(Enter city)_ Zip Code: _(Enter zip code)_

Allergies: _None Known_

I agree and give consent that, in case of accident, injury, or illness of a serious nature, my child will be given medical attention/emergency care.  I understand I will be contacted immediately, or as soon as possible if I am away from the numbers listed on this form.

### PERMISSION TO LEAVE PREMISES

I hereby give the school/center _Somersett Heights_ permission to take my child

on neighborhood walks using a _baby buggy_ (state equipment, e.g. a

baby buggy that seats six children & has safety straps). YES _SM_ (INITIAL)

NO, I do not give permission at this time: _____ (INITIAL)

Parent/Guardian's Signature: _Mrs. Rust_

Parent/Guardian's Signature: _Mr. Jackson_

Date: _04/01/20XX_

**Figure 3–7** Enrollment Application example *(Continued)*

AUTHORIZED
PERSON
CARD

_Reverend James_
Name of Authorized Person

May pick up my child _Joseph_

on my behalf.

_[signature]_                    _3/16/xx_
Parent/Guardian Signature        Date

USE HEAVY CARD STOCK (FRONT OF CARD)    USE HEAVY CARD STOCK (BACK OF CARD)

**FIGURE 3–8** Authorized Person Card

## TWO-YEAR-OLD DAILY OBSERVATION SHEETS

Two-year-olds are unable to discuss their daily activities with their families. Accurate recording provides the family with a clear picture of that day. Figure 3–9 provides a completed example of a *Twos Daily Observation Checklist.*

Consider making a copy of each completed *Twos Daily Observation Checklist.* Give one copy to the parents or guardian when they pick up the child. File the second copy for 2–3 months, keeping at least the past 2 months at all times. Check with your local licensing agency for the required period of storage.

### OUR DAYS, EATING AND NAPPING PATTERNS SHEETS

At age two, some centers are mandated by licensing rules to create individual records for each child. Many centers choose to reduce paperwork by recording daily information as a class group, rather than individually. If your center opts not to create *Twos Daily Observation Checklists,* then other types of reports will serve your purpose. The *Our Day* (see Figure 3–10) form is used to provide information for the parents regarding the final outcome of their child's day. Although lesson plans are available, the *Our Day* provides actual details of events that occurred on that day. Nap time often provides a quiet time for the teacher to complete the majority of the information. *Our Day,* communicated in a cheerful, informative, legible manner, provides the parents with information they can enjoy discussing with their child. A form called *Eating Patterns* (see Figure 3–11) provides a space for each child's name and whether they ate a partial or complete meal that day. The *Nap Time* (Figure 3–12 sample) sheet provides a space for every child's name and a place to record when they fell asleep and when they awoke. You can gather information, using the suggested records, and post it on the Twos Current Events Bulletin Board covered in detail later in this chapter.

It is very helpful to make written observation documents, whether they are individual reports or class reports. Occasionally, parents express concerns. Use this observation material to provide helpful information, or to review if a family conference is warranted. For example, parents might be concerned that their child's appetite seems to be fluctuating at home and might want to explore how their child's appetite levels at home compare to those at the center. A series of daily sheets will help track any unusual patterns the two-year-old might be exhibiting. Documented information will provide helpful specifics needed to answer parents' questions. The director or program manager is encouraged to  review all records at least monthly to look for consistent recording practices or to spot areas requiring intervention, where education on a matter is warranted.

## Twos Daily Observation Checklist

Child's name: _____Caden_____ Date: __1/27/2005__

Arrival: ___7:30 am___ Departure: ___4:30 pm___

| | Ate Partial | Ate Complete | Water Juice Oz |
|---|---|---|---|
| Breakfast | | ✓ | |
| Snack | ✓ | | |
| Lunch | ✓ | ✓ | 8 oz W |
| Snack | | ✓ | |
| Mini Snack | | ✓ | |
| Dinner | | Home | |
| Evening Snack | | | |
| | | | |

| | Medications * | Treatments * |
|---|---|---|
| Time | 8:00 am Eye drops | None |
| Time | 12:30 pm Eye drops | None |
| Time | 4:45 pm | Asthma Treatment |

* see daily medication sheets for details

| Diaper Changes | | | | |
|---|---|---|---|---|
| Time | Wet | BM | Dry | Initials |
| 1:55 pm | | | ✓ | L.S. |
| | | | | |
| | | | | |
| | | | | |

Nap Times: ___11:45 – 1:45 pm___      Other: _____

### Toilet Training Progress

| Time | Wet | Dry | Bowel Movement | Accident Clothing Change | Seemed confused upset/resisted/refused re-evaluate readiness |
|---|---|---|---|---|---|
| 8:00 am | ✓ | | ✓ | | |
| 9:30 am | ✓ | | | | |
| 11:30 am | ✓ | | | | Nap time diaper applied |
| 2:15 pm | Refused | | | | Didn't want to leave water table |
| 2:30 pm | ✓ | | | ✓ | |
| 4:20 pm | ✓ | | | | |

**Moods / Activity Level:**
*Circle all that apply*
Busy • Curious •
(Adventurous) •
Active • Cheerful •
Quiet • Content •
Cuddly • Drowsy •
Bubbly (Verbal) •
Assertive •
(Focused) •
Frustrates Easily

Today's Play Center Choices: ___Water table___      ___Sandbox – Swings___

Comments: ___Caden has adopted the "potty time" book and won't part with it. He might enjoy his own copy.___

Lead Teacher: ___Mrs. Lois___
Shift Time: _8 – 5_
Teacher: ___Ms. Caroline___
Shift Time: _6:30 – 3:30_
Teacher: ___Ms. Becky___
Shift Time: _____
Teacher: ___Mr. Bill___
Shift Time: _4:45 – 6:00_
Teacher: _____
Shift Time: _____

**FIGURE 3–9** Daily Observation Checklist

# OUR DAY

DATE _January 14th_      **Day of Week** _Monday_

**Early morning activities/centers**:    (Beginning the day during morning arrival)

_Set up airport and city toys_

_Housekeeping corner—Rocked our babies & fed them_

_Played with our new puzzles_

**_KIDEX: Fun with Language and Telling Tales_: Activities to build our vocabulary were:**

_Winter word pictures with flannel board_

**Finger plays & songs we sang today were:**

_Three Little Kittens Lost Their Mittens Song_

**Our morning outdoors activity was:**

_Rolled & chased our snowballs (balls)_

**_KIDEX: My Body is Wonderful_: Activities to exercise our fine and large muscles were:**

_Marching to the music during our winter parade_

**Our morning project was:**

_Matched mittens_

**AFTERNOON**

**_KIDEX Exploring My World/Creating My Way_: Our creative/sensory activities were:**

_Painted with sponges_

_Played with Blocks_

**The story we read was:**

_"Dear Rebecca Winter's Here"_

**Our afternoon outdoor activity was:**

_Chased snowflakes (bubbles)_

_Swinging and sliding_

**Late afternoon activities/centers: (Ending the day during departures)**

_Washed our chairs while we listened to our favorite music. Jungle Book_

_Brushed and combed our hair_

_Lined up our boots and shoes_

**Extra activities today were:**

**FIGURE 3–10** Documenting a Day

# EATING PATTERNS

| Classroom: *Bananas* | Week of: *January 6* | | | | |
|---|---|---|---|---|---|
| Child's Name | Mon | Tues | Wed | Thur | Fri |
| *Katie* | *C* | *C* | *C* | *C* | *P* |
| *Andre* | *C* | *P* | *Absent* | *P* | *C* |
| *Ellen* | *P* | *C* | *C* | *C* | *C* |
| *Collin* | *C* | *C* | *C* | *C* | *C* |
| *Kara* | *P* | *P* | *C* | *P* | *C* |
| *David* | *C* | *C* | *C* | *C* | *C* |
| *Joseph* | *C* | *C* | *C* | *P* | *C* |
| *Hannah* | *P* | *C* | *P* | *Home Early* | *C* |
| *Hunter* | *P* | *C* | *C* | *P* | *C* |
| *Cedrick* | *C* | *C* | *C* | *C* | *P* |
| | | | | | |
| | | | | | |
| | | | | | |
| | | | | | |
| | | | | | |
| | | | | | |
| | | | | | |
| P = Ate Partial | | | | | |
| C = Complete | | | | | |

**FIGURE 3–11** Documenting Eating Patterns

# Nap Time

**Classroom** *Bananas*     **Week of:** *January 6*

| Name | Monday | | Tuesday | | Wednesday | | Thursday | | Friday | |
|------|--------|--------|---------|--------|-----------|--------|----------|--------|--------|--------|
| | Asleep | Awake | Asleep | Awake | Asleep | Awake | Asleep | Awake | Asleep | Awake |
| Katie | 12:15 | 2:00 | 12:00 | 2:00 | 11:50 | 2:00 | 12:10 | 2:00 | 11:50 | 2:00 |
| Andrea | 12:00 | 2:00 | 12:05 | 1:55 | Absent | | 12:00 | 2:05 | 11:45 | 1:50 |
| Ellen | 12:05 | 1:55 | 11:50 | 2:00 | 12:10 | 2:00 | 11:55 | 1:55 | 12:00 | 2:00 |
| Collin | 11:50 | 2:00 | 11:45 | 1:50 | 12:00 | 2:05 | 12:15 | 2:10 | 12:10 | 2:00 |
| Kara | 11:45 | 1:50 | 12:00 | 2:00 | 11:55 | 1:55 | 12:15 | 2:00 | 12:00 | 2:05 |
| David | 12:00 | 2:00 | 12:10 | 2:00 | 12:15 | 2:10 | 12:00 | 2:00 | 11:55 | 1:55 |
| Joseph | 12:10 | 2:00 | 12:00 | 2:05 | 12:15 | 2:00 | 12:05 | 1:55 | 12:15 | 2:10 |
| Hannah | 12:00 | 2:05 | 11:55 | 1:55 | 12:00 | 2:05 | Home | Early | 12:00 | 2:00 |
| Hunter | 11:55 | 1:55 | 12:15 | 2:00 | 12:05 | 1:55 | 11:45 | 1:50 | 11:50 | 2:00 |
| Cedrick | 12:15 | 2:10 | 11:45 | 1:50 | 11:50 | 2:00 | 12:00 | 2:00 | 12:00 | 2:05 |

**FIGURE 3–12** Documenting Nap Time

## DIAPER CHANGING RECORD

If your center opts to collect information as a group, post a *Diaper Changing Schedule* (see example Figure 3–13) near the changing table to collect pertinent information regarding each individual child's diaper change. Even if you only use *Twos Daily Observation Check-lists*, consider using this handy record to gather information during changes and transferring the information to the individual reports later. Refer to the Forms and Templates appendix for a reproducible blank template.

## CHILD REPORT

Most children experience separation anxiety when they are first enrolled. Everything and everyone is new to them. They often exhibit confusion, fear or lack of trust until they have had adequate time and positive experiences that help bonding to their new friends, teachers, and surroundings. Some children exhibit their fears through tears, temper tantrums, or the need for constant reassurance until their family returns. Younger children respond to a welcome lap to sit on or cuddling a favorite stuffed animal or blanket. For the most part children usually begin to adjust to the group within a two-week period or sometimes a bit longer if they attend on a part-time basis.

Use the *Child Transitioning Report* to provide the new family with daily information until their child has established an initial bond of trust. Discontinue its use when the little one has adjusted to the new routines. An example of a *Child Transitioning Report* can be

## Diaper Changing Schedule

**Day:** _Thursday_   **Date:** _November 10_

| Child's Name | 8:00 am–9:00 am | | | 11:00 am–12:00 pm | | | After Nap | | | 5:00 pm–6:00 pm | | | Bedtime | | | Wake up | | |
|---|---|---|---|---|---|---|---|---|---|---|---|---|---|---|---|---|---|---|
| | BM | WET | DRY | BM | WET | DRY | BM | WET | DRY | BM | WET | DRY | BM | WET | DRY | BM | WET | DRY |
| 1. Jacob | | | CM | MA | MA | | | CM | | BS | BS | | | | | | | |
| 2. Madison | CM | CM | | | | MA | CM | CM | | | BS | | | | | | | |
| 3. Matt | | CM | | MA | MA | | | CM | | Home | | | | | | | | |
| 4. Olivia | | CM | | | MA | | CM | CM | | | BS | | | | | | | |
| 5. Daniel | | CM | | | MA | | | | CM | | BS | | | | | | | |
| 6. Ashley | CM | CM | | MA | MA | | | CM | | | | BS | | | | | | |
| 7. Samantha | | | CM | MA | MA | | | CM | | BS | | | | | | | | |
| 8. Christopher | CM | CM | | | MA | | | CM | | | | BS | | | | | | |
| 9. Emma | CM | CM | | | | MA | | CM | | BS | | | | | | | | |
| 10. Ethan | | CM | | | MA | | CM | CM | | | | BS | | | | | | |
| 11. | | | | | | | | | | | | | | | | | | |
| 12. | | | | | | | | | | | | | | | | | | |

Initial the appropriate box when diapering is completed.

**FIGURE 3–13** Diaper Changing Schedule

found in Figure 3–14. The template to reproduce, with instructions for completing, are found in the Forms and Templates Appendix.

## HOW TO CREATE A CURRENT EVENTS BULLETIN BOARD

In a busy two-year-old room, time is of the essence. A *Current Events Bulletin Board* will provide a centrally located place to post ongoing messages. It is an important center for communications. The Current Events Bulletin Board will provide a means for communication between the program, current participating families, and future families touring your facility. It will save busy teachers the task of repeating information to each individual family, and will reduce the chance that information will not be disseminated to everyone. Look at Figure 3–15 for an example of the Current Events Bulletin Board. Please check your center's requirements for respect of families and children's confidentiality.

Create a bulletin board and decorate it with a seasonal theme. This will reduce the need to change the overall board every month, and will only require changing daily and monthly communication pieces. Hang the bulletin board near the room's entrance, where everyone passes by. If the board is located at the back of the room, there's a chance that busy parents won't take the opportunity to read it every day. The following lists are *suggested* items to post on the class Current Events Bulletin Board. Add items you feel are vital to your room's operation.

# Child Transitioning Report

Name ___Justin (Enter last name)___     Teacher ___Ms. Rose___

Date of Report ___March 17___     Teacher ___Mr. Michael___

Day  1  2  3  4  5  6  7  8  9  10  11  12  13  14  15

|                          | SOME | A LOT | NOT YET |
|--------------------------|------|-------|---------|
| Played with toys         | ✓    |       |         |
| Participated in activities |    |       |         |
| Played with the children |      |       |         |

| **Appetite**       | COMPLETE | PARTIAL |
|--------------------|----------|---------|
| Breakfast appetite |          | ✓       |
| AM snack appetite  | ✓        |         |
| Lunch appetite     | ✓        |         |
| PM snack appetite  | ✓        |         |
| Dinner appetite    |          |         |

**Naptime**

Indicate time                    From ___12:00 pm___ To ___2:00 pm___

**Bowel & bladder pattern** (See diaper changing sheet if applicable)

**Overall day**

Great! _____ *Seemed comfortable with new environment*

Fair ___✓___ *Adjustments to the new group and environment will improve as your child grows accustomed to the new environment*

Staff Comments: ___Justin only cried for 2 minutes after you left this morning! He enjoyed___ ___library time and outdoor activities!___

Parent's Comments or Questions (If any): ___He told us about the "pet hamster" last night___

- Use for 1-3 weeks until the new child feels comfortable with the group.

**FIGURE 3–14** Child Transitioning Report

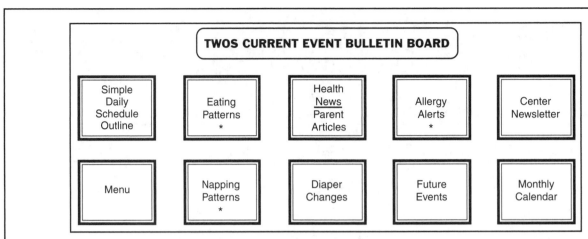

**FIGURE 3–15** Current Events Bulletin Board

| | |
|---|---|
| Daily Outline | Use this area to post the general schedule for the group. |
| Future Events | Here is a great place to post future events, for example, a scheduled visit from Charlie the pet pig, or a celebration of the monthly birthdays. |
| Health News | Choose articles from Chapter 8 to explain a recent exposure to a communicable disease and types of symptoms to watch for. |
| Nutrition & Menu Information | To reduce writing, duplicate information, post a copy of your menu for the day, week, or month. Many families find this information helpful for planning home meals that compliment the center meals. Refer to Figure 3–16 for an example of a daily menu. |
| Parent Articles | Post information relevant to two-year-olds, such as toilet training, or a schedule of parenting classes offered in the community. |
| Calendars & Center Newsletter | If your center creates a monthly newsletter or calendar, post current copies here. Find examples of both in Figures 3–17 & 3–18. |
| Allergy Postings | Post a listing of each child's name and known allergies. Collect this information from the KIDEX *Individual Monthly Profile.* |
| Our Day | Post these to tell parents about the day and the activities the children completed. |
| Eating Patterns | (Used to describe each individual child's appetite pattern each day, that week, on a group form.) |
| Napping Patterns | (Used to describe each individual child's napping pattern that day, for the week, on a group form.) |
| Diaper Changing Record | (Used to record each individual child's diaper change for the day in a group format.) |

## BIRTHDAY BULLETIN BOARD

Creating a Birthday Bulletin Board is a wonderful way to spotlight a special quality each child possesses. Create a theme for the year, and a list of each child's birthday month, and

**OUR MENU TODAY**

Date *Thursday, July 6*

Breakfast
- *Milk 2% (1/2 cup)*
- *Syrup (1 tsp)*
- *Apricot halves*
- *Margarine (1 tsp)*
- *French Toast (1/2 slice)*

Snack
- *Cheese (1/2 oz.)*
- *Apple Juice 100% Vitamin C (1/4 cup)*
- *Crackers (1/2 serving/0.5 oz.)*

Lunch
- *Milk 2% (1/2 cup)*
- *Baked Chicken (1/2 oz.)*
- *Diced Mixed Vegetables, Carrots*
- *Fruit Cocktail (1/4 cup)*

Snack
- *Blueberry Yogurt (2 oz.)*
- *Graham crackers (1 square)*
- *Water (2–4 oz.)*

Mini Snack
- *Saltines (2 squares)*
- *Water (2–4 oz.)*

**FIGURE 3–16** Our Menu Today

add names as children join your group. An example of a Birthday Bulletin Board can be found on Figure 3–19.

## NOTES HOME/STAFF COLLABORATION

The director is responsible for the overall well-being of the staff, parents, and children. The director must be kept informed with regard to any unusual changes, challenges, or problems that occur during the course of a shift. It can be very disconcerting for an emotionally upset client to communicate with the center when the director is completely uninformed. Discuss any written communication with the director prior to sending notes home, other than requests for personal supplies, or each child's daily record. After discussing the problem at hand, together you can devise a plan of action. Sharing your concerns with the director will facilitate problem-solving and will keep information flowing between staff and director. The director has encountered many of these situations before, and often has workable solutions that will be beneficial to all.

## FRAGILE FAMILY RELATIONSHIPS

Experienced early care and education professionals are well aware that newly-enrolled families are most fragile within the first several weeks of their child's attendance. For some families, this is the first time they have been separated from their child for any length of time. They might experience sadness, anxiety, and for some, feelings of guilt. This is

# January

| Sunday | Monday | Tuesday | Wednesday | Thursday | Friday | Saturday |
|---|---|---|---|---|---|---|
| Theme:<br><br>"Winter" | 1<br><br>Happy New Year Center Closed | 2<br><br>Lead Teacher Meeting 7:00 pm | 3 | 4 | 5<br><br>Happy 1st Birthday Rory | 6 |
| 7<br><br>Theme:<br><br>"Ways We Travel" | 8 | 9<br><br>Happy 1st Birthday Natalie | 10 | 11<br><br>First Aid Class | 12<br><br>Happy 4th Birthday Andrew | 13<br><br>Happy 5th Birthday Keegan |
| 14<br><br>Theme:<br><br>"Alphabet-orama" | 15 | 16<br><br>Happy 2nd Birthday Gregory | 17 | 18 | 19 | 20 |
| 21<br><br>Theme:<br><br>"Tropical Vacation" | 22 | 23<br><br>Happy 3rd Birthday Amanda | 24 | 25<br><br>Director/ Parent Round Table 7:15 pm | 26<br><br>Beach Party! | 27 |
| 28<br><br>Theme:<br><br>"People Who Work" | 29 | 30<br><br>Fire Extinguisher Safety Week | 31<br><br>Happy 1st Birthday Davis | | | |

**Figure 3–17** Center Calendar

a hand-holding stage while a trusting relationship is established. It is human nature, once we become familiar with our routines, to easily forget how it feels to be brand-new to the center setting. Challenge yourself to look at each new family and recollect how you felt on your first day.

For a successful liaison, it is imperative to establish trust and rapport quickly. New families appreciate an extra-big welcome in the morning, and it is your role to include them in discussions while establishing care. Show them where to store their child's belongings, where to sign in for the day, and where they can find the child's daily sheets. Offer them information about the daily routines or invite them to visit before their child's first day at the center. Introduce them to other parents so that they quickly begin to feel a part of the group. As rapport builds, a level of trust will begin to develop, and families will naturally settle into a familiar, comfortable routine. It will become easier for the family to move in and out when they drop off their little one.

Other times a client might be considered fragile are usually when the family experiences an upsetting situation involving their child. If a family does not feel that the staff

**CLASS NEWSLETTER**

**Enriching the Lives of Children Since 1979**

# HIGHLIGHTS

## OUR MONTHLY NEWSLETTER
## FOR JANUARY

Dear Parents,

Thank you for the special gifts, cards, and holiday wishes we received throughout the holiday season. We all want to wish you and your loved ones a prosperous New Year!

The snow, ice, and low temperatures have made the New Year a memorable one. Because we are all housebound, I thought an indoor family activity would be helpful. All of our groups participate in cooking projects each week. I would like to share our most popular recipe.

Play Dough
Ingredients:

- 2 cups flour

- 2 cups water

- 1 cup salt

- 2 tablespoons salad oil

- 4 teaspoons cream of tartar

- food coloring

Mix together and cook over medium heat until a soft, lumpy ball forms. It happens quickly! Knead for a few minutes until dough is smooth. Store dough in an airtight container and store in the refrigerator. Have fun & enjoy!

I do have a few reminders that I think will be helpful to start off the New Year. The reminders are listed on the next page.

Sincerely,
Ms. Niehoff, Director

**Figure 3–18** Class Newsletter

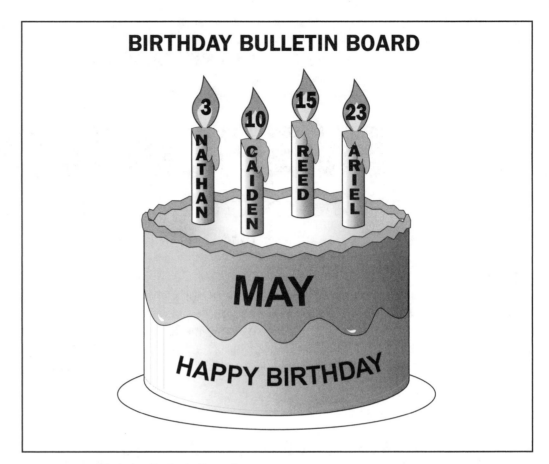

**FIGURE 3–19** Birthday Bulletin Board

views their concerns as legitimate, their trust is compromised. Examples of some fairly common scenarios are a situation in which a family's recently healthy child now is experiencing frequent bouts of illnesses, or concerns about their child's relationship with another child who is biting. Again, this is a time to make extra efforts to reassure the family that you are very committed and sympathetic to their concerns. Share whatever information you can to assist their understanding. If a situation can be improved, outline the plan of action you have put into place to prevent a reoccurrence of the situation or incident.

Sometimes the concerns do not involve classroom situations. For example, the issue may be an error with a family's billing, or how their billing has been handled. Because families naturally bond with classroom teachers through positive daily contact, they sometimes feel more comfortable sharing their concerns with the classroom personnel, rather than with administrative personnel. At times, they may experience some dissatisfaction in other center matters. If you consistently hear a parent voicing a concern, it is very helpful to share these observations with the director. Doing so provides an opportunity to proactively alleviate any misunderstandings, or clear up whatever frustrations the client may be experiencing. It takes a whole team to make the center a pleasant and positive experience for everyone, and it is very important to keep the lines of communication open on all levels. With the center manager's vast array of experience, matters can often be smoothed out, and mutually-accepted outcomes reached quickly.

## REFERENCES

*Accreditation criteria & procedures table* 6 p. 47. Retrieved January 27, 2005, from http://www.naeyc.org

Reisser, P. C. (1997). *Baby & child care.* Wheaton, IL: Tyndale House.

## RECOMMENDED RESOURCES

*Caring for our children: National health and safety performance standards* (2nd ed.), available online at http://nrc.uchsc.edu

Jurek, D. (1995). *Teaching young children.* Morristown, NJ: Fearon.

Shelov, S. P. & Hannemann, R. E. (1998). *Caring for your baby and young child: Birth to age 5* (Rev. ed.). New York: Bantam Books.

## HELPFUL WEB SITES

High/Scope Educational Research Foundation, 1-800-407-7377, http://www.highscope.org

CHAPTER

# 4

To find your specific
State's Licensing, Rules
and Regulations go to:

http://nrc.uchsc.edu

# Hygiene, Cleaning, and Disinfecting

Proper cleaning, disinfecting, and hygiene practices consistently employed in an early care and teaching environment will significantly reduce the spread of infection and disease. Disinfecting and cleaning are two distinctly different procedures used to prevent the spread of germs, and they each require specific measures to achieve their intended results. *Cleaning* is a *less* rigorous procedure designed to remove dirt, soil, and small amounts of bacteria. It *does not eliminate all germs.* Soap, detergents, and cleaners are examples of cleaning products. *Disinfecting* procedures are *more rigorous* and refer to cleaning surfaces with the use of chemicals, *virtually eliminating all germs.* Diaper tables are an example of items that should be disinfected. For a disinfectant solution to work effectively, the instructions must be adhered to rigorously. To be effective, disinfecting products require a certain concentration of solution and must remain in contact with the contaminated item for a specific time period. The Environmental Protection Agency (EPA) regulates the use of disinfectants. To avoid confusing a cleaning agent with a disinfecting agent, look on the label. Products possessing properties capable of disinfecting will state so on the label and will also show EPA approval.

If you are mixing your own disinfecting solutions, the National Health and Safety Performance Standards for Child Care recommends ¼ cup of bleach in 1 gallon of water. Mix fresh daily. To avoid creating a poisonous gas, never mix bleach with anything other than water.

Chlorine bleach solutions have been known to aggravate asthma or other respiratory conditions. Some care providers are concerned with the potential toxic effects of common household products used abundantly in an early care environment. There are several effective natural disinfecting products on the market. Check your local health food stores for a variety of products currently available, or refer to the recommended resource section at the end of this chapter.

## DIAPER CHANGING PROCEDURES

Frequent changing assures comfort and prevents skin irritations. Check each child's diaper status upon arrival. Two-year-old children require a diaper change at least four times during an 8–9 hour shift to assure comfort and prevent skin irritations. Absolute cleanliness during diaper changes is of primary importance. Do not use areas that come in close contact with children during play, such as couches, play room floor areas, etc. Many viruses and infections are easily spread from child to child. Diseases can be carried by people who are completely without symptoms and be passed on to another, causing severe diarrhea to the point of dehydration, hospitalization, and lengthy illness. Employing the procedures outlined in Figure 4–1 for disposable diaper changes and Figure 4–2 for cloth diaper changes will ensure that you and the little ones will remain healthy.

Diaper changing time is a wonderful opportunity for sharing one-on-one moments. This is a repetitive routine performed many times a day and can be a great opportunity for

## Diaper Changing Procedures for Disposable Diapers

**Supplies:** Disposable nonabsorbent gloves, nonabsorbent paper liner, disposable wipes removed from container, child's personally labeled ointments (under medical direction), diapers, cotton balls, plastic bags, tissues, physician-prescribed lotions, lidded hands-free plastic-lined trash container, soap, disinfectant, and paper towels.

Use a nonabsorbent changing surface. Avoid dangerous falls: keep a hand on baby at all times and never leave alone. In emergency, put child on floor or take with you.

| | **Steps for Changing Disposable Diapers** | | | | |
|---|---|---|---|---|---|
| 1 | Wash hands with soap and water. | 2 | Gather supplies. | 3 | Put on disposable waterproof gloves (if used). |
| 4 | Cover diapering surface with nonabsorbent paper liner. | 5 | Place baby on prepared diapering area (minimize contact: hold baby away from your body if extremely wet or soiled). | 6 | Put soiled clothes in a plastic bag. |
| 7 | Unfasten diaper. Leave soiled diaper under the child. | 8 | Gently wash baby's bottom. Remove stool and urine from front to back, and use a fresh wipe each time. Dispose directly in designated receptacle. | 9 | Fold soiled diaper inward and place in designated receptacle followed by the disposable gloves (if used). |
| 10 | Use disposable wipe to clean surface of caregiver's hands and another to clean the child's. | 11 | Check for spills on paper. If present, fold over so fresh part is under buttocks. | 12 | Place clean diaper under baby. |
| 13 | Using a cotton ball or tissue, apply skin ointment to clean, dry area if indicated/ordered. | 14 | Fasten diaper and dress with fresh clothing. | 15 | Wash baby's hands with soap and water between 60°F and 120°F for 15–20 seconds and dry. Turn faucet off with a paper towel, then place baby in a safe location. |
| 16 | Clean and disinfect diapering area, leaving bleach solution in contact at least 2 minutes. Allow table to air dry, or wipe it after 2 minutes. | 17 | Wash your hands with soap and water for at least 15–20 seconds. Turn off faucet with paper towel. | 18 | Chart diaper change and any observations. |

Adapted from: Standard 3.014 Diaper Changing Procedure. *Caring for our children, National health and safety performance standards* (2nd ed.). Used with permission, American Academy of Pediatrics.

**FIGURE 4–1** Diaper Changing Procedures for Disposable Diapers

### Diaper Changing Procedures for Cloth Diapers

**Supplies:** Disposable nonabsorbent gloves, nonabsorbent paper liner, disposable wipes removed from container, child's personally labeled ointments (under medical direction), diapers, cotton balls, plastic bags, tissues, physician-prescribed lotions, lidded hands-free plastic-lined trash container, soap, disinfectant, and paper towels.

*Soiled Diapers:Contain in a labeled and washable plastic-lined receptacle that is tightly lidded and hands-free only. Don't require separate bags. However, any soiled diapers sent home are to be secured in a plastic bag, separately bagged from soiled clothing. Clean and disinfect receptacle daily and dispose of waste water in toilet or floor drain only.*

Use a nonabsorbent changing surface. Avoid dangerous falls: keep a hand on baby at all times and never leave alone. In emergency, put child on floor or take with you.

| Steps for Changing Cloth Diapers | | | | | |
|---|---|---|---|---|---|
| 1 | Wash hands with liquid soap and water. | 2 | Gather supplies. | 3 | Put on disposable waterproof gloves (if used). |
| 4 | Cover diapering surface with nonabsorbent paper liner. | 5 | Place baby on prepared diapering area (minimize contact: hold baby away from your body if extremely wet or soiled). | 6 | Put soiled clothes in a plastic bag. |
| 7 | Unfasten diaper. Leave soiled diaper under the child. Close each safety pin immediately out of child's reach. Never hold pins in mouth. | 8 | Gently wash baby's bottom. Remove stool and urine from front to back, and use a fresh wipe each time. Dispose directly in designated receptacle. | 9 | Fold soiled diaper inward and place in designated receptacle followed by the disposable gloves (if used). |
| 10 | Use disposable wipe to clean surface of caregiver's hands and another to clean the child's. | 11 | Check for spills on paper. If present, fold over so fresh part is under buttocks. | 12 | Place clean diaper under baby. |
| 13 | Using a cotton ball or tissue, apply skin ointment to clean, dry area if indicated/ordered. | 14 | Fasten diaper with pins, placing your hand between the child and the diaper on insertion, and dress with fresh clothing. | 15 | Wash baby's hands with soap and water between 60°F and 120°F for 15–20 seconds and dry. Turn faucet off with a paper towel, then place baby in a safe location. |
| 16 | Clean and disinfect diapering area, leaving bleach solution in contact at least 2 minutes. Allow table to air dry, or wipe it after 2 minutes. | 17 | Wash your hands with soap and water for at least 15–20 seconds. Turn off faucet with paper towel. | 18 | Chart diaper change and any observations. |

Adapted from: Standard 3.014 Diaper Changing Procedure. *Caring for our children, National health and safety performance standards* (2nd ed.). Used with permission, American Academy of Pediatrics.

**FIGURE 4–2** Diaper Changing Procedures for Cloth Diapers

a special visit to talk one-on-one about things the two-year-old is experiencing in his or her day. Meaningful experiences with the child can be missed if care is not taken to be fully present during this time. Use this occasion to listen, talk, or sing with each two-year-old. Plan specific *Sharing Time* subjects to discuss with the two-year-old, or choose interesting pictures, and change them often. Post them near the diaper changing table for all staff to use. Describe your actions to the child, such as "Tom, you love to have your diaper changed. A dry diaper will feel so nice!" This can be a very vulnerable time for children, and how we treat them communicates our attitude toward them. They will develop feelings of acceptance and security in a kind and respectful climate.

The suggested diaper changing equipment and details for creating a diaper changing area are listed in Chapter 2, "Creating and Organizing a Two-year-old Room." Requirements for diaper changes vary from state to state. Some states, for instance, allow caregivers to change diapers in the infant's personally assigned crib; others allow caregivers to choose whether to use disposable gloves. According to *Standard 3.014 Diaper Changing Procedure, Caring for Our Children National Health and Safety Performance Standards 2nd edition*, the following diaper changes should be posted in the changing area and shall be used as part of staff evaluation of caregivers who do diaper changing:

- Child caregivers shall never leave a child alone on a table or countertop, even for an instant.
- A safety strap or harness shall not be used on the diaper changing table.
- If an emergency arises, caregivers shall put the child on the floor or take the child with them.

**Step 1:** Get organized. Before you bring the child to the diaper changing area, wash your hands, gather and bring what you need to the diaper changing table:

- Nonabsorbent paper liner large enough to cover the changing surface from the child's shoulders to beyond the child's feet;
- Fresh diaper, clean clothes (if you need them);
- Wipes for cleaning the child's genitalia and buttocks removed from the container or dispensed so the container will not be touched during diaper changing;
- A plastic bag for any soiled clothes;
- Disposable gloves, if you plan to use them (put gloves on before handling soiled clothing or diapers);
- A thick application of any diaper cream (when appropriate) removed from the container to a piece of disposable material such as facial or toilet tissue.

**Step 2:** Carry the child to the changing table, keeping soiled clothing away from you and any surfaces you cannot easily clean and sanitize after the change.

- Always keep a hand on the child;
- If the child's feet cannot be kept out of the diaper or from contact with soiled skin during the changing process, remove the child's shoes and socks so the child does not contaminate these surfaces with stool or urine during the diaper changing;
- Put soiled clothes in a plastic bag and securely tie the plastic bag to send the soiled clothes home.

**Step 3:** Clean the child's diaper area.

- Place the child on the diaper change surface and unfasten the diaper but leave the soiled diaper under the child;

■ If safety pins are used, close each pin immediately once it is removed and keep pins out of the child's reach. Never hold pins in your mouth;

■ Older two-year-olds are very active and mobile and sometimes they would rather wrestle than have their diaper changed; A great technique that will often calm them involves giving them an object that is easy to sanitize, to hold and manipulate while you accomplish your mission;

■ Lift the child's legs as needed to use disposable wipes to clean the skin on the child's genitalia and buttocks; Remove stool and urine from front to back and use a fresh wipe each time; Put the soiled wipes into the soiled diaper or directly into a plastic-lined, hands-free covered can.

**STEP 4:** Remove the soiled diaper without contaminating any surface not already in contact with stool or urine.

■ Fold the soiled surface of the diaper inward . . .

■ Put soiled disposable diapers in a covered, plastic-lined, hands-free covered can. If reusable cloth diapers are used, put the soiled cloth diaper and its contents (without emptying or rinsing) in a plastic bag or into a plastic-lined, hands-free covered can to give to parents or laundry service.

■ If gloves were used, remove them using the proper technique and put them into a plastic-lined, hands-free covered can.

■ Whether or not gloves were used, use a disposable wipe to clean the surfaces of the caregiver's hands and another to clean the child's hands, and put the wipes into the plastic-lined, hands-free covered can.

■ Check for spills under the child. If there are any, use the paper that extends under the child's feet to fold over the disposable paper so a fresh, unsoiled paper surface is now under the child's buttocks.

**STEP 5:** Put on a clean diaper and dress the child.

■ Slide a fresh diaper under the child.

■ Use a facial or toilet tissue to apply any necessary diaper creams, discarding the tissue in a covered, plastic-lined, hands-free covered can.

■ Note and plan to report any skin problems such as redness, skin cracks, or bleeding.

■ Fasten the diaper. If pins are used, place your hand between the child and the diaper when inserting the pin.

**STEP 6:** Wash the child's hands and return the child to a supervised area.

■ Use soap and water, no less than 60° F and no more than 120° F, at a sink to wash the child's hands, if you can.

■ If a child is too heavy to hold for hand washing or cannot stand at the sink, use commercial disposable diaper wipes or follow this procedure:

■ Wipe the child's hands with a damp paper towel moistened with a drop of liquid soap.

■ Wipe the child's hands with a paper towel wet with clear water.

■ Dry the child's hands with a paper towel.

**STEP 7:** Clean and sanitize the diaper-changing surface.

■ Dispose of the disposable paper liner used on the diaper changing surface in a plastic-lined, hands-free covered can.

- Clean any visible soil from the changing surface with detergent and water; rinse with water.

- Wet the entire changing surface with the sanitizing solution (e.g., spray a sanitizing bleach solution of ¼ cup of household liquid chlorine bleach in one gallon of tap water, mixed fresh daily).

- Put away the spray bottle of sanitizer. If the recommended bleach dilution is sprayed as a sanitizer on the surface, leave it in contact with the surface for at least 2 minutes. The surface can be left to air dry or can be wiped dry after 2 minutes of contact with the bleach solution.

**STEP 8:** Wash your hands and record the diaper change in the child's daily log.

Record the diaper change and detail any skin irritation, loose stools, unusual odors, blood in the stool or elimination concerns on the Child's Transitioning Report and/or the Diaper Changing Schedule. If you are concerned with any of your findings, share this information with the director or lead teacher.

## PRACTICING DIAPER RETURN DEMONSTRATIONS

In a medical setting it is common for the personnel to employ the use of *return practice demonstrations* for procedures requiring sterile or hygienic techniques. Sterile and hygienic practices require a specific order when carrying out the procedures. Cutting corners by leaving out parts of a routine procedure will compromise the integrity of the hygienic practice.

Although most child care programs are not medical programs, the adoption of some notable medical practices makes sense. Diaper changing sessions consume a large part of every day in a two-year-old room. The very nature of repeating a task over and over can become monotonous at times, thus lending itself to a break in procedure. A breakdown in procedure will seriously compromise the hygienic practices necessary for positive health promotion in the two-year-old group.

Adopt the habit of observing all child care personnel perform a return practice demonstration for diapers on a regular basis for an observation record to be used during the return practice demonstration procedure. In smaller program settings, observation could be practiced on a quarterly basis. In larger centers involving a broader range of staffing, or one that is experiencing high turnover rates, employ once per month return practice demonstration procedures. The practice will keep everyone's diaper changing techniques sharp. It will also help shy personnel build their demonstration confidence for those occasional visits and observations conducted by the licensing agencies.

## TOILET TRAINING

Most early care and education professionals and medical experts agree that many two-year-old children are beginning to show an interest in toileting, and by age 2½, most are ready to master the task of toilet training. In past generations, it was expected of parents to have their children trained before two years of age. Parents are often pressured by older family members to conform to these outdated ideas, and this often becomes the driving force behind initiating toilet training before the two-year-old is ready. By age two, many children have developed sphincter control for urine and bowel movement. The teacher and their families might notice the children experiencing longer periods of dryness. Some children might begin to notice other children using the toilet, and express an interest to copy their behavior. Two-year-old children learn a great deal through imitation.

# Return Practice Demonstration for Disposable Diapering Procedures

Name: _____Tyra (Enter last name)_____     Date: ____01-24____

Observer: _____Ms. Kendall_____

*Procedure:*

____✓____  Wash hands with liquid soap and water.

____✓____  Gather supplies.

____✓____  Put on disposable waterproof gloves (if used).

____✓____  Cover diapering surface with nonabsorbent paper liner.

____✓____  Place baby on prepared diapering area (to minimize contact: hold baby away from your body if extremely wet or soiled).

____✓____  Put soiled clothes in a plastic bag.

____✓____  Unfasten diaper, leave soiled diaper under the child.

____✓____  Gently wash baby's bottom. Remove stool and urine from front to back, and use a fresh wipe each time. Dispose directly in designated receptacle.

____✓____  Fold soiled diaper inward and place in designated receptacle followed by the disposable gloves (if used).

____✓____  Use disposable wipe to clean surface of your hand, and another to clean the child's.

____✓____  Check for spills on paper. If present, fold over so fresh part is under buttocks.

____✓____  Place clean diaper under baby.

____✓____  Using a cotton ball or tissue, apply skin ointment to clean, dry area if indicated/ordered.

____✓____  Fasten diaper and dress baby with fresh clothing.

____✓____  Wash baby's hands with soap and water between 60°F and 120°F for 15–20 seconds and dry. Turn faucet off with a paper towel, then place baby in a safe location.

____✓____  Clean and disinfect diaper surface, leaving bleach solution in contact for at least 2 minutes. Allow table to air dry, or wipe after 2 minutes.

____✓____  Wash your hands with soap and water for at least 15–20 seconds. Turn off faucet with paper towel.

____✓____  Chart diaper change and any observations.

**FIGURE 4–3** Return Practice Demonstration for Disposable Diapering Procedures

# Return Practice Demonstration for Cloth Diapering Procedures

Name: _____Tyra (Enter last name)_____     Date: ____01-24____

Observer: ____Mrs. Kendall____

*Procedure:*

___✓___  Wash hands with liquid soap and water.

___✓___  Gather supplies.

___✓___  Put on disposable waterproof gloves (if used).

___✓___  Cover diapering surface with nonabsorbent paper liner.

___✓___  Place baby on prepared diapering area (to minimize contact, hold baby away from your body if extremely wet or soiled).

___✓___  Put soiled clothes in a plastic bag.

___✓___  Unfasten diaper, leave soiled diaper under the child. Close each safety pin immediately and place out of child's reach. Never hold pins in your mouth.

___✓___  Gently wash baby's bottom. Remove stool and urine from front to back, and use a fresh wipe each time. Dispose directly in designated receptacle.

___✓___  Fold soiled diaper inward and place in designated receptacle followed by the disposable gloves (if used).

___✓___  Use disposable wipe to clean surface of your hand, and another to clean the child's.

___✓___  Check for spills on paper. If present, fold over so fresh part is under buttocks.

___✓___  Place clean diaper under baby.

___✓___  Using a cotton ball or tissue, apply skin ointment to clean, dry area if indicated/ ordered.

___✓___  Fasten diaper with pins, placing your hand between the child and the diaper on insertion, and dress the baby with fresh clothing.

___✓___  Wash baby's hands with soap and water between 60°F and 120°F for 15–20 seconds and dry. Turn faucet off with a paper towel, then place baby in a safe location.

___✓___  Clean and disinfect diaper surface, leaving bleach solution in contact for at least 2 minutes. Allow table to air dry, or wipe it after 2 minutes.

___✓___  Wash your hands with soap and water for at least 15–20 seconds. Turn off faucet with paper towel.

___✓___  Chart diaper change and any observations.

**FIGURE 4–4** Return Practice Demonstration for Cloth Diapering Procedures

It is worthwhile to note that some young two-year-olds might express a curiosity, but are not ready to make the commitment yet. In other words, their play time might be a bigger priority to them than preserving a clean and dry diaper. Two and one-half-year-old Alexander was very interested in his new potty chair. For the first few days he ran to his teacher every time she called the children over for toilet time. He beamed a smile as he received a great deal of praise for accomplishing his toilet task like a big boy. Soon after his initial success, he seemed to lose interest. Now, when the teacher called him from the block section or his art activity, he ignored her and would cry loudly if she attempted to coax him to the toilet. After a few days of this behavior, Ms. Adrienne, with permission from Alexander's mother, had a frank conversation with Alex. She asked him if he would rather resume wearing diapers again for a while and try toilet training another time. Little Alex seemed relieved and happily accepted his diaper. Close to his third birthday, his mother and father asked Alex if he would like some superhero underwear. He seemed excited. Within in one week Alexander mastered the use of his potty chair, without any tears, and no longer needed diapers.

When to begin toilet training is not always a clear-cut decision. Many parents and teachers often choose a season of year when the children can wear clothes that are easy for them to manage. If you live in a climate where the cold weather season is lengthy, this might not be a practical solution. It is important to pay attention to the signs of readiness and be prepared to encourage the child once he or she exhibits a desire to try. As noted in the example, the process can be stopped at any time and begun at a later date if the child changes his or her mind, or isn't developmentally mature enough to accept the responsibility. When parents feel frustrated that their child is not interested, show them additional materials about toilet training. If their frustration continues, they can discuss the issue with their child's pediatrician. Set aside a time to discuss a plan with the two-year-old's family. This is a great topic to discuss at a two-year-old parenting class, parent-teacher conference, or parent round table. Such a class will provide families with helpful information and generate active discussions. Advanced preparation increases the probability of more positive toilet training experiences and, in the long run, saves the staff and the families the time and frustration caused by unrealistic expectations for the two-year-old.

Toilet training is a collaborative effort that requires an open line of communication between home and the center. If at any time the toilet training is met with resistance, it bears slowing the process or stopping completely until the two-year-old has time to mature. Encourage parents to bring several changes of clothing, socks, training pants, and plastic pant covers. Disposable training pants are available and are constructed for the two-year-old to pull up and down with ease. Some programs and licensing agencies require the use of disposables, to protect other children from harmful exposure brought on by an "accident." Disposables are well-padded and will contain accidents during the course of training. Disposable training pants are the most expensive option, but most parents already use disposable diapers and feel the added expense and laundry time makes them a reasonable choice. Sometimes the absorbent materials used in the disposable training pants mask the feeling of wetness and reduces the two-year-old's ability to distinguish between wet and dry. Choose clothing that is easy to remove or manage during toilet breaks.

An example of a typical toilet training sheet used to record progress can be found on Figure 4–5. Duplicate the blank *toilet training sheet* template provided in the Forms and Templates Appendix. You can use it to record the daily progress of each child. Review this sheet with the parents over the course of the next few weeks to determine if the two-year-old continues to demonstrate interest, and is progressing. It is very normal to expect a two-year-old to experience occasional accidents for the next few years.

# TOILET TRAINING

**Child's Name:** _Grace (Enter last name)_

**Lead Teacher:** _Mrs. Carla_       **Date:** _June 3_

| Time | Wet | B.M. | Dry | Refused | Seemed Confused | Comments |
|---|---|---|---|---|---|---|
| 6:00 – 6:30 | | | | | | |
| 6:30 – 7:00 | | | | | | |
| 7:00 – 7:30 | | | | | | |
| 7:30 – 8:00 | | | | | | Arrived |
| 8:00 – 8:30 | ✓ | | | | | |
| 8:30 – 9:00 | | | ✓ | | | |
| 9:00 – 9:30 | | | ✓ | | | |
| 9:30 – 10:00 | | | ✓ | | | |
| 10:00 – 10:30 | ✓ | ✓ | | | | |
| 10:30 – 11:00 | | | ✓ | | | |
| 11:00 – 11:30 | | | ✓ | | | |
| 11:30 – 12:00 | | | | | | Nap time Diaper |
| 12:00 – 12:30 | | | | | | |
| 12:30 – 1:00 | | | | | | |
| 1:00 – 1:30 | | | | | | |
| 1:30 – 2:00 | | | | | | |
| 2:00 – 2:30 | | | | | | Awake |
| 2:30 – 3:00 | ✓ | | | | | |
| 3:00 – 3:30 | | | | ✓ | | |
| 3:30 – 4:00 | | ✓ | | | | Accident Changed Clothing |
| 4:00 – 4:30 | | | | | | |
| 4:30 – 5:00 | | | ✓ | | | |
| 5:00 – 5:30 | | | | | | Home at 5:10 |
| 5:30 – 6:00 | | | | | | |
| 6:00 – 6:30 | | | | | | |
| 6:30 – 7:00 | | | | | | |
| 7:00 – 7:30 | | | | | | |
| 7:30 – 8:00 | | | | | | |

**FIGURE 4–5** Toilet Training

## STORING PERSONAL BELONGINGS/SANITATION STORAGE

If the parents are supplying diapers and disposable training pants, ask them to also provide disposable diapers in unopened packages to maintain proper sanitation. Avoid storing the diapers on the floor. Store clothing, diapers, training pants, and personal items for each child in an individual container or cubby locker. Do not allow one child's personal belongings to touch another child's. This habit will reduce the potential cross-contamination of other children's personal items, from germs or infestation, caused by contagious conditions such as head lice (pediculosis) or scabies.

## HANDLING WET AND SOILED CLOTHING

When the child's clothing becomes wet or soiled, remove the soiled item and replace it with something clean and dry. Secure the soiled article of clothing in a plastic bag and store it where the parents will find it at the time of departure. If the item is a soiled cloth diaper, secure it in a bag separate from the other articles of clothing. In order to ensure that the clothing is not damaged or misplaced, do not launder any of the soiled clothing you remove from the two-year-old. Each parent has his or her own personal way of laundering clothing. To avoid mildew or permanent stains, send soiled clothing home promptly. To prevent future misunderstandings with parents when items are returned to them soiled, share this policy and rationale with them at the time of enrollment.

## HAND WASHING PROCEDURES

Frequent hand washing is a cornerstone for a healthy early care and education program. Proper hand washing prevents the spread of many communicable diseases such as E. coli (found largely in feces), hepatitis, giardia, pinworms, and a host of many more common ailments. All are spread through a fecal–oral route (anus to mouth).

Giardiasis and pinworms are the two most common parasitic infections among children in the United States; its prevalence among children in daycare centers may range from 17 percent to over 50 percent during outbreaks (Bartlett and others, 1991). Wong (1999) notes "Hand washing is the single most effective and critical measure and control of hepatitis in any setting" (p. 1577).

The best defense for reducing the spread of illness is consistent hand washing habits. Hand washing procedures (see Figure 4–6) are recommended for staff and children in such circumstances as: before and after playing in the sand and water table; after playing with pets; after playing outdoors; before and after preparing bottles or serving food; before and after diapering or toileting; before and after administering first aid; before and after giving medication; before working with children and at the end of the day; before leaving the classroom for a break; after wiping nose discharge, coughing, or sneezing. Check with your local licensing agency for any other requirements in your area.

Install liquid soap with a pump or a dispenser, and disposable paper towels near the sink. The National Center for Infectious Diseases (2000) encourages us to "turn on the warm water [regulated by an anti-scald device] and adjust accordingly to achieve a comfortable temperature. Wet hands and apply liquid soap. Rub hands vigorously for approximately 15–20 seconds. Be sure to wash under rings and the nails. It is the soap combined with the scrubbing action that helps dislodge and remove germs. Rinse hands well and dry hands with a clean disposable paper towel. Use a disposable paper towel to turn off the faucet to avoid recontamination of your clean hands. Dispose of the paper towel in a lidded trash receptacle with a plastic liner. A trash can operated with a foot mechanism is

**Posted Hand Washing Procedures**

| 1 | Turn on warm water and adjust to comfortable temperature. | 2 | Wet hands and apply soap. | 3 | Wash vigorously for approximately 15–20 seconds. |
|---|---|---|---|---|---|
| 4 | Dry hands with paper towel. | 5 | Turn off faucet with paper towel. | 6 | Dispose of paper towel in a lidded trash receptacle with a plastic liner. |

Use hand washing procedures for staff and children

- before and after preparing bottles or serving food.
- before and after diapering or toileting.
- before and after administering first aid.
- before and after giving medication.
- before working with the children and at the end of the day.
- before leaving the classroom for a break.
- after wiping nose discharge, coughing, or sneezing.
- before and after playing in the sand and water table.
- after playing with pets.
- after playing outdoors.

Reprinted with permission from the National Association of Child Care Professionals, http:www.naccp.org.

**FIGURE 4–6** Posted Hand Washing Procedures

an expensive option, yet the hands-free action reduces the possibility of recontaminating clean hands.

Install sinks with running hot (regulated by an anti-scald device) and cold water, installed at the children's height to promote frequent use. Two-year-olds can move about the room quickly, and they are fascinated with a source of water at a sink or in a toilet. Install an *off* and *on* water valve at the teachers' height to prevent curious infants from unscheduled water play. Close bathroom doors when not in use and, to avoid a potential drowning, do not leave buckets of water unattended.

Disinfect toilet seats, diapering areas, and water fountains with 10 percent solution of bleach and water (one part chlorine bleach to 9 parts water), or any registered EPA disinfectant prepared according to instructions. Registered EPA approval is displayed on the product label.

## EMPLOYING UNIVERSAL PRECAUTIONS AND THE PROPER USE OF GLOVES

In 1991, the Occupational Safety and Health Association (OSHA) established a blood-borne pathogen standard mandating measures to protect employees from exposure to potentially infected blood pathogens. *Hepatitis B (HBV)* and *Human Immunodeficiency Virus (HIV)* are the two most common sources of blood-borne pathogens. HBV is a disease of the liver contracted by exposure to contaminated blood, causing inflammation and destruction of the liver and, if not cured, eventually leading to death. HIV is a disease that is contracted by contaminated body fluids, and has the potential to lead to AIDS, which destroys the human immune system.

Center staff is commonly exposed to body fluids in the form of urine, feces, vomitus, sweat, saliva, breast milk, and nasal secretions. It is difficult to stress the importance of using universal precautions without sounding a fear alarm. Contracting a case of HIV/AIDS is highly unlikely; in fact, Kinnell reports, "the Center for Disease Control and Prevention stated 'we have never documented a case of HIV being transmitted through biting.'" Because it is impossible to know when a person is infected with such a disease, *all* body fluids or secretions *must* be treated as if they are infected with disease.

If a situation occurs that involves exposure to another persons' body fluids, put on a pair of disposable, moisture-proof gloves before making contact with the contaminated source. To avoid delaying immediate intervention and increasing risk for the child, yet protect yourself from harmful exposure, place gloves in several convenient areas so they can be retrieved in a moment's notice. To avoid contaminating yourself with soiled gloves, you must take care to remove them properly. Instructions for proper gloving procedures are located in the Forms and Templates Appendix. Post this next to the first aid directives for a quick reference. Follow your center's policies for disposal of contaminated supplies and equipment.

## DENTAL HYGIENE

The Center for Disease Control and Prevention offers several recommendations for tooth care for young children. It is recommended to begin cleaning teeth early with a small, soft toothbrush. Young children are not capable of holding a brush and will require assistance. Until they are two years of age, avoid fluoride toothpastes unless the child's dentist recommends it. Use only a small pea-sized amount of toothpaste. Teach children to spit out and rinse after brushing. The toothbrushes need to be stored in a properly ventilated individual container, and labeled with each child's name. In some states, the toothbrushes are to be stored so they can air dry. The brushes should not touch each other, to avoid cross contamination. Children need to brush at least twice a day to remove food particles and prevent plaque buildup. Discard and replace the toothbrush each time a child experiences a serious cold, flu, fever or other communicable disease in order to avoid a cycle of recontamination. Involve the parents when planning a schedule. It might be more feasible to have their two-year-old brush in the morning before coming to the center, and in the evening after their family dinner. The center staff can promote positive oral care habits by providing water for the little children to rinse with after eating. Refer to the American Dental Association (ADA) www.ada.org Web site to find helpful information to share with the children's families that promotes positive dental hygiene habits.

## CLEANSING THE TOYS AND EQUIPMENT

A great deal of activity occurs in an early care and teaching environment. The equipment and toys are handled by many little hands every day. Establishing regular cleaning routines that employ general hygiene practices will reduce the spread of germs and infectious diseases. Wash the surfaces of soiled equipment and toys with soap and water. Disinfect the toys with a sanitizing solution such as bleach solution 50 parts per million (approximately ½ teaspoon of chlorine bleach to one gallon of water). Submerge the toys in the bleach solution and air dry them. Make a fresh supply of solution every day to maintain the effectiveness of the disinfecting bleach agent. Once the toys have completely dried, they are ready for use again. Use this same preparation to sanitize high chairs, cribs, tables, and chairs.

## REFERENCES

American Academy of Pediatrics, American Public Health Association, National Resource Center for Health and Safety in Child Care (2002). *Stepping stones to using caring for our children, 2nd Edition.* Elk Grove Village, IL.: American Academy of Pediatrics.

National Center for Infectious Diseases. (2000). *An ounce of prevention: Keeps the germs away.* Retrieved August 3, 2005 from http://www.cdc.gov/ncidod/op/handwashing.htm

Wong, D. L. (1999). *Whaley & Wong's nursing care of infants and children.* St. Louis, MO: Mosby.

## RECOMMENDED RESOURCES

Church, D. S. (2004). *The wellness guide* (8th ed.). RM Barry Publications.

**CHAPTER**

# 5

## Health

To find your specific
State's Licensing, Rules
and Regulations go to:

**http://nrc.uchsc.edu**

## SICK BAY AND ISOLATION AREAS

Centers need to prepare a sick bay and an isolation area for sick children to rest until their parents or guardians can call for them. Equip a space or room (depending on state regulations) with a bed or cot, and a crib in an area where constant supervision can be administered. Sometimes space is very limited, and a cot in the director's office will have to suffice. If a bed is used, provide several changes of linens, each to be used for one child only. Select a variety of toys and books to offer the little ones until their departure. Provide a thermometer to measure body temperatures and a container large enough to catch emesis, in case the child vomits. Place a child-size chair in the area so the child can sit while you administer first aid. Medication is most conveniently stored close to the sick bay and isolation area, in a medication/first aid cabinet and a small refrigerator. The refrigerator should hold a container and lid labeled "refrigerated medications only," along with ice in baggies or cold packs, popsicles (for mouth and lip injuries), juice boxes, and fresh drinking water.

## FIRST AID CABINET AND FIRST AID KITS

Minor injuries are common in a center setting. Children will experience scratches and bumps as they go about their activities of daily living. Prepare a first aid cabinet and kits to use in the event of an accident. As previously mentioned, it is convenient to provide a first aid cabinet near the sick bay area used to isolate sick children. The first aid cabinet must remain locked at all times so it is not accessible to the children, but is accessible to the staff in a moment's notice. If your center transports by bus or van, then provide a complete first aid kit in the vehicle. Stock the first aid cabinet with disposable nonporous gloves, the American Red Cross first aid manual or American Academy of Pediatrics (AAP) standard first aid chart, or an equivalent first aid guide. Other items to include are a non-glass thermometer, bandages, band aids, sterile gauze pads, triangular cloth splint, plastic splint for immobilizing a limb, scissors, tweezers, safety pins, adhesive strips, disposable apron, protective glasses, and a pocket mouth-to-mouth resuscitation mask to open an airway.

Causing vomiting when a caustic or corrosive substance has been swallowed can cause further physical damage; for this reason, best practices no longer recommend the use of syrup of ipecac in child care facilities.

Provide a source of running water and soap near the first aid station to cleanse wounds. The playground is another area that should have a convenient source of first aid supplies. Some centers find it convenient to hang a fanny pack in each classroom near the door so the teacher can wear it on the playground; use it in the classroom for minor injuries and on field trips. Because accidents on the playground often involve blood, the teacher will need to immediately employ universal precautions before handling the child.

If a fanny pack is not used, another option on the playground can be to install a mailbox on a post and stock it with items such as disposable nonporous gloves, tissues, wipes, plastic trash bags, sterile gauze pads, and band aids. The mailbox will keep the items dry until they are needed.

## MANAGING MEDICATIONS

Administering medications in a center is a common practice, one that requires special attention to detail. In some states, all personnel distributing medication must take a special class and earn a certification. Check your local regulations for your area mandates.  Instruct all personnel to always wash their hands before beginning, make sure they have the correct child by name, and match the name to the label on the prescription. Double-check the proper dose. Always use a medication spoon or measuring spoon to be certain the proper dosage is administered. Check the expiration date on the label. Follow the instructions for how frequently the medication should be given, and if it should be given before or after eating. Once the medication is given, document it on the Daily Medication record. The details for using the Daily Medication record are explained further in this chapter, and an example is provided in Figure 5–2.

Medications prescribed for an individual child must be kept in the original container bearing the original pharmacy label that shows the prescription number, the date it was filled, the physician's name, directions for use, and the child's name. Send medication back home every day with the child. If the child requires a repeat dosage the following day, begin  with fresh instructions from the family. Do not rely on information from the previous day. For the protection of the child and yourself, do not give any over-the-counter medications without prior written approval from both the child's physician and the parents. Written permission from the parents and the child's physician is a standard required by most states. Check with your licensing consultant.

Occasionally, a child will develop symptoms of illness such as high fever, persistent cough, or ear pain caused by an infection. Although most programs are not equipped to provide continuous sick care, there often is a lapse in time before the parent or guardian can arrive to attend to the ill child. It takes time to locate working parents, especially if they are out in the field. Sometimes parents are delayed waiting for a suitable replacement at their place of work, for example, if the parent is a nurse or a firefighter. Before such a situation occurs, collect pre-signed medically approved physician orders for fever-reducing medications, using the Medical Authorization for Nonprescription Medications form (see Figure 5–1 for an example). Make sure this complies with your state rules and regulations.  Only give medications with this pre-approved authorization and under the written directions of the parents. Use the Daily Medication sheet to document the administration of medications throughout the day (see Figure 5–2 for an example). The sheet includes the date, child's name, the type of medication, how much medication should be administered, and the route of administration, such as by mouth, in the eyes, ears, or rectum, and how often to repeat it. Sign the record with your full name and the time you administer the medication to maintain an accurate medication history. Store all medications requiring refrigeration in a container with a secure lid labeled with the words "refrigerated medications only." Store any medications that do not require refrigeration in a locked cabinet that is inaccessible to the children.

Figure 5–3 provides a flowchart for creating a file box in which to store copies of the Medical Authorization for Nonprescription Medications form. Since you will need to refer to the permission slips quite frequently, it is helpful to store them where there is easy

## Medical Authorization
## for Nonprescription Medication*

Name of Child: _____ Jessie (Enter Last Name) _____          Date: _____ 09-18-2009 _____

The staff is authorized to dispense the following medications as ordered by your physician and directed by the parents/guardian.

**Please indicate specific medication, route it is to be given, dosage, and frequency.**

| Type | Medication | Route | Dosage | Frequency |
|---|---|---|---|---|
| Nonaspirin Preparation | Tylenol | By mouth | .4cc | Every 4 hours over 101° as needed Send Home |
| Aspirin Preparation | | | | |
| Cough Preparation | Robitussin | By mouth | 1/2 tsp | Every 6 hours for persistent cough |
| Decongestant | | | | |
| Skin Ointment | Desitin | On perineum | Thin layer | Every diaper change when redness develops |
| Diaper Wipes | Any brand | As directed | | As needed |
| Sunscreen | Any brand | On skin | Small amount | Before outdoor play |
| | | | | |
| | | | | |

_____ Dr. Randall _____          _____ Dr. Randall _____          _____ XXX-XXX-XXXX _____
Print Name of Physician                 Signature of Physician                     Phone Number

_____ Mr. Howard _____
Parent/Guardian Signature

*Complete this form on admission and update annually.  Store medical authorizations in an index box and place in or near locked cabinet for quick referencing.

**FIGURE 5–1** Medical Authorization for Nonprescription Medication

**Daily Medication Sheet**

| Child's Name | RX Number & Type of Medication | Amount & Route Administered | Date | Time | Given By: | |
| --- | --- | --- | --- | --- | --- | --- |
| | | | | | First Name | Last Name |
| Camela (Enter Last Name) | RX 652201 Amoxicillin 250 Milligrams | 1 tsp by mouth | 02-22 | 11:00 am | Mrs. | Hoffriah |
| | | | | 5:00pm | Ms. | Szalay |
| | | | | | | |
| | | | | | | |
| | | | | | | |
| | | | | | | |
| | | | | | | |
| | | | | | | |
| | | | | | | |
| | | | | | | |
| | | | | | | |
| | | | | | | |
| | | | | | | |
| | | | | | | |
| | | | | | | |
| | | | | | | |
| | | | | | | |
| | | | | | | |
| | | | | | | |
| | | | | | | |

**FIGURE 5–2** Daily Medication Sheet

access, such as the locked medicine cabinet. Place the Daily Medication record on a clipboard near the Beginning the Day clipboard discussed in Chapter 7, "Facilitating Two-Year-Olds and Their Families." Place the clipboard at the entrance to your room or facility to enable the parents or guardian to record daily medication instructions.

Since most medications are required every 4–6 hours, or on schedules 3 or 4 times a day, create a schedule to administer the majority of medications at specific times. Specifying the times that medications are usually administered guides the parents to pick a schedule that makes sense for the center and also adheres to the proper time regimen advised for medications. Encourage the parents to administer the first dose in the morning before arriving. Mornings typically are very busy and the center staff is occupied with so many details already that a medication dosage can easily be missed. It is not uncommon, during the winter months, for the number of children on medications to increase substantially. Suggest that the center can be responsible for the midday dose, administered typically around lunchtime, and again around 4:00 or 5:00 PM, leaving the evening dose for the parents to administer. Adjust the dosing times if you are open for nontraditional hours. There will always be occasional exceptions to the scheduled times, such as a sudden need for an asthma treatment. By scheduling the majority of medication administration at the same time, the risk of missing treatments and doses is decreased, and the accuracy of administration is increased. In some states, it is a requirement that only one person administer medications and that this person must have received specific training before they assume that responsibility.

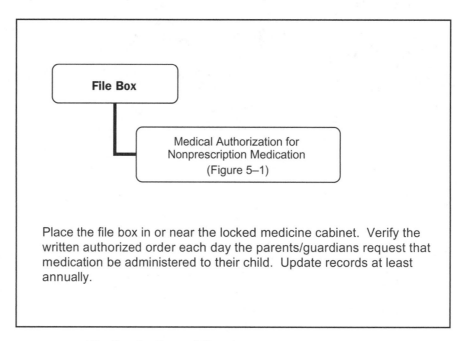

**FIGURE 5–3** File Box for Record Keeping

On a final note, if your program provides care for infants, medication schedules are better served by providing the infant room with a separate Daily Medication record. There are a myriad of reasons for this, including that infants' demand schedule for eating and sleeping is quite different from the other age groups. Unless you have a very small number of children in your program, separate the infants, Daily Medication record from the two-year-old through school age Daily Medication record.

## MEASURING BODY TEMPERATURES

If you suspect a child is overly warm or has an elevated temperature, measure and record the body temperature. The safest method for recording a child's temperature is to place the thermometer under the arm, also known as an *auxiliary* temperature. The average normal temperature for an auxiliary temperature is 97.4° F or 36.3° C. If you are using a plastic (non-glass) thermometer, be sure to shake the mercury reading below 98° F before measuring the baby's temperature. Hold the thermometer under the child's arm for ten minutes. Mercury is extremely toxic and can be a high risk hazard if the thermometer breaks and the mercury escapes. If that ever occurs, call Poison Control to receive specific instructions. To save time and provide convenience, many centers opt for a more expensive route and use either thermometer strips for the forehead or electronic thermometers. If you use an electronic thermometer, then hold it in place until you hear a beeping sound.

Report an elevated body temperature immediately. Initiate an illness report and notify the attending supervisor so that the parents/guardians can be contacted. Medicate if instructed by the parents, guardians, or physician. Record the child's temperature reading on a Suggested Illness record (see example on Figure 5–4). Continue checking the temperature every half hour to monitor any drastic changes. Children who have experienced elevated temperatures should not return to the group for 24 hours following the return to

## SUGGESTED ILLNESS

Child's name: ___*Courtney (Enter Last Name)*___    Date: ___*10/04/05*___

SYMPTOMS ARE:

___*102°*___    Body Temperature (under arm, add 1 degree)

_____    Vomiting

_____    Diarrhea

_____    Exhibiting signs of a communicable illness

_____    Skin condition requiring further treatment

Other: _____*Complaining her left ear hurts*_____

Report initiated by: _____*Mr. Eagle*_____

Were parents notified? Yes __✓__ No _____ By whom? *Ms. Gilreath*

Time parents notified:    1st Attempt _*1:30 pm*_    ___*Dad*___
                                                      Which Parent Notified

                          2nd Attempt _*1:35 pm*_    ___*Mom*___
                                                      Which Parent Notified

                          3rd Attempt _____    _____
                                                Which Parent Notified

Time child departed: ___*1:50 pm*___

Director's signature: _____*Mrs. Niehoff*_____

Children exhibiting a temperature that exceeds 100°F, symptoms of vomiting (1–3 forceful rushes), diarrhea (defined as watery, mucous, foul-smelling bowel movement), or an unrecognized rash shall not return to group care for a minimum of 24 hours after treatment or before symptoms subside.

1. Office Copy    2. Parent/Guardian Copy

**FIGURE 5–4** Suggested Illness Report

a normal range, unless advised differently by their physician. Review this written policy with the children's guardian(s) prior to an illness so they can prepare for substitute care in advance.

## IMMUNIZATIONS

To protect all children attending the center, medical authorities require they all have current immunizations. Since the recommended dosages and types of immunizations continually fluctuate, you can refer to the American Academy of Pediatrics Web site http://www.aap.org for the most recent schedule, or contact your state licensing representative. Sometimes a center encounters children who do not have current immunizations for a variety of reasons, such as medical conditions or religious preferences. If immunizations are withheld for either reason, obtain the specific reason in writing from the parent or legal guardian, the child's physician, and/or religious leader and keep it in the child's record. Special care should be taken to notify and exclude under-immunized children from the program if an active vaccine-preventable disease occurs in the facility.

## ALLERGIES AND POSTING ALLERGY NOTICES

Allergies are caused by a variety of culprits known as allergens. Some can be triggered by a range of substances, including: venom, nuts, latex, drugs, stings, pollen, dust, mold, animal dander, and shellfish. A severe reaction can occur quickly, usually within a few minutes. Severe reactions are usually dramatic, with symptoms such as swelling on the face, tight and difficult breathing, or hives that look like a red, blotchy rash on the skin. Mild allergic reactions are more common than severe ones. Milder allergic reactions display the same symptoms, but in much weaker forms, and take longer to develop. Local reactions such as swelling of an entire arm or leg can be severe, but are not commonly lethal. If the allergy is severe, recommend that the child wear a Medical Alert bracelet for immediate identification of the allergen if an exposure ever occurred. Severe reactions can be life-threatening. Anaphylactic shock will interfere with the child's ability to breathe very quickly. If a child is attending the center with a known anaphylactic shock history, then a kit for epinephrine injections should remain on premises and all staff should be familiar with how to administer it. Call 9-1-1 or the appropriate number if the two-year-old is exposed to a known allergen or is beginning to exhibit signs of a severe reaction. Milder reactions, although not life-threatening, will need a doctor's care, especially if the reaction has not occurred before.

On the KIDEX Individual Monthly Profile and Introduce Us to Your Two-Year-Old forms, a space is provided for listing and recording any allergies a child might have. Always post a list of all children and their known allergies in the KIDEX Class Book.

## ILLNESS RECORDS AND TRACKING ILLNESS REPORTS

Begin each day with a general health assessment of each child. Familiarity with each child will assist you in becoming a reliable detector of unusual physical symptoms. If a child has a pre-existing medical condition or a physical handicap, become familiar with that child's particular needs.

Minor illnesses are often exhibited by a change in a child's general appearance or behavior such as glassy eyes, flushed cheeks, swollen glands, or sluggish movements. Remove and isolate sick children from the group if they have a temperature that exceeds 100 degrees, symptoms of vomiting (1–3 forceful rushes), diarrhea (defined as watery, mucous, foul-smelling bowel movement), or an undiagnosed rash. If you suspect a child is exhibiting any of these symptoms, then complete an illness report with details and give to the director to initiate the next step. Once the director confirms the child is sick then take action to notify their parents.

Parents often feel frustration and guilt, coupled with anxiety, about missing work and having a sick child. Be certain the child is ill before disturbing the parents. If at any time a child is exposed to a communicable illness such as chicken pox, measles, etc., then post a notice on the current events bulletin board to properly notify parents and guardians. Descriptions for some common communicable illnesses and symptoms can be found in Chapter 7.

A local pediatrician once mentioned how much she appreciated written documentation accompanying a sick child who just arrived from the center. She indicated that, all too often, parents would bring the child to be examined with little or no information with regard to the symptoms the child had been experiencing. Provide the parents with a copy of the Suggested Illness report so they will have details in hand when they see the physician. Track reports of illnesses on a daily basis to help identify potential outbreak patterns that might be developing in the center. An example of how to track illnesses is shown in Figure 5–5.

| Illness Tracking Report | | | | | | | |
|---|---|---|---|---|---|---|---|
| **Name of Child** | **Time** | **Type of Illness** | **Person Reporting Illness** | **Director Notified** | **Report Filed** | **Parent Notified** | **Time Called** |
| Emily (Enter Last Name) | 12:30 pm | Fever 101° | Ms. Willis | ✓ | ✓ | ✓ | 1:30 pm |
| Jaden (Enter Last Name) | 11:00 am | Diarrhea | Ms. Sutton | ✓ | ✓ | ✓ | 11:15 am |
| Olivia (Enter Last Name) | 2:00 pm | Vomiting | Mr. Thurmond | ✓ | ✓ | ✓ | 2:30 pm |
| Marta (Enter Last Name) | 7:30 am | Ear Ache | Ms. Hiland | ✓ | ✓ | ✓ | 8:00 am |
| Chen (Enter Last Name) | 8:15 am | Headache | Ms. Day | ✓ | ✓ | ✓ | 8:45 am |
| Joshua (Enter Last Name) | 4:00pm | Split Lip | Mr. Law | ✓ | ✓ | ✓ | 4:30 pm |
| Andrew (Enter Last Name) | 4:30 pm | Fever 100° | Ms. Lane | ✓ | ✓ | ✓ | 4:45 pm |
| | | | | | | | |
| | | | | | | | |
| | | | | | | | |
| | | | | | | | |
| | | | | | | | |

**FIGURE 5–5** Illness Tracking Report

## HOW TO PREVENT A HEAD LICE INFESTATION

Whenever children are cared for in groups, an infestation of head lice is possible. Children with head lice infestation usually have older siblings that attend elementary school and unsuspectingly carry it home to their family. Head lice are a potential problem that can happen to anyone. Head lice can be picked up anywhere, at places such as movie theaters, on a bus, or airline seat. In a child care setting, a head lice infestation is more likely to occur if infested clothing touches other clothing.

To reduce the possibility of a head lice epidemic in your center, the program will need to be proactive and employ weekly head checks for every child. Figure 5–6 is an example of a completed Head Check sheet. Take measures to ensure that head check information remains confidential. Head checks need to occur on a different day each week to include all children attending, especially those with a part time schedule. Plan to administer head checks right after a nap period, when hair brushing and combing is already occurring. Make sure you are in a well-lit area. You might see a louse, but they move very quickly and you might only detect their eggs (nits). As you comb the hair, examine the hair roots for any nits. They often attach about ¼"–½" from the hair root. They are very tiny and translucent, and you can sometimes see through them. It is easy to distinguish between a nit and a hair flake. A nit will not move very easily because it is more firmly attached than a hair flake.

A head louse does not live very long without a warm-blooded host, in this case a human being. A head lice infestation can be treated by using special shampoos formulated to destroy the live nits and their eggs. Check with your local pharmacist for recommendations. Send all the bedding home with all the families.

### Head Lice Checklist

Group Name: _____The Peaches_____

| Name | Sunday | Monday | Tuesday | Wednesday | Thursday | Friday | Saturday |
|------|--------|--------|---------|-----------|----------|--------|----------|
|  |  | April 29 | May 1 | May 10 | May 18 | May 21 |  |
| Baily (Enter Last Name) |  | A | C | C | A | A |  |
| Emily (Enter Last Name) |  | C | C | C | C | C |  |
| Jared (Enter Last Name) |  | C | C | C | C | C |  |
| Jenni (Enter Last Name) |  | C | C | A | C | C |  |
| Mary (Enter Last Name) |  | C | C | C | C | C |  |
| Robert (Enter Last Name) |  | C | C | C | C | C |  |
| Kellie (Enter Last Name) |  | C | A | C | C | C |  |
| Erin (Enter Last Name) |  | C | C | C | C | C |  |
| Ian (Enter Last Name) |  | C | C | C | C | C |  |

C = Clear,               A = Absent               P = Possible

(**Reminder:** Please check weekly on different days of the week.)

**Figure 5–6** Head Lice Checklist

If you discover a child with a potential problem, contact the parent or guardian immediately and isolate the child from other children until the affected child departs. Send home all of the children's blankets, soft toys, pillows, hats, coats, and any other personal items that might harbor head lice or their eggs. Instruct the parents to launder all washable items in hot water and dry them at a high heat for at least twenty minutes. Non-washable items can be bagged in plastic trash bags and left for a week or so before using them again. Sprays are available to kill the lice and eggs if a quicker turn around is needed, such as for a favorite stuffed bunny. The center will need to follow similar measures to cleanse potentially contaminated items. Immediately sanitize all items, including dress-up clothing and hats. Do not allow the infested child to return to the program until all evidence of nits has been removed from his or her hair. To prevent the spread of head lice and reduce the possibility of an epidemic, check every child's head for the next five days following the last discovery.

Cross contamination can be a challenge if measures are not employed to separate personal items, such as hair combs and brushes. It is tempting to discourage children from bringing combs and brushes to the center. Yet, positive opportunities to interact with each child during grooming far outweigh the measures required to reduce such occurrences. The children need to be touched in positive ways during the day and hair brushing and combing is a wonderful way to do this. Separate and store hair items in individual closed containers. Plastic zip bags, available at the grocery store, are inexpensive and work very well. Label each storage container, comb, and brush with the child's name.

A diligent effort to maintain stringent hygienic practices and regular head checks will thwart the possibility of an epidemic in your program.

## RECOMMEND RESOURCES

Aronson, S., & Shope, T. (2004). *Managing infectious diseases in child care and schools.* Elk Grove Village, IL: American Academy of Pediatrics.

Kemper, K. J. (1996). *The holistic pediatrician.* New York: HarperCollins.

## RESOURCES FOR FIRST AID SUPPLIES

Coastal Training Technologies, 500 Studio Dr., Virginia Beach, VA 23452; 1-800-725-3418; http://www.coastal.com (videos and other products about bloodborne pathogens)

Conney Safety Products, 3202 Latham Dr., P. O. Box 44190, Madison WI 53744; 1-888-356-9100; http://www.conney.com

## HELPFUL WEB SITES

Health and Safety Tips, *Daily Health Checks,* http://nrc.uchsc.edu

Health and Safety Tips, *Immunizations,* http://nrc.uchsc.edu

*Immunizations,* http://www.nrc.uchsc.edu/tips/immunizations.htm

National Resource Center for Health and Safety in Child Care: Health and Safety Tips, *Medication Administration in the Child Care Setting,* http://nrc.uchsc.edu

## POSTING FIRST AID DIRECTIVES

Early care and education professionals who are adequately trained in cardiopulmonary resuscitation (CPR), artificial respiration, and first aid procedures are an asset to the children they care for. It is advisable for all child care personnel to receive and maintain current CPR, artificial respiration, and first aid training.

Post first aid directives in each room to serve as a quick reminder of what steps to follow in case of an emergency. First aid directives are a brief review of what to do if an emergency does occur. There are many different emergencies. Figure 6–1 outlines directives for some of the most common emergencies, such as poisoning, bleeding, choking, convulsions, shock, nosebleeds, and situations requiring artificial respiration. Place the directives next to each phone, along with phone numbers for the poison control center, fire department, emergency help, medical, dental, ambulance, and the police station. When pertinent information is readily available in an emergency situation, it can help the staff to remain calm in order to perform at an optimum level.

## LEAVING THE ROOM UNATTENDED

Child/adult ratios are established and maintained for classroom safety. A room with children present should *never* be left unattended by an adult! Leaving children unattended puts them in a potentially dangerous situation. Open your door and alert someone, or pick up the telephone (if near by) and page for help. When it becomes necessary to leave your room, arrange for another adult to cover for you.

## SAFETY AND ACCIDENT PREVENTION

Two-year-old children remain in a high-risk category for accidents and will require a close eye. They are very curious about everything in their environment. Their curiosity often exceeds their life experiences. For example, they might really enjoy eating blue ice cream and place window cleaner in the same category if they are thirsty. Medicine might be mistaken for candy their mother occasionally shares with them. Center staff must keep vigilance for safety in mind at all times in caring for small children. Purses should be stowed out of reach, preferably in a locked locker, cabinet, or closet. Cleaning fluids such as bleach solutions must be safely stowed at all times. Always ask the question, "What is the potential outcome of an action?" For example, "Can that large branch fallen from the tree become an eye-poking weapon in a curious two-year-old's hands?" And, finally, form the habit of performing quick safety checks every morning before the

# SUGGESTED FIRST AID DIRECTIVES

## CHOKING

*(Conscious)* - Stand or kneel behind child with your arms around his waist and make a fist. Place thumb side of fist in the middle of abdomen just above the navel. With moderate pressure, use your other hand to press fist into child's abdomen with a quick, upward thrust. Keep your elbows out and away from child. Repeat thrusts until obstruction is cleared or child begins to cough or becomes unconscious.

*(Unconscious)* - Position child on his back. Just above navel, place heel of one hand on the midline of abdomen with the other hand placed on top of the first. Using moderate pressure, press into abdomen with a quick, upward thrust. Open airway by tilting head back and lifting chin. **If you can see the object**, do a finger sweep. Slide finger down inside of cheek to base of tongue, sweep object out but be careful not to push the object deeper into the throat. Repeat above until obstruction is removed or child begins coughing. If child does not resume breathing, proceed with artificial respiration (see below).

**Infants** - Support infant's head and neck. Turn infant face down on your forearm. Lower your forearm onto your thigh. Give four (4) back blows forcefully between infant's shoulder blades with heel of hand. Turn infant onto back. Place middle and index fingers on breastbone between nipple line and end of breastbone. Quickly compress breastbone one-half to one inch with each thrust. Repeat backblows and chest thrusts until object is coughed up, infant starts to cry, cough, and breathe, or medical personnel arrives and takes over.

## POISONING

Call Poison Control Center (1-800-382-9097) immediately! Have the poison container handy for reference when talking to the center. Do not induce vomiting unless instructed to do so by a health professional. Check the child's airway, breathing, and circulation.

## HEMORRHAGING

Use a protective barrier between you and the child (gloves). Then, with a clean pad, apply firm continuous pressure to the bleeding site for five minutes. Do not move/change pads, but you may place additional pads on top of the original one. If bleeding persists, call the doctor or ambulance Open wounds may require a tetanus shot.

## SEIZURE

Clear the area around the child of hard or sharp objects. Loosen tight clothing around the neck. Do not restrain the child. Do not force fingers or objects into the child's mouth. After the seizure is over and if the child is not experiencing breathing difficulties, lay him/her on his/her side until he/she regains consciousness or until he/she can be seen by emergency medical personnel. After the seizure, allow the child to rest. Notify parents immediately. If child is experiencing breathing difficulty, or if seizure is lasting longer than 15 minutes, call an ambulance at once.

## ARTIFICIAL RESPIRATION *(Rescue Breathing)*

Position child on the back; if not breathing, open airway by gently tilting the head back and lifting chin. Look, listen, and feel for breathing. If still not breathing, keep head tilted back and pinch nose shut. Give two full breaths and then one regular breath every 4 seconds thereafter. Continue for one minute; then look, listen, and feel for the return of breathing. Continue rescue breathing until medical help arrives or breathing resumes.

If using one-way pulmonary resuscitation device, be sure your mouth and child's mouth are sealed around the device.

(Modification for infants only)  Proceed as above, but place your mouth over nose and mouth of the infant. Give light puffs every 3 seconds.

## SHOCK

If skin is cold and clammy, as well as face pale or child has nausea or vomiting, or shallow breathing, call for emergency help. Keep the child lying down. Elevate the feet. If there are head/chest injuries, raise the head and shoulders only.

**FIGURE 6-1** Suggested First Aid Directives

children arrive. Scan the room for items inadvertently left behind by the evening cleaning crew or maintenance staff.

### SAFETY PLUG COVERS

For the safety of all the children, check electrical outlets for safety plug covers on a daily basis. *It is important for safety plug covers to be in place at all times.* Two-year-olds are curious, and an unprotected electrical outlet is a potential for electrocution.

According to Standard 5.048 of *Caring For Our Children National Health And Safety Performance Standards* (2nd Ed.), the best safety practice is to use safety plug covers—the type that are attached to the electrical receptacle by a screw or other means—to prevent easy removal by a child. Avoid using outlet covers that a child can remove by extraction of a plug from the socket. All newly installed electrical outlets accessible to children must be protected by GFCI (grand-fault circuit-interruptes) shock protection devices or safety receptacles that require simultaneous contact with both prongs of a plug to access the electricity. If you are planning new construction, consider placing the electrical outlets at least 48 inches from the ground. Several new safety plug outlets are now available for consumers. Form a regular habit of checking your electrical outlets for missing safety devices.

### TOY SAFETY

Toy safety is another important concern. Too many toys on the floor at once can be overwhelming and create a tripping hazard. Limit the amount of toys that are on the floor at a given time. Select toys that do not present a strangulation hazard. Steer clear of small removable parts, knobs, or beads. Avoid stuffed animals or dolls with detachable eyes, such as button eyes. Stuffed animals are best if they are individually labeled and used by one child only during their resting period. Purchase a *no-choke testing tube* at better toy stores. If the object fits in the tube, then it is considered potentially dangerous and should not be used by children under age three. Small balls or latex balloons are dangerous and should be avoided. Mylar balloons are a safer choice. Avoid using toys with long cords or strings in order to avoid strangulation. Shorten cords or strings on push pull toys or clothing to no longer than 12 inches. Avoid items with sharp edges. Sharp edges and broken pieces on toys are a potential danger: remove them immediately. Heed warning labels on toys. They are placed there by law in the United States. The Consumer Product Safety Commission (CPSC) has the authority to recall dangerous toys and products from the market. Also, the mission of the state Public Interest Research Groups (PIRGs) is to help educate toy purchasers to avoid the most common hazards in toys. For a complete list of toy tips and safety e-mail alerts, go to http://www.toysafety.com.

### LATEX BALLOONS AND SMALL OBJECT HAZARDS

Latex balloons are very dangerous toys for young children. Because they explore with their mouths, it is not uncommon for young children to bite a balloon, causing it to burst. Young preschool children will attempt to inflate the balloons, and run the risk of them deflating and blocking their airways. Best practices strongly discourage latex balloons; they should not be permitted in the child care facility when young children are present. If the center shares playground space with school age children at different times during the day, be very careful to clean up any latex pieces left by the older children. The same advice remains true for toy lending and swapping. If older children borrow a set of the younger group's building blocks to help construct their block city, double-check the returned items for any errant small objects, such as marbles or puzzle pieces, that could present a hazard for the younger group.

## INDIVIDUAL ACCIDENT REPORT AND ACCIDENT TRACKING REPORT

If a child is injured during the course of the day, complete an Incident/Accident form (see example Figure 6–2). The accident report will describe the type of injury, its location on the body, and what time it occurred. Was blood present? If so, were universal precautions employed? What type of treatment was rendered and who witnessed the accident? After you have completed this report, send it to the director for review. Contact the family and inform them of the injuries so they can decide, with the center personnel, if they desire further treatment for their child. Some are more likely to seek medical treatment than others, and it is a decision they are entitled to make. Some states require the center/teacher to submit a copy of the accident report to their licensing consultant if the injury required medical intervention with the doctor or clinic or hospital. This form is a legal document so great care must be exercised to complete it accurately. Describe the injury rather than assign a diagnosis. An example of the nature of injury: A "purple mark the size of a dime on the right cheek," rather than a "bruise" or "contusion on the face." If you are unsure of how to describe it accurately, it is best to obtain assistance from a supervisor.

In centers it is helpful to track trends of illness or accidents. Create a binder specifically to collect and record all accident and illness reports. On a daily basis, log accidents and illnesses, using the Accident and Illness Tracking Reports (see Figure 6–3). It will only require a few moments. The director can use it as a handy reference to track possible illness trends, such as influenza, RSV, etc., or perhaps a pattern of accidents occurring within a specific group, such as biting or falls. If your center maintains a copy of Individual Incident/Accident Reports or Suggested Illness reports discussed in Chapter 5, it is advisable to store them in the binder with the Illness and Incident/Accident tracking reports so they do not become part of the child's permanent record. Figure 6–4 is a flowchart that provides guidance for creating a binder in which to keep emergency and safety information. Although it is not a regular occurrence, it is not uncommon for government agencies such as OSHA, local fire marshals, firefighting personnel, or staff from program licensing agencies to visit and request to see this type of information.

## POSTING EMERGENCY EVACUATION PLANS AND EMERGENCY PHONE NUMBER LISTS

Place a list of emergency contacts next to every phone for quick reference when needed (see Figure 6–5). If you need to dial a number to reach an outside line (e.g., #9), be sure to specify that on the emergency numbers list. Conduct emergency drills at least on a monthly basis. Every room where children are cared for requires a very specific outline of instructions and procedures that are to be followed in an emergency. Post this in a visible location. The instructions must identify which exits to use in a situation that requires the children to be removed from the building (see Figure 6–6).

# Incident/Accident

Child's Name: ___David (Enter Last Name)_____

Date of accident/injury: ___09/26/2005_____ Time: ___10:30 am_____

Brief description of accident/injury: _____David tripped over his_____

_____napping cot and bumped his right elbow causing small purple mark_____

_____about the size of a dime._____

Was first aid given? ___Yes_____ If so, describe: ___applied cold compress___

_____

Was blood present in accident? ___No___ How much? ___N/A_____

Were Universal Precautions employed? _____Not needed_____

Was medical intervention required?* ___No___ If yes, describe: _____

_____

Person initiating this report: ___Ms. Brown___ Witness: ___Ben_____

Name of parent contacted: ___Mr. Allen___ Time contacted: ___10:40 am___

Director's signature: ___Mrs. Neihoff_____

* In some states it is required to file a copy of this report with the child care licensing department if medical intervention is required.

**Figure 6–2** Incident/Accident Report

## Accident/Incident Tracking Reports

| Name of Child | Date | Time | Type of Accident | Person Reporting Accident | Director Notified | Report Filed | Parent Notified | Time Called |
|---|---|---|---|---|---|---|---|---|
| David (Enter Last Name) | 1/26 | 10:30 am | Fell & hurt right elbow | Ms. Runisfeld | ✓ | ✓ | ✓ | 11:00 am |
| Agnes (Enter Last Name) | 1/27 | 3:15 pm | Tripped & fell down, she scraped her left elbow & right knee | Mr. Meda | ✓ | ✓ | ✓ | 3:30 pm |
| | | | | | | | | |
| | | | | | | | | |
| | | | | | | | | |
| | | | | | | | | |
| | | | | | | | | |
| | | | | | | | | |
| | | | | | | | | |

**FIGURE 6–3** Accident/Incident Tracking Report

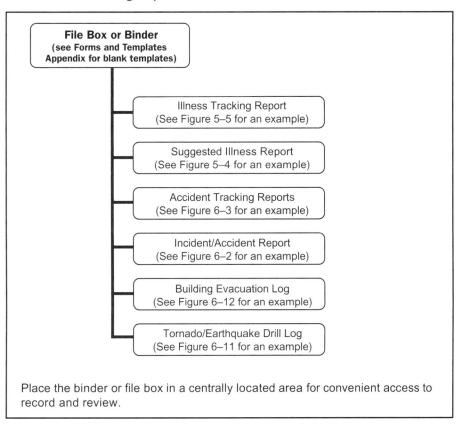

**FIGURE 6–4** File Box for Record Keeping

**Emergency Contacts:** *Post Near Every Telephone*

Your Facility Address: _____
*(Enter Street # / Apt. #)*

_____
*(Enter City)*

Nearest Main Intersection: _____
*(Enter Street # / Apt. #)*

Your Facility Phone Number: _____
*XXX-XXX-XXXX*

| Contact | Phone Number |
|---|---|
| Operator | *XXX-XXX-XXXX* |
| Emergency | *XXX-XXX-XXXX* |
| Fire | *XXX-XXX-XXXX* |
| Police | *XXX-XXX-XXXX* |
| Consulting Dentist | *XXX-XXX-XXXX* |
| Poison Control | *XXX-XXX-XXXX* |
| Local Hospital Emergency Dept | *XXX-XXX-XXXX* |
| Other | |
| Other | |

**FIGURE 6–5** Emergency Contacts

## CONDUCTING EMERGENCY EVACUATION DRILLS

Familiarize yourself with this information long before a drill occurs.

It is helpful to have a large blanket available and an emergency bag of supplies in case reentry into the building is delayed (see Figure 6–7). Replenish and maintain the emergency bag at all times so it is available in a moment's notice. Schedule drills to be conducted on a regular basis. Two-year-olds are often very afraid of the loud sound of an alarm. Talk to them and prepare them for the drill ahead of time.

## Emergency Evacuation Plan

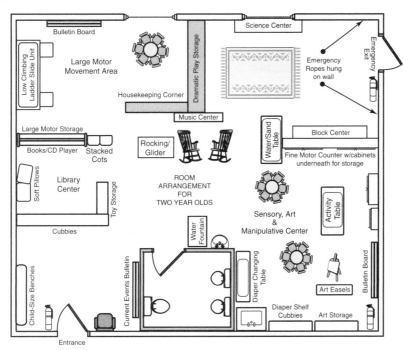

Draw First Choice Escape Route, Draw Second Choice Escape Route

In Case of Fire Call:  *XXX-XXX-XXXX*

In Case of Bomb Threat Call:  *XXX-XXX-XXXX*

In Case of Gas Leak Call:  *XXX-XXX-XXXX*

Fire Extinguisher expires Date:  *11-05-2009*

Emergency Bag and Blanket are located:  *in closet of main hallway*

For two-year-olds – Stretch the evacuation rope out on the floor. Have each child grab a knot and hold tight. Account for all children in attendance.  If the door is cool, open door slowly, make sure fire or smoke isn't blocking your escape route. If your escape is blocked, close the door and use an alternative escape route.  Smoke and heat rise. Be prepared to crawl where the air is clearer and cooler near the floor. Move as far from the building as possible.  In case of a real fire, do not re-enter the building until it is cleared by the proper authorities.

How to create an emergency evacuation rope:
Create an emergency evacuation rope by using a rope long enough for 5–7 children. Tie a knot every 12" for them to hold onto and guide them to a safe area.

**When the rope is not in use, place it on a hook out of reach to avoid a potential strangulation accident.**

**12"**     **12"**     **12"**     **12"**     **12"**     **12"**     **12"**

**FIGURE 6–6** Emergency Exit Evacuation

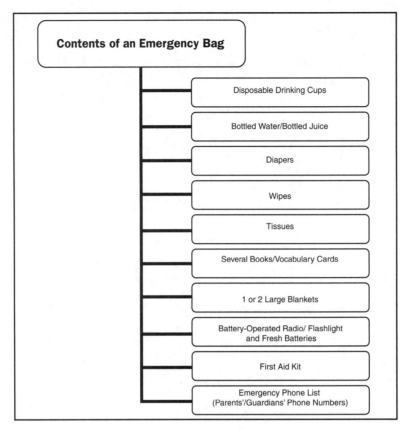

**FIGURE 6–7** How to Assemble an Emergency Bag

---

**Hurricane Emergency Instructions**

**Hurricane/Tropical Storm Watch:** indicates conditions are possible in the specified area within 36 hours.

**Hurricane/Tropical Storm Warning:** conditions are expected within 24 hours.

Send the children home.
Learn your specific evacuation route.
Secure your facility.
Close storm shutters.
Turn utilities off at main valves if instructed by authorities.
Take emergency phone numbers with you.

Your Evacuation Route: _____ *turn right on West 86th Street, drive 2 blocks to* _____

_____ *Meridian, turn right, go a mile to Interstate 465 West for two miles, to Interstate 865 to* _____

_____ *Interstate 65 to North Carolina* _____

**FIGURE 6–8** Hurricane Emergency Instructions

---

**Tornado Emergency Instructions**

Your county or region is: _____ *Marion County* _____

**Tornado Watch**: A tornado is possible. Remain alert for approaching storms. Tune your portable (battery-operated) radio to a local weather station.

**Tornado Warning**: A tornado has been sighted. Activate your emergency shelter plan immediately.

Grab your emergency bag and blanket. They are located: _____ *in main hallway closet* _____

_____

For two-year-olds – Stretch the evacuation rope out on the floor. Evacuation rope is located: _____ *in main hallway closet* _____
Have each child grab a knot and hold on tight. Account for all children in attendance. Move children calmly and quickly to an interior room or hallway.
Your best location is: _____ *Main hallway past library* _____

_____

_____

_____

_____

_____

Cover the children with heavy blankets or cushions, if available, in case of flying glass or debris. Avoid windows, doors, outside walls, and corners of rooms.

---

**FIGURE 6–9** Tornado Emergency Instructions

## RECORDING EMERGENCY EVACUATION DRILLS

Keep a record of the day and time the emergency drill takes place, and how long it takes for the center to completely evacuate all the children *safely* to their designated areas. Evacuation drill examples are provided on the individual emergency instruction forms for hurricanes, tornados, and earthquakes (see Figures 6–8, 6–9, and 6–10). Use them to customize a drill that is suitable for your specific circumstances. Figures 6–11 and 6–12 provide examples for creating the tornado/earthquake drill and building evacuation logs. Forms for all of these examples are located at the back of the book in the Forms and Templates Appendix.

## Earthquake Emergency Instructions

Prior to an earthquake:
- Brace high and top-heavy objects.
- Fasten cubbies, lockers, toy shelves to the wall.
- Anchor overhead lighting fixtures.
- Install flexible pipe fitting to avoid gas or water leaks.
- Know when and how to shut off electricity, gas, and water at main switches and valves.
- Locate safe spots in the room to protect yourself from dropping debris such as under a sturdy table or crib.

Your safest location is: _____*in the hallway under library tables*_____

The shutoff for gas is located: _____*in the basement next to furnace*_____

The water main is located: _____*in the kitchen next to large sink*_____

Your emergency bag is located: _____*top shelf of toy cabinet*_____

During an earthquake:

- Stay inside until shaking stops and it is safe to go outside.
- Move the children to your safe location (inside a crib on an inside wall).
- Describe where: _____*Move children under the large library table located in hallway*_____

- Place a heavy blanket or lightweight mattress over the crib.
- If you are on the playground, move away from the building.

When the shaking stops be prepared for aftershocks.  Check for injuries and administer first aid as indicated.  Use flashlights if electricity is out.  DO NOT light candles or matches in case of gas leakage.

**FIGURE 6–10** Earthquake Emergency Instructions

**Tornado / Earthquake Drill Log**

| Date | Time of Drill | Time Needed to Seek Cover | Comment | ull Name of  er on in Charge |
|------|---------------|--------------------------|---------|------------------------------|
| 2/14 | 2:30 pm | 2 minutes | Well Done! | Mrs. Ferdahard - Director |
| | | | | |
| | | | | |
| | | | | |
| | | | | |
| | | | | |
| | | | | |
| | | | | |
| | | | | |

**FIGURE 6–11** Tornado/Earthquake Drill Log

# Building Evacuation Log

| Date | Time of Drill | Evacuation Time | Comments | Full Name of Person in Charge |
|------|---------------|-----------------|----------|-------------------------------|
| 05-11 | 8:30 am | 1 min 50 sec | Great Job! | Mrs. Ferrie Director |
| 06-24 | 2:45 pm | 2 min 10 sec | | Mrs. Ferrie Director |
| 07-08 | 3:45 pm | 2 min 5 sec | | Mrs. Ferrie Director |
| | | | | |
| | | | | |
| | | | | |

**FIGURE 6–12** Building Evacuation Log

## REFERENCES

American Academy of Pediatrics, American Public Health Association, National Resource Center for Health and Safety in Child Care. (2000). *Stepping stones to using caring for our children* (2nd Ed.). EIk Grove Village, IL: American Academy of Pediatrics.

Indiana State Board of Health. (2002). *Health care program for child care centers suggested first aid directives.* Retrieved December 21, 2004, from http://www.in.gov/icpr/webfile/formsdiv/45877.pdf

To find your specific
State's Licensing, Rules
and Regulations go to:

http://nrc.uchsc.edu

## CHAPTER 7

# Facilitating Two-Year-Olds and Their Families

This chapter provides in-depth information about subjects introduced earlier in the book, such as:

- Tips for completing daily schedules
- Facilitating the children's arrival at the center
- Recording observations about the children's daily activities
- Creating lesson plans
- Early childhood development milestones
- Choosing classroom supplies
- Planning and leading stimulating classroom activities

## BEGINNING THE DAY: ARRIVAL

Everyone appreciates a warm hello and welcome upon arrival. Make an effort to greet your children and their families as they arrive. At this age, many two-year-olds experience separation anxiety, especially if they are a new member of your group. During this phase it is sometimes difficult for two-year-olds to allow their parents or guardians to leave without tears. Every parent and child has an individual style for sharing a goodbye. Some parents will appreciate if you take their child from them so they can leave, and others will spend time with their child, hanging up belongings, assisting him or her in joining others at the breakfast table, or selecting a toy the child will enjoy. It is important to discuss with parents how you can best assist with the morning arrival and a smooth separation.

Collecting pertinent information during morning arrival allows the teachers to provide optimum care for each two-year-old. The Beginning Our Day form will help teachers gather specific information about each child, such as the time the child awoke, last ate, had his or her last diaper change or toileted, and any comments that will assist with each child's care for that day. Morning arrivals are a very busy time. Place the Beginning the Day Sheet on a clipboard near the Medication Sheet (see Chapter 5) or in an area easily accessible to the parent for convenient recording.

## CREATING A DAILY OUTLINE

For an example of how to create the daily schedule, see Figure 3–3 in Chapter 3.

| Beginning Our Day | Date: July 8 | | | |
|---|---|---|---|---|
| **Welcome** | | | | |
| Child's Name | Time Awoke | Last Meal/Snack | Last Diaper Change or Toilet Break | Comments, if any |
| Nanci (Enter Last Name) | 5:30 am | Breakfast | 5:45 am | Dr. appt will pick up at 2 |
| Hailey (Enter Last Name) | 6:00 am | Juice | 6:15 am | |
| Caden (Enter Last Name) | 7:00 am | Graham crackers | 7:15 am | |
| Harriet (Enter Last Name) | 7:15 am | | 7:40 am | Meeting downtown Mrs. Smith 848-5267 |
| Carter (Enter Last Name) | 6 ish | English muffin, eggs, juice | 6:15 am | Up early - probably tired |
| Jackson (Enter Last name) | 8:30 am | | 8:45 am | |
| Paul (Enter Last Name) | 6:50 am | Muffin | 7:15 am | May want more breakfast |
| Tasha (Enter Last Name) | 5:45 am | Breakfast | 6:00 am | Grandpa Brown will pick up today |
| Annette (Enter Last Name) | 7:30 am, | Dinner | 7:45 am | Hungry |
| | | | | |

**FIGURE 7–1** Beginning Our Day

## ESTABLISHING AN EXCELLENT PATH FOR COMMUNICATION

As you will note in Figure 3–3, the Daily Outline Schedule only *briefly* lists the planned day's activities with the corresponding times noted, but does not offer any specific details. This schedule is primarily used for a quick overview and reference for the two-year-olds' planned day. You will be asked to complete a Daily Schedule Details form, which does cover the details in the next section.

Typically, the Daily Outline Schedule is updated at least every season, especially in climates that warrant a change from outdoor activities because of rough weather. The Forms and Templates Appendix provides a template for creating your own classroom's *Daily Outline Schedule.* Fill in the blanks to reflect the typical schedule you have developed for the two-year-old children you care for. Maintain this schedule so that a substitute or assistant teacher will always have a current version of the two-year-olds' planned day.

## CREATING A DAILY SCHEDULE DETAILS

For an example of the Two-Year-Old Daily Schedule Details, see Figure 3–4 in Chapter 3, "Establishing an Excellent Path for Communication." Detailed descriptions of the daily activities are suggested here, as well as specific information for children with special considerations such as allergies; or early arrival time for a child on a particular day necessitating his eating breakfast. Record specifies such as, Jack and Lisa eat breakfast every day or Max has a milk allergy. Paint a picture with words describing the children's whole day. The information provided *in detail* will promote consistent and *safe* care, in your absence, the two-year-olds will experience the familiar routines you have established and will certainly provide the substitute teacher with the confidence needed to fulfill his or her tasks.

A Daily Classroom Schedule Details template for your use can also be found in the Forms and Templates Appendix. Make a duplicate of the template and fill in the blanks to accurately reflect the detailed schedule you have planned for your group of two-year-olds.

## LESSON PLANS

Once the Daily Classroom Schedule Details are completed, the weekly lesson plan is the next endeavor. An example of Weekly Lesson Plans is provided in Figure 7–2. Lesson plans are your blueprint for each day. Lesson planning is a crucial element for achieving an enriching environment and a satisfying experience for the two-year-olds in your care. A Lesson Plans template has been provided in the Forms and Templates Appendix. Use this template to create lessons plans for the two-year-old group. Many books are available to assist with lesson plan ideas. Check the resource guide for a list.

Keep a copy of your current lesson plan in this section of the KIDEX Class Book for your handy reference and all staff members who care for the children. Two-year-olds are not yet able to discuss their day with their parents, so post the lesson plan on a special parents bulletin board, or somewhere easy for them to see.

## RECORDING OBSERVATIONS OF THE TWO-YEAR-OLD CHILD'S DAY

Once children reach age two some centers decide to record daily information as a class group rather than individually, while other centers are mandated by licensing rules to create an individual record for each child. Two options are offered here for daily record keeping.

In Chapter 3, "Establishing an Excellent Path for Communication," a completed example of the Twos Daily Observation Checklist is provided in Figure 3–10. A blank template for the Twos Daily Observation Checklist is supplied for your daily use in the Forms and Templates Appendix. Keep a written daily record for each two-year-old. Accurate, timely record keeping gives the family a clear understanding of their child's day. Adopting a routine for record keeping assures all important aspects are covered. Provide the parents or guardians with a copy of this record so they, too, will have a record of their child's napping patterns, toileting patterns or diaper changes, eating patterns, and the two-year-old's overall mood and activity level for that day. Consider making a copy of the Twos Daily Observation Checklist. Provide one copy for the parents or guardians at departure, and file the second one for at least a couple of months, or longer if your state requires.

The other method of providing observations of the children is to post it on the current events bulletin board. Examples of the charts Our Day (Figure 3–10), Eating Patterns (Figure 3–11), and Nap Time (Figure 3–12) were provided in Chapter 3. Use these charts instead of the individual Twos Daily Observation Checklist. You will find these forms in the Forms and Templates Appendix so that you can make copies of them as needed. You can document all the pertinent information about the children by duplicating the templates and updating the current events bulletin board daily. This information is very helpful to parents, as it may well affect the way they plan dinner for their child or schedule their bed-time hour. For example, if lunch didn't appeal to a child, he or she may need to eat dinner early or have a light snack before dinner. The parents will appreciate the time you

## Twos Weekly Lesson Plans

**Stage of Play Development:** Parallel (dominant) (emerging) Cooperative

**Group Name:** Bananas
**Theme:** Winter
**Lead Teacher:** Ms. Laura

**Week of:** Jan 3–9

| Activities | Sun | Mon | Tues | Wed | Thurs | Fri | Sat |
|---|---|---|---|---|---|---|---|
| **Concept** | | Signs of Winter | Plants & Animals | What We Wear | Winter Activities | Winter Magic | |
| **Sharing Time** | | Talk about signs of winter | This is how the wind blows | My coat, my hat, my mittens | Sledding, igloos, snowballs | I am hot / I am cold | |
| **Language Skills** | | | | | | | |
| **KIDEX Fun with Language & Telling Tales Activities** | | Puppet talks about winter | Noise-maker rhythms | Sing "Did You Ever See a Snowman" | Musical instruments | Winter picture words | |
| **Songs/Finger Plays** | | "I'm a Little Ice Cube" | Pictures of animals that hibernate | "3 Little Kittens Lost Their Mittens" | "Frosty the Snowman" | "Are You Sleeping Little Bear" (song) | |
| **Reading/Stories (Flannel Board/ Vocabulary/ Puppets)** | | Dear Rebecca, Winter's Here | A Hat for Minerva | Br-r-r | Katy and the Big Snow | Prize in the Snow | |
| **KIDEX: Exploring Our World Activities** | | Weather Outside | Hang bird feeder & watch | Gelatin blocks | Fragrant snow balls (cotton) | Winter puzzles | |
| **Cognitive / Sensory / Pre-Math / Science** | | Line up our boots or shoes | The plants, trees, and animals are asleep | Match the mittens | Different colored hats | Float ice cubes in water table | |
| **KIDEX: Creating My Way Activities / Arts Exploration/ Crafts** | | Paint with sponges | Make peanut butter bird feeder | Color with white crayon on dark paper | Finger paint with pudding | Black construction paper/white chalk | |
| **KIDEX: My Body Is Wonderful Activities – Large Muscle Practice** | | Walk on snow cushions | Riding toys sleigh ride | Catch the snowflakes bubbles | March to winter music | Sleigh ride in a box (scooting) | |
| **Small Muscle Practice** | | Snap & button | Brush/comb our hair | Dump & load the snow blocks | Practice z-ipping | Stacking rings | |
| **Indoor/Outdoor Activities** | | Toss snowballs in big basket–rolled socks | Throw snowballs ping pong ball | Scarf dance | Roll the big snowball ball | Make pretend snow angels & ice skating | |
| **Daily Play Centers** | Housekeeping / Dramatic Play / Toys Center | Fine Motor / Art / Eating / Water Table | | Library / Music / Quiet Play / Block Center / Computer | | Active Play / Music Movement / Toys | |

**Self-Help Skills/Social Skills**
25–36 Months: Integrate and encourage the development of skills during this 12-month span

- Managing Clothing with help
- Wash & dry hands
- Feed self/use of fork & spoon & cup
- Toilet training practice (18 months & older only)
- Help with cleanup
- Practice please & thank you
- Learning basic self-control skills
- Verbal skills-building
- Refining body movements
- Body/Self awareness
- Safety awareness
- Follow basic instructions
- Building imagination

**FIGURE 7–2** Weekly Lesson Plan example

take to provide this information. For some children, it may remain fairly routine. For others, it may even affect the next day if they haven't had a good nap the day before and didn't get enough sleep that night. Be sure to check with your center's requirements to ensure confidentiality, respecting families and children.

Because many two-year-old children are often in varying stages of toilet training, their families appreciate an individual update of their daily progress.

Regardless of how you choose to report the daily observations, maintain a copy of the written observations to review in the event questions occur or a conference is warranted. Occasionally, parents or guardians express concerns—for example how their child's appetite seems to fluctuate—and want to know how much the child is eating at the center. The recorded observations provide you with the information you need to address their concerns and reach a mutually acceptable outcome. The director is encouraged to review all records at least monthly to look for consistent recording practices, or to spot areas where intervention or education is warranted. Before you leave for lunch, or at the end of your shift, check the charts for accuracy. Remember: after your shift ends, your observations provide pertinent information for each parent about his or her child's care. An accurate record is essential to facilitate open communication!

## COMPLETING A NEW CHILD TRANSITIONING REPORT

The detail of how a new child is adjusting to the program is of primary importance to his/her family and the director of the center. Typically a child attending two weeks fulltime will bond with the center, staff, and children even in the most difficult circumstances. It may take a little longer for some or if they attend on a part-time basis. An example of the completed New Child Transitioning Report can be found in Figure 3–14 in Chapter 3. Although some of this information is already recorded on the class listings, the families will find an individual copy helpful to share with other family members during this period of transition.

Make a duplicate copy of the blank template called New Child Transitioning Report and complete a report for each new child in your group. Indicate the day they are in attendance, if they played with the toys, and how much they participated in activities (some, a lot, or not yet). How was the child's appetite today? Indicate whether it was light, partial, or complete for all applicable meals. Record the times the child fell asleep and when he or she awoke from a nap. If the child is using diapers, record the bowel and bladder patterns. If the child is toilet training, attach a copy of the Toilet Training Sheet to the New Child Transitioning Report. Record whether the child had a fair day or great day. If you have any questions about care, this is a good place to communicate the need for clarification. If the child cried most of the day, it is important to record, but not dwell on the subject. It's important to share an honest account, yet it can be beneficial to focus on the positive progress, such as the child did not cry as often or seemed to observe more. Perhaps the child did not join in group activities yet, but did seem interested and curious. Using this approach is more comforting to a parent racked with guilt, rather than hearing "Oh, (he or she) just cried all day long!"

## TRACKING DEVELOPMENTAL MILESTONES

Figures 7–3, 7–4, 7–5, and 7–6 provide a guide for observing and recording developmental milestones for each two-year-old. Observe the behavior expected at or about the two-year-old's current age in each area of development. *It is very important to understand from*

# 25-27 Months

## DEVELOPMENTAL MILESTONES

**TWOS CAN:**

___N___ DEVELOP A VOCABULARY OF 50 OR MORE WORDS

___Y___ BEGIN UNDERSTANDING MORE ABSTRACT CONCEPTS (e.g. BIG/LITTLE; COLD/HOT; UP/DOWN)

___Y___ BEGIN TO COMBINE WORDS & ANSWER SIMPLE QUESTIONS

___S___ DEVELOP AN INTEREST IN NAMING PICTURES IN BOOKS

___Y___ UNDERSTAND & FOLLOW SIMPLE DIRECTIONS

___Y___ BEGIN SELF-HELP SKILLS, SUCH AS WASHING HANDS & BRUSHING TEETH WITH ASSISTANCE

___Y___ ABLE TO USE CUP & EATING UTENSILS

___N___ CAN IMITATE BUILDING A STACK OF CUBES

___Y___ BUILD WITH NESTING BLOCKS

___Y___ USE SIMPLE STACKING TOYS

___Y___ PLAY SIMPLE MUSICAL INSTRUMENTS

___Y___ JUMP UP & STEP UP TO HIGHER SURFACE

___Y___ BEGIN TO ROLL AND THROW LARGE BALLS

___Y___ IMITATE SOUNDS

___Y___ PARTICIPATE IN MUSIC

> *Important Note: Children will develop at similar rates but each in a unique pattern. If you find a child is not exhibiting the majority of characteristics listed, there could be many plausible reasons ranging from premature birth to a more reserved and cautious personality. This list is a broad overview and not all-inclusive of developmental milestones two year olds experience.*

| Y = YES | S = SOMETIMES | N = NOT YET |
|---------|---------------|-------------|

Child's Name: _____Tina (Enter Last Name)_____     Teacher: _____Ms. Jones_____

Date Initiated: _____2/12_____     Date Completed: _____12/16_____

**FIGURE 7–3** 25–27 Months Developmental Milestones

# 28-30 Months

## DEVELOPMENTAL MILESTONES

**TWOS CAN:**

___Y___ BEGIN TO SOLVE PROBLEMS MENTALLY

___Y___ MATCH FAMILIAR ITEMS TO SOUNDS OR PICTURES

___Y___ SING ALONG WITH FAMILIAR SONGS AND FINGER PLAYS

___Y___ LISTEN TO A FIVE-MINUTE PICTURE BOOK AND IDENTIFY 3–4 PICTURES BY NAME

___S___ PARTICIPATE IN PRETEND PLAY

___Y___ BEGIN TO USE PLEASE AND THANK YOU

___Y___ MORE AWARE OF OTHERS' FEELINGS

___N___ PARTICIPATE IN SAND AND WATER PLAY

___Y___ BEGIN TO UNDERSTAND SAFETY RULES

___Y___ DEVELOP AN AWARENESS OF SELF (INCLUDING BODY PARTS) AND OTHERS

___S___ BEGIN TO TAKE SHOES AND SOCKS (OR OTHER ARTICLE OF CLOTHING) ON AND OFF

___N___ WASH AND DRY HANDS

___Y___ HELP WITH CLEAN UP TIME

___Y___ JUMP DOWN OFF A SURFACE, LAND ON TWO FEET

___Y___ WALK ON TIP-TOE

___N___ BALANCE ON ONE FOOT

___Y___ USE SMALL MUSCLE SKILLS (e.g. STRING LARGE BEADS/COMPLETE PUZZLES OF 3–4 PIECES/DRAW SCRIBBLES ON PAPER)

___S___ REFER TO SELF BY NAME

> *Important Note: Children will develop at similar rates but each in a unique pattern. If you find a child is not exhibiting the majority of characteristics listed, there could be many plausible reasons ranging from premature birth to a more reserved and cautious personality. This list is a broad overview and not all-inclusive of developmental milestones two-year-olds will experience.*

| Y = YES | S = SOMETIMES | N = NOT YET |
|---|---|---|

Child's Name: _____Sherry (Enter Last Name)_____ Teacher: _____Mr. Conroy_____

Date Initiated: _____1/15_____ Date Completed: _____9/20_____

**FIGURE 7–4** 28–30 Months Developmental Milestones

# 31-33 Months

## DEVELOPMENTAL MILESTONES

**TWOS CAN:**

___Y___ MAKE CHOICES AND DECISIONS

___Y___ UNDERSTAND USE OF FAMILIAR OBJECTS

___Y___ NAME FAMILIAR ITEMS AND PICTURES

___Y___ UNDERSTAND CONCEPTS OF SAME/DIFFERENT; ONE/MANY; SOFT/HARD

___Y___ IDENTIFY SIX BODY PARTS

___Y___ DESCRIBE THEIR ACTIVITIES

___N___ MANAGE SIMPLE CHORES

___S___ PARTICIPATE IN PARALLEL PLAY

___Y___ IDENTIFY SOME FRIENDS BY NAME

___N___ CLEAR EATING IMPLEMENTS FROM THE TABLE

___N___ COMPLETE 4–5 PIECE PUZZLES

___Y___ SORT SIMPLE COLORS AND SHAPES

___Y___ MATCH OBJECTS BY COLOR/SHAPE/SIZE

___N___ PEDAL A RIDING TOY

___Y___ BALANCE RIGHT, LEFT FOOT

___S___ BUTTON AND ZIP OWN CLOTHING

___N___ ENJOY SMALL GROUP ACTIVITIES

___N___ IDENTIFY SELF WITH CHILDREN OF SAME GENDER

___Y___ SHOW INTEREST IN TOILET TRAINING

___Y___ SHARE SOMETIMES

> *Important Note: Children will develop at similar rates but each in a unique pattern. If you find a child is not exhibiting the majority of characteristics listed, there could be many plausible reasons ranging from premature birth to a more reserved and cautious personality. This list is a broad overview and not all-inclusive of developmental milestones two-year-olds experience.*

| Y = YES | S = SOMETIMES | N = NOT YET |
|---|---|---|

Child's Name: ___Mike (Enter Last Name)___  Teacher: ___Ms. Stiles___

Date Initiated: ___1/2___  Date Completed: ___4/18___

**FIGURE 7–5** 31–33 Months Developmental Milestones

# 34-36 Months

## DEVELOPMENTAL MILESTONES

**TWOS CAN:**

_S___ HELP TELL A STORY

_Y___ DEVELOP A VOCABULARY OF 300 TO 1000 WORDS

_Y___ USE DESCRIPTIVE WORDS

_S___ USE 2 OR 3 SENTENCES IN CONVERSATION

_N___ BECOME MORE ATTENTIVE TO ART ACTIVITIES AND STORIES

_S___ USE PREPOSITIONS (e.g., IN, BY, FOR, WITH, TO)

_Y___ FOLLOW A TWO- OR THREE-PART COMMAND

_Y___ NAME BASIC COLORS

_S___ BEGIN TO UNDERSTAND NUMBER CONCEPTS (SHOW 2 FINGERS)

_N___ DRAW A SIMPLE DESIGN AND COPY HORIZONTAL/VERTICAL LINE AND CIRCLES

_S___ RUN SMOOTHLY, CAN STOP AND START

_N___ GALLOP AND TROT

_Y___ BEND OVER WITHOUT FALLING

_S___ PEDAL AND STEER RIDING TOY

_S___ WALK BACKWARDS

_Y___ BEGIN TO MASTER SNAPS, LARGE BUTTONS AND ZIPPERS

_Y___ USE PEG BOARDS

_Y___ FIT LIDS ON JARS

_N___ THROW A BALL OVERHAND

_S___ BEGIN TO DRESS HIMSELF OR HERSELF

_Y___ INCLUDE OTHER CHILDREN DURING PLAY

_N___ BEGIN USING SCISSORS

_Y___ USE TOILET WITH HELP

> *Important Note: children will develop at similar rates but each in a unique pattern. If you find a child is not exhibiting the majority of characteristics listed, there could be many plausible reasons ranging from premature birth to a more reserved and cautious personality. This list is a broad overview and not all-inclusive of developmental milestones two-year-olds will experience.*

| Y = YES | S = SOMETIMES | N = NOT YET |
|---------|---------------|-------------|

Child's Name: ___Sarah (Enter Last Name)___     Teacher: _____Ms. Roja_____

Date Initiated: _____2/18_____     Date Completed: _____6/15_____

**FIGURE 7–6** 34–36 Months Developmental Milestones

*the beginning that all children are individuals.* Every child will develop at similar patterns but at a unique rate. Each child has a unique personality and will develop at a slightly different pace. The milestone checklist provided describes a broad spectrum of developmental states, suggesting developmental milestones that can be expected to occur approximately as outlined for each month. If you find that a child is not exhibiting the majority of characteristics listed, there could be many reasons. Remember that children may cross stages of development according to their particular growth pattern. For example, the child who is using more energy in physical growth may not be as advanced in language development. If a child was born prematurely, then he or she would not be expected to follow the average suggested milestones and might lag a few weeks behind. A child who is reserved might avoid certain activities and prefer others, but this would not necessarily be to the child's detriment. If you have a child who consistently does not exhibit signs of achieving the majority of the outlined milestones, with a lag of 5–7 weeks, then perhaps more exploration is in order, and it would be advisable to share your concerns with the director or your program supervisor for consideration.

Review the developmental milestones at the beginning of each quarter and complete the checklist at the end of the quarter. Completing the form at end of the quarter will provide each two-year-old time to achieve mastery of each skill outlined.

1. Check the behaviors with a (Y) for yes if the child demonstrates an action regularly.
2. Mark (S) for sometimes if the two-year-old is just beginning to do the action or only does it sometimes.
3. Mark (N) for not yet if the two-year-old doesn't demonstrate this action yet.
4. Place the chart for the current month's age on an individual clipboard, in a separate mailbox slot, or individual notebook for each child, along with the Activities and Play Opportunities, two-year-old's Individual Monthly Profile (Chapter 3, Figure 3–6), and the Twos Daily Observation Checklist (Chapter 3, Figure 3–10) for handy reference when time permits.

## PLANNING ACTIVITIES AND PLAY OPPORTUNITIES

At age two, children are growing, learning, and developing in so many ways that you cannot expect them to become an expert at most things. Since each child develops at their own individual pace, familiarize yourself with activities that are appropriate for each stage of development. Figures 7–7, 7–8, 7–9, and 7–10 provide a variety of planned activities that assist with building large and small muscle control, language skills, sensory responses, mental cognition, and social growth. The activities and play opportunities provide a variety for play in all the aforementioned areas.

Choose activities from five sections: *Fun with Language, Telling Tales, My Body is Wonderful, Exploring My World,* and *Creating My Way.* For maximum practice, choose one activity from each of the five sections when planning daily activities on the lesson plan. This will provide plenty of variety. How long each activity lasts will depend solely on the child's level of interest. Feel free to repeat activities. Two-year-old children are comforted by repetition, and enjoy the feeling of success in practicing their new skills. Some days children are not in the mood for new activities. Use your best judgment and select one with which they are already familiar.

### FUN WITH LANGUAGE AND TELLING TALES

A teacher has a very important influence in the development of language and the introduction of books for two-year-olds. It is essential to remember that children understand a great deal of spoken language before they are able to use it themselves. At the beginning of

# 25-27 Months

## ACTIVITIES

| | |
|---|---|
| **Category 1** | **Telling Tales – Simple Picture Books – Language Activities**<br>• Using small sandwich bags, insert one picture in each bag, punch two holes, and connect with yarn; then name the pictures.<br>• Provide commercially purchased <u>cardboard</u> or <u>plastic</u> books w/simple pictures to name.<br>• Ask parents to bring in "family photo albums"—these can be made from single pictures in plastic bags, and can include grandmother and grandfather, family pets, pictures of the house, the child's favorite toy, etc.<br>• Use a book with simple pictures of animals. Look at each picture, name the animal, and see if the child can imitate the sound the animal makes.<br>• Make a book of the child's favorite toys, pets, foods, etc. Review the book with him or her and other children.<br>• Make a book of pictures of simple things a child uses, and ask him or her to find a picture by identifying its use: e.g., *We eat with this; We brush our teeth with this; We use this when we play outside.*<br>• Look at a picture book and collect matching real objects to pull out of a box as you name the pictures in the book. |
| **Category 2** | **Fun With Language Activities**<br>• Match picture cards of toys and the actual toy.<br>• Play chanting or singing games whenever possible, when starting an activity or finishing one.<br>  a. *We are sitting in our chairs one by one... We are washing both our hands to eat our lunch... (To the tune of "If you're happy and you know it")*<br>  b. *We are eating with our spoons and drinking with our cups and pretty soon we'll have eaten everything up.*<br>• Use puppets to tell simple stories and as a gimmick to help a child talk. A child will sometimes talk to a puppet or other inanimate object before talking to the teacher.<br>• Talk or sing or chant quietly to children when things have become a little too chaotic and use their attention to redirect their behavior or progress to the next activity.<br>• Help the children learn to use words to express emotions and get along with others. Show pictures of people displaying various emotions and discuss familiar situations where the children would have positive and negative feelings. Give examples of ways to handle different emotions and ask the children for suggestions. Try to avoid telling them they are wrong if they suggest hitting, for example, ask what might happen if they did that and if they have another way to manage the situation. Use the book for reminders occasionally, and direct the children to the book in conflict situations to see if you can get them to talk about acceptable behavior. |

Child's Name: ___*Nasim (Enter Last Name)*___   Teacher: ___*Ms. Doyle*___

Date Initiated: ___*6/9*___   Date Completed: ___*11/1*___

**FIGURE 7–7** 25–27 Months Activities

# Continued 25–27 Months Activities

| | |
|---|---|
| **Category**<br><br>**3** | **My Body Is Wonderful — Large & Small Muscle Activities**<br>• Children at this age enjoy wheeled riding toys which they can push with their feet. This is an important stage for progressing to toys that require pedaling. You can make up a course with tape or obstacles to contain "the little drivers" and control the number of crashes! Wagons are also great fun for *pulling* and *pushing, loading* and *unloading*. Pushing boxes around is great fun, too.<br>• Big, soft balls (6" –10") can be rolled back and forth. Teach children to push the ball to guide it in the right direction. Retrieval also provides muscle exercise and release of energy.<br>• Children this age like to move in various ways around a large object. Talk about & model the different ways of moving around, stressing the word *around*. Use other words for spatial relations and movement – *under, over....*<br>• Make climbing and obstacle games. Bean-bag chairs and pillows can be arranged or piled to create inside climbing areas. A blanket draped over chairs provides a tunnel; big foam blocks can make steps for practice in stepping up and down.<br>• Children love to chase bubbles. Change the height of the bubbles so children can stretch and reach, or bend over to pop them *(Bubble recipe included in Figure 7–12).*<br>• Talk about different types of walking and use them to move to specific areas. *Tiptoe* to the cots for nap time; *march* to the playground; *walk with hands behind you* with big steps to the lunch table; *hop* to the centers; *hands on waist* to the bathroom.<br>• Use a 6" or 8"-wide board flat on the carpet to give children practice for the balance beam. It does not need to be long, and can be covered with fabric to prevent ankle injury. |
| **Category**<br><br>**4** | **Creating My Way — Creative Exploration**<br>• Model building towers with blocks; create shapes, trains, a structure for small cars, etc.<br>• Play dough provides many experiences for fine muscle control. Edible play dough can be used for those who just can't resist tasting (recipe included in Figure 7–12).<br>• Finger paint with pudding. Use different colors of pudding to add to the experience.<br>• Take tubs of water outside and let the children "paint" the sidewalk or the outside of the building.<br>• Color and draw on dark construction paper with large pieces of chalk.<br>• Part one — Glue pictures about your weekly theme, e.g., animals, to paper plates, talk about each one, and then hang to dry.<br>• Part two — Cut paper plates into 2–3 pieces — use as a puzzle. |
| **Category**<br><br>**5** | **Exploring Our World — Activities to Explore Cognitive, Pre-Math, Sensory and Science**<br>• Put some small sturdy toys like beads or Legos in a bowl or plastic bin. Give the children several plastic bottles with tops of varying circumferences. As they find a fit and put all the toys in bottles, they can dump them out and start again.<br>• Create your own small water table with a plastic bin or baby tub. Use pouring cups and pitchers and basting tools, and talk about pouring, the feel of the water, etc. Use sponges (can cut to different shapes and sizes) and show children how to squeeze the water out.<br>• Tissue boxes make great hiding and sorting boxes—paint or cover them with printed sticky shelf paper.<br>• Use a large spoon to transfer cubes from one container to another.<br>• Explore objects that float and sink in water table or dishpans.<br>• Separate and sort different–shaped large beads in muffin tins and bowls according to the color.<br>• Sort a box of gloves or socks and match up pairs or colors.<br>• Cover toilet paper rolls or cut paper towel cardboard tubes in half. Cover with peanut butter, roll in seed, and then hang on tree outside. Watch the birds enjoy them from the window. |

Child's Name: ___*Nasim (Enter Last Name)*___ Teacher: ___*Ms. Doyle*___

Date Initiated: ___*6/9*___ Date Completed: ___*11/1*___

**FIGURE 7–7** 25–27 Months Activities *(Continued)*

# 28-30 Months

## ACTIVITIES

| | |
|---|---|
| **Category 1** | **Telling Tales — Simple Picture Books — Language Activities**<br>• Box book — Tape simple pictures to the outside of an oatmeal box and cover with sticky shelf paper. Let the child roll it and name the pictures. You can create several with themes, and also make up simple stories together about the pictures.<br>• Glue several pictures to pages of your book to make "peek-a-boo" books. Alternate picture pages with pages cut into three strips. Let the child turn one strip at a time to discover the picture. Discuss what he or she is seeing while turning each strip.<br>• As you are reading a short story, change your voice to mimic that which might be appropriate (e.g., child's high voice; Daddy's low voice; animal sounds). Or, use a simple picture book and tell a story. Ask the children to imitate the voices.<br>• Show the children how to handle books and how they are replaced on shelves.<br>• Practice turning pages and even finding a quiet place to enjoy a book.<br>• Use a puppet to tell a simple story. Tell it again and see if the children can help with words or simple details.<br>• Introduce short finger plays and simple songs. Make a book to illustrate a song/finger play and the children can look at it by themselves and perhaps remember the chant or song. |
| **Category 2** | **Fun With Language Activities**<br>• Discuss the routine activities with the children before they happen (e.g., *We are going to have a cracker now. Let's go over to the sink and wash our hands. Now let's sit on the mat and when you are sitting, I will get a cracker for you;* or, *We are going to sit on a cushion and look at a book. Can you find a cushion and sit down?).*<br>• Think of things that the children can find on their own and give them directions to get them for you. Discuss what they did.<br>• Take a small group of children on a walk through the center. Listen for sounds and talk about the sounds you are hearing.<br>• Gather a few items from places the children can identify. Place them in a box so they can't be seen. Remove one item at a time and hold it up for all to see. Make a game of returning it to its correct location (e.g., pretend you don't know where it goes and ask for help, or put it in the wrong place and let the children correct you). This can be done with different routines during the day (e.g. cups set at each place at the table or art supplies, so that children can help set up activities and help with routine tasks).<br>• Try to spend a few minutes talking individually with each child shortly before she or he leaves. Talk about progress that child is making, especially if you are working hard on a specific activity or improvement of a social interaction skill.<br>• Show the children pictures of people "in action." Talk about and imitate the action (e.g., *clapping, walking, sitting with legs crossed, waving, sleeping*).<br>• Collect objects that demonstrate big and little (2 plastic glasses, for example), sort them, and tell whether big or little. |

Child's Name: _Katrine (Enter Last Name)_    Teacher: _Mr. Sveinbjornsson_

Date Initiated: _3/15_    Date Completed: _9/1_

**FIGURE 7–8** 28–30 Months Activities

## Continued 28–30 Months Activities

| | |
|---|---|
| **Category 3** | **My Body Is Wonderful — Large & Small Muscle Activities** <br> • Move like the animals: *flap wings; crawl and squirm; tiptoe; stand on one leg.* Use a quiet animal last to calm down the children. Tell a story about the animal to get the children to move in different ways (e.g., *I see a little turtle; he's sleeping on a rock; now he's going to slide into the water and swim around; brrr, it is cold and he wants to sun himself on the rock again, so he slips back up on the rock and stretches in the sun and falls asleep again*). <br> • Follow the leader games are good for attention; following verbal directions; moving from one place to another with no noise when requested *("we will have to stop if I hear noise")*; as well as exercise of muscles. Falling and getting up is one of the favorite exercises for children. <br> • Create a throwing corner: use soft toys like crochet balls, nerf balls, beanbags, and yarn balls. <br> • Jumping activities are great fun. If a child is having difficulty, hold hands and jump with him to help him learn. Jump on leaves or targets made with tape on the floor. <br> • A large inner tube provides good experience for climbing in and out, bouncing up and down while straddling it, etc. <br> • Use carpet squares for a game like musical chairs. Start and stop the music and tell the children to find a square. Do not remove squares—simply play until children are tired of it. <br> • Show the children how to "scoot" around the floor on their carpet squares—using their heels to propel themselves or lie on their stomachs and pull themselves with their arms. <br> • Practice balancing on one foot, initially holding on to something. |
| **Category 4** | **Creating My Way — Creative Exploration** <br> • Shape boxes are good for picking up and turning shapes to place in the correct hole. You can make one with any round container with a plastic lid into which shape holes are cut. <br> • Fun with cotton balls. Use a plastic bin filled with cotton balls and discuss their color and softness. Give the children cups to fill with cotton balls and later toast tongs to enhance the difficulty. These could also be stuck to a mural for snow or buds on trees. You should control the glue and watch that children do not taste the cotton balls! Painting with cotton balls and cotton swabs is also great fun. <br> • Trace each child's hand and let them "color" it with a crayon. <br> • Cut and glue differently shaped macaroni or cereal pieces, such as Toasty O's, to paper. <br> • Use chalk to draw on sidewalks outdoors. <br> • Roll and pound play dough. <br> • Spread and explore shaving cream on the table. Have damp paper towels ready to wipe little faces. <br> • Place an object under paper, e.g., a large leaf, ribbons or yarn, construction squares. Tape paper over it and allow children to scribble new textures. |
| **Category 5** | **Exploring Our World — Activities to Explore Cognitive, Pre-Math, Sensory and Science** <br> • Collect sets of pictures that show big and little. Make a picture book with these pictures to discuss (add other concepts you are teaching e.g., *up and down*). <br> • Put several inches of rice in a sturdy dishpan. Provide cups, spoons, other containers. You may want to put an old shower curtain or a piece of vinyl under the rice container. Hide small cars or other small items to find. <br> • Find a variety of squeezable items and place in a bin. Try to use different types of items to offer a variety of experiences. Some may be easier to squeeze than others (examples: sponge block, infant squeeze toy, nerf balls, large scraps of cloth; a softball, crumpled paper). Discuss how soft the items are and verbalize what the children are doing: one hand, two hands; soft. <br> • Provide squeeze bottles (old dish detergent containers). Let the children "clean" the tables or mats or make interesting spray patterns on the sidewalks. <br> • Make a "track" on the wall with colored masking tape. Let the children run a small wheeled car or their finger on the track — be sure to use curves, V's and even circles. <br> • Hang a shoe bag on the wall or door. Let children put things in and take things out of the pockets. You can tape pictures to the outside of the pockets to add a sorting activity (put all the red things in the red row; all the animal pictures in the zoo row). <br> • Show the children how to use one finger (vs. fist or palm) to push the levers or buttons on a push toy. |

Child's Name: _Katrine (Enter Last Name)_    Teacher: _Mr. Sveinbjornsson_

Date Initiated: _3/15_    Date Completed: _9/1_

**FIGURE 7–8** 28–30 Months Activities *(Continued)*

# 31-33 Months

## ACTIVITIES

| | |
|---|---|
| **Category 1** | **Telling Tales — Simple Picture Books — Language Activities**<br>• Read short books to small groups of children. All children may not be ready for a story. Find pictures in the story when you are finished. (Do you remember that the boy was looking for something? Can you show me or tell me what it was? Or what happened next?)<br>• Make picture books of opposites to elicit the words (e.g., same/different, one/many, tall/short).<br>• Make a class photo album of children doing different things inside and outside. Discuss what is going on in the picture, and perhaps what could happen next, or what happened before.<br>• Find pictures of places children might go (e.g., grocery store, movie theater, park). Ask what they might do there; if it would be fun; if they would sleep or eat there.<br>• Play the find it game with books: Find the airplane or the thing that is flying. Find two boys in this picture.<br>• Make your own (large) book about an activity the children completed. Remember simple steps and create simple drawings to illustrate the activity. Use this later to discuss the activity again. |
| **Category 2** | **Fun With Language Activities**<br>• Talk about the clothes they're wearing; names of items; colors; clothes specific for weather conditions; types of shoes; long socks/short socks, etc.<br>• Hide something small in a place all the children can reach. Ask one child to help you find it, giving one direction at a time (e.g., Chris, can you help me find the bear puppet? Look over by the blocks. Good. Now find a blue bucket. Look in the bucket. You found it! As the children progress, your directions can become more complex).<br>• Make a habit of talking to children about what they are doing and about what other children are doing. This is a good activity to orient a new child or while cuddling one who is having a hard day. The child just might become interested in one of the activities as you are discussing it.<br>• Talk about what just happened, what is to happen next, or the preparation needed for a specific activity. We sure have been playing hard outdoors. I'll bet you feel hot and I think it would be nice to have a nice cool drink of ____. Before we go outdoors, we need to do something. What is it? Before we eat our snack, we need to... What did we just do? Right, we ate our snack. Now we need to put our napkins and cups in the trash basket.<br>• Some children will respond well to a puppet. Let the puppet "tell a story" about something familiar to the children and they can fill in specific words. Let the puppet "give directions" of things to do. Let the puppet "orient" the shy child and "talk" about feelings.<br>• For a good mouth and tongue exercise, make silly sounds and ask the children to imitate you. Make faces and use your tongue and mouth to form sounds in isolation. (Exaggerate the sound and mouth movements.) |

Child's Name: _____Ushi (Enter Last Name)_____ Teacher: _____Ms. Delfaco_____

Date Initiated: _____5/15_____ Date Completed: _____11/15_____

**FIGURE 7–9** 31–33 Months Activities

## Continued 31–33 Months Activities

| | |
|---|---|
| **Category**<br><br>**3** | **My Body Is Wonderful — Large & Small Muscle Activities**<br>• Set up a target area for kicking balls (8" – 10"). You can use a long piece of vinyl (long, to provide a wide target area) and hang it low on the playground fence. Let the children try to kick the balls into the target.<br>• Music generally elicits movement. Children will often bounce up and down or move side to side, changing weight from one foot to the other. Creative movement to music is fun and beneficial and you can teach children many ways to move their bodies and to stop when the music stops (or fall down, which is much more fun).<br>• Batting beach balls around is great fun and provides movement, eye-hand coordination, jumping up— and may also cause crashes, so you will want to limit the number of balls and children.<br>• Make walkways for the children with chalk outside, or tape on the floor inside. Tell the children to walk between the lines, trying not to step on either one. Limit the length of the walkway or they will want to run!<br>• Create a bowling area with plastic bowling pins, plastic bottles or plastic milk bottles. Each child should stand about 3' away from the pins and roll a large ball at them. Show the children how to re-set the pins! (You can fill the bottles with sand to make it easier to "re-set" them.)<br>• On the playground, watch how things around them move. Imitate the leaves blowing; the wheels on the cars going around; the flag flapping; birds flying.<br>• Running and jumping into a pile of pillows is great fun. Watch carefully that there is no open floor space between pillows and that the children go one at a time.<br>• Cut some footprints out of colored contact paper and make a path to the bathroom or places to stand when lining up to go outside. Make sure to space footprints closely together for short legs, but provide enough space between each set to prevent conflict. |
| **Category**<br><br>**4** | **Creating My Way — Creative Exploration**<br>• Peg boards with large pegs (or smaller if the child is ready) provide good fine muscle exercise, and you can direct a child to colors, simple patterns and shapes, etc. Use these when you can supervise. It is very tempting to check out how the pegs taste!<br>• Let the children practice tearing all kinds of paper. You will need to show them how to grasp the edges with their fingers and pull in opposite directions. Use different thicknesses of paper and show them how to put the torn bits into a plastic bin. This can be used for collages later on or for falling confetti (limited amounts) which they can try to catch and then pick up and give to you to toss again. Picking up the paper will be tedious (though good for small muscles), so use the larger, thicker pieces and limit the number for this game.<br>• Play different types of music during creative activities.<br>• Spread a small amount of paint on construction paper, have children explore making paint tracks on their paper with toy car wheels.<br>• Play with oatmeal instead of water in the table. Talk about full and empty.<br>• Have children spread non-toxic glue or homemade paste (flour and water) on a piece of construction paper. Sprinkle sand on it, pieces of yarn, pieces of scrap paper to create a collage of textures.<br>• Hang several feet of Contact paper on wall at their height. Have children stick different colors and sizes of construction squares to it. |
| **Category**<br><br>**5** | **Exploring Our World — Activities to Explore Cognitive, Pre-Math, Sensory and Science**<br>• Go on a hunt for soft and hard objects in the room. Talk about how you can squeeze a soft object, but not a hard one.<br>• Finger plays offer lots of good practice and chanting and repetition are good for memory development and rhythm. Open hands and close in a fist; wave with one hand up and down, sideways; wave with one finger; feather fingers; put fingertips together; point with one finger.<br>• Create garages for toy cars and trucks. Cover a shoe box with contact paper and cut out a door or two. Use an equal number of cars and boxes and introduce the child to one-to-one correspondence.<br>• Play a quiet game with large stickers or pieces of colored contact paper. Have them imitate where you put the sticker—hand, nose, chin, leg, and forehead.<br>• Part I: Glue rough pieces to paper (burlap, sand paper, pieces of course netting) and talk about textures.<br>• Part II: Glue smooth pieces to paper (velvet squares, aluminum foil, wax paper) and talk about smooth textures.<br>• Part III: Glue soft pieces to paper (cotton balls, tissues, feathers) and discuss soft textures.<br>• Part IV: Glue hard pieces to paper (popsicle sticks, small blocks) and talk about hard textures.<br>• Part V: Stack all pictures together, punch a hole and tie together loosely, creating a texture book for each child. |

Child's Name: _____Ushi (Enter Last Name)_____ Teacher: _____Ms. Delfaco_____

Date Initiated: _____5/15_____ Date Completed: _____11/15_____

**FIGURE 7–9** 31–33 Months Activities *(Continued)*

# 34-36 Months

## ACTIVITIES

| | |
|---|---|
| **Category 1** | **Telling Tales — Simple Picture Books**<br>• Make a story book for your room.  Take pictures of children involved in different activities.  Ask the children to help write the story, telling about what is happening in each picture.  Use this book to remind the children silently that it is time to get ready for lunch, nap, center time, etc.; to show new parents that their children are happily involved in activities; to orient a new child (be sure to take a picture soon after he or she starts!); to help someone "tour" the room, etc.<br>• Make felt books with 5–6 felt pages.  Glue simple pictures (e.g., sun, pond, house, etc.) on each page and put a figure or an animal in a pocket on the front.  Let the child remove the felt figure and go through the book telling a story as she goes.  Other felt shapes and pictures can be added from a boxed collection to increase the complexity of the activity.<br>• Make a book with simple pictures and outlines of two pictures on the opposite page.  Ask the child which page shows the outline or shadow of the picture, and why.  Use metal binder rings and change the pictures around and add/delete for new challenges.<br>• Find books to use in the classroom that provide a purpose other than a story (e.g., a book about a specific concept, which can be read several times until the children can say and use the concept.  Find a book that shows spatial relations and ask questions about what is on, under, beside, between, after you have talked about these concepts with real objects.)<br>• Once you have read a story to the children a few times: read it and leave out key words for them to fill in; stop and ask them what happens next; choose a different ending; remember the characters' names; use puppets or act out the story with assistance; make a set of flannel board characters so they can "tell" the story on their own.  Let them change and add to the story, as this is natural at this age. |
| **Category 2** | **Fun With Language Activities**<br>• Show pictures of things that make sounds and practice the sounds (tea kettle, race car, train, squeaky door).<br>• Talk about the recent past and future.  Ask children if they can remember the art project or snack they had this morning and/or tell them what might be happening in the afternoon or tomorrow.<br>• Make simple language mistakes in ways that a child can correct; e.g. *Here is a book for you to read, when handing the child something else.*  Let the child correct you.  This can also be a gimmick for directing a child to something he or she doesn't want to do — *"let's go wash our hands in the toy box."*  The silly nature of the request may be the catalyst to urge the child in the right direction.<br>• Make some matching cards with simple pictures. Gather 2 or 3 children and ask who has the picture of the ball.  Give that child your picture of the ball and when all are matched, trade cards and start again.<br>• Sing hello, hello _____ (child's name) how are you today?<br>• Look at animal pictures and match their sounds. |

Child's Name:  _Serenka (Enter Last Name)_   Teacher:  _Ms. Gomoll_

Date Initiated:  _1/1_   Date Completed:  _12/1_

**FIGURE 7–10** 34–36 Months Activities

## Continued 34–36 Months Activities

| Category **3** | **My Body Is Wonderful — Large & Small Muscle Activities**<br>• Use instrumental music to create rhythmic movement; show children how to march; tiptoe walking to quiet music; swaying from side to side; bending up and down; moving head in various ways; patting parts of the body as well as clapping; shoulders up and down, etc.<br>• Make a safe balance beam by covering a smooth board with heavy fabric or vinyl. Show the children how to move forward and back, sideways, one foot close to the other, tiptoe, etc.<br>• Make plastic bag balls. Stuff one plastic bag with several others. Tie the outer bag in tight knots and you have a ball you can throw as hard as you want without hurting anyone.<br>• Make a hanging target for the children to jump up and touch. This could be a large ball in a cloth bag. You can also hang the target lower and use foam batting forms.<br>• Create a walking path to follow with chalk on the sidewalk, or tape on the floor inside. Make zig-zags and curves and shapes and show the children different ways to move on the path (e.g., forward, backward, side-stepping, hopping, on tiptoe, swimming, rocking, bending, swaying, swinging arms and marching; one foot close in front of the other, scooting, skating, galloping, etc.)<br>• Create a stepping stone path or obstacle course with carpet squares—spaced so the children have to stretch to reach the next one. They can move in various ways on the path or course—walking, crawling, jumping with one leg out, etc.(You may need to use double-sided sticky tape to secure "stepping stones.")<br>• Move like the animals—show pictures of various animals and discuss how they move—then imitate the movements and add variations—fast and slow/stop when music stops/high and low/big and small (for baby or momma animals).<br>• Show children how to roll across a mat or a row of pillows set in a line. |
|---|---|
| Category **4** | **Creating My Way — Creative Exploration**<br>• Make your own lacing cards by gluing appealing pictures (or in relation to your weekly theme) to cardboard and covering with contact paper. Punch holes for the child to use in threading a shoelace. The pattern the child follows is not important.<br>• Plastic bottles and jars with screw tops can provide the same experiences as noted in letter A.<br>• Let the children cut their snacks into bite-sized portions before eating or preparing for a cooking activity.<br>• Play dough: cut different sizes of plastic straws and let children explore sticking the straw pieces in the dough.<br>• Paint with feathers and Q-tips.<br>• Make circle pictures: cut out round fruit—lemon, oranges—to dip in paint and stamp on paper.<br>• Practice spreading icing on a cookie and decorate it for a special snack.<br>• Wash dishes today in the water table. |
| Category **5** | **Exploring Our World — Activities to Explore Cognitive, Pre-Math, Sensory and Science**<br>• Make a simple roadway on a piece of vinyl. Show the child how to "trace" the roadway with one finger, or a toy vehicle. You can add obstacles to go around, under, over.<br>• Show the children how to pretend that their hands are insects, with the fingers "crawling" up their arms or down their legs; up the sides of their faces to the top of their heads (a good activity for "waiting" time).<br>• Surprise bags—Put small familiar objects (e.g., toy car, block, Lego, sponge, etc) in a fabric bag with a drawstring top. Let the child put a hand in and touch and describe the object. The child can then guess what it is, or ask the other children if they can guess from his or her "clues."<br>• A variety of boxes and other containers with lids offers many good experiences: matching size and developing dexterity and small muscles; matching patterns on the outside of containers; the delight of finding something inside (e.g., a picture glued to the bottom; a small toy to move around inside the box on the track; a small soft ball to toss back into the box).<br>• Toilet paper, paper towel, and wrapping paper tubes make great tunnels for cars. Paint or cover with printed sticky paper. The children can run the cars through them; create an obstacle course; combine two or more to make longer tunnels; run the cars over the top.<br>• Large metal clips (the type used for hanging clothes) make for good muscle exercise. Show the children how to squeeze them and attach to a cup or other container. You can also sort colors and introduce the concept of one-to-one correspondence with one clip per cup.<br>• Use a muffin tin to sort several different kinds of color cubes by color, by shape, etc.<br>• A variation on peg boards: Use a plastic bowl (like one for whipped topping) with a lid, etc. and punch holes around the lid with a paper punch. File the points off golf tees, and the children can put the tees into the holes in the lid. The container is used for storing, and another dimension can be added by using different colored tees and identifying the container with a colored paper tee held onto the top with contact paper.<br>• Explore water in different forms: make ice cubes — watch them melt. What happens when ice cubes float in warm water? |

Child's Name: _Serenka (Enter Last Name)_   Teacher: _Ms. Gomoll_

Date Initiated: _1/1_   Date Completed: _12/1_

**FIGURE 7–10** 34–36 Months Activities *(Continued)*

language development, children first understand spoken language and then they associate words to objects. At about 24–30 months, they start to combine two or three words (e.g., no play now). This is the time they really start blossoming and expanding their vocabularies. At about 30–36 months, children begin to express tenses such as "I played dolls," vs. "I play dolls." Their use of sentence structure begins to grow. They may start to carry on conversations of two or three sentences.

Because children learn language by listening to the sounds other humans make, they need to hear talking and the use of descriptive language around them. The basic rule to use is *talk, talk, and talk* to the children. Children need to be surrounded by language in order to become fluent by the age of three. Talk about what you are doing together; speak to each child about his or her special qualities; talk about situations; share what you're going to do next. Use a variety of means to expose two-year-olds to language development opportunities.

Early care and education professionals are well aware that reading helps develop children's attention span, builds vocabularies, enhances self-esteem, increases the ability to visualize and imagine, and provides many opportunities to understand words and how they create spoken language. The introduction of books is an essential element in your overall language program.

Reading to children for as little as 15–20 minutes per day from an early age contributes to a myriad of positive brain developments. Two-year-old children are very interested in learning. They love to look at books and hear stories read to them. They are especially fond of books that describe stories they can relate to in their own lives. For example, stories such as grocery shopping, visiting grandparents, taking a bath, learning to use the toilet are all stories they delight in hearing. Simple little books with pictures and photos allow them to read stories to themselves. Provide them with sturdy books made of heavy cardboard construction (board books). Stories with rhyming words and repetitive phrases appeal to young children. There is a vast selection of books available to use. Many centers have access to public libraries and bookmobile programs that can come to the child care site. Several books are listed at the end of this chapter of authors who compiled books to help you choose appropriate material. The box below lists examples of books that have been enjoyed by two-year-olds for years.

Don't be surprised if the children want you to read the same books repeatedly. Two-year-olds are comforted by repetition. They often will insist on the exact story and will object

---

### Suggested Books for Two-Year-Olds

*My Family* by D. Bailey Willowdale

*Franklin's Blanket* by P. Bourgeois and B. Clark

*Clifford's Spring Clean-Up* by N. Bridwell

*Arthur's Tooth* by M. Brown

*Clap Your Hands* by L. B. Cauley

*No More Baths* by B. Cole

*Carl Goes to Day-Care* by A. Carl Day

*Bye-Bye, Pacifier* by L. Gikow

*Finders Keepers* by W. Lipkind and N. Mordvinoff

*I Make a Cake* by M. Murphy

*Shopping Trip* by H. Oxenbury

*Joseph Had a Little Overcoat* by S. Taback

*Little Bill* by K. Watson

if the reader deviates from the written word. Their appetite for exact duplication of reading, songs, and rhymes at this stage of development mirrors their expectations in every area of their current existence. Ames and Ilg (1976) note "the world is large and confusing to the child this age…[the] rituals help him avoid the conflict of having to make a choice" (p. 13).

Stories are complemented with flannel pieces that bring the story alive, and the two-year-olds can easily participate. Cut pictures from magazines and place them in a Plexiglas display board, found in school supply catalogues, that attaches to the wall. Hang pictures or picture cards by the diaper-changing station, or in places at their eye level to encourage discussions with you. Change the pictures regularly.

Singing and playing songs on a regular basis is another excellent opportunity for practicing language skill development. Music and singing offer opportunities to explore sound and to assist with building and mastering language skills. Musical activities are a vital part of any curriculum and promote many positive environmental influences for young children. Nursery rhymes are also an enjoyable activity to incorporate into the day. Many nursery rhymes are very old and date as far back as the fourteenth century. Most children love being told nursery rhymes. There are a multitude of books on the market, found in libraries and bookstores. You will find an extensive list of the most popular nursery rhymes at the Web site http://www.rhymes.org. Click on *Lost Lyrics of Old Nursery Rhymes 112 Additional Online Nursery Rhymes, History and their Origins!*

### My Body is Wonderful

The two-year-old experiments and begins to discover his physical abilities and relate to his body and his world through sensory motor play (activities that use senses and muscles). *My Body Is Wonderful* encourages the two-year-old child's budding small and large muscle skills. *My Body Is Wonderful* includes large muscle activities that work the large muscles in arms, legs, and body, and small muscle skills that provide fine motor activities for the children to develop hand and finger movements and eye-hand coordination. The children are relating physically to their environment and learning words like "over," "under," and "around." A child begins to learn a sense of identity and uniqueness through these activities. Large muscle and small muscle activities will provide practice for refining children's rapidly developing mobility.

It goes without saying that the two-year-old children will explore their muscles on their own, and that they need redirection at times. If a child is climbing on the stove in the housekeeping center (discovering his or her own leverage), redirect the child to the climbing apparatus, or the foam blocks, which can be used as steps. Sand and rice play need to be closely watched, and sometimes guided. Obviously, toys with small pieces need teacher supervision.

One last hint on these activities: Be sure that the space is appropriate for the activities. *If children are crowded or made to wait a long time for a turn, they may become aggressive.* If too much open space is available, children are tempted to run from one end to the other. Also, ensure that enough choice is available for activities involving small muscle activity and, ideally, that activities are rotated so that children are presented with new and different experiences.

### Creating My Way

*Creating My Way* provides a variety of art and creative activities for the children. Art activities are opportunities for children to explore materials and colors, and offer a variety of open-ended experiences involving the senses. Art can be enjoyed by children who are functioning at different levels. Art is not created for the parents' benefit. It is created for the development of the child's creative abilities. To that end, you can help parents understand that the art work coming from your room will not have so-called teacher-produced parts, nor color-inside-the-line projects.

Keep teacher-made materials and models at a minimum. Prepare the materials and offer simple explanations for their use. Observe the activities so that you can provide guidance, if necessary. Replenish materials and assist with writing the child's name for displaying. Offer children the choice to participate in the art activity or to wait until they are ready. Given a variety of materials and the opportunity to explore, children will become involved as their interest and ability levels dictate. At first, the art experience is simply cause and effect. For example: "If I do this with the paint brush, I will make a colored mark on the paper." Or "This feels a certain way in my hands and I can move it in different ways." Next, the children will get more involved in the exploration and creation with the materials. When the work is completed and ready to display, hang the children's work at their eye level so they can see it and feel proud. They also can locate it to show it to others. Cover the art display area with a large piece of thick plastic, available in discount or fabric stores, and it won't matter how often the children touch the art work. Let the child determine if he or she wants to save the work, hang it, take it home, or throw it away.

Activities planned in the *Creating My Way* are located in Figure 7–11, which provides a variety of ideas and tips for sensory, creative, and discovery activities. Basic ideas, alternative uses for materials, and suggestions for expanding the basic activities are also provided. Tips for setting up materials and suggestions for ensuring their safe use are noted in Figure 7–11, as well as ideas for painting and using crayons and markers, and basic information on collages, sticker designs, chalk drawings, carpentry, and feely art bags.

A collection of recipes for sensory and creative expressions is available in Figure 7–12. Often, it is much less expensive to make basic materials than to purchase them. Included are recipes for different types of paint and play dough, bubble mix, paste, and instructions for making chunky crayons and chalk, which are easier for children this age to grasp.

Figure 2–1 provides a list of supplies and equipment appropriate for two-year-olds. This list is not intended as all-inclusive or as required equipment and supplies. The list does include items for the ideas suggested throughout *KIDEX for Twos* and the variety of equipment that supports a well-planned interest center. Many of the activities listed require supplies that can be made by the teacher, using found or donated items. Costs can be kept lower, and parents often like to help, by collecting such materials as old milk cartons, egg containers, expired magazines, etc. The opportunity to contribute will promote family involvement, and the children are often quite proud when their families collect and donate helpful materials to their class.

### EXPLORING MY WORLD

*Exploring My World* entices two-year-old children to experience and explore the world they live in. The five senses are used for sensory exploration and learning about the world. Although sensory elements are essentially integrated in all of the KIDEX planned activities, they are grouped in this section to assist with planning a balanced program. Using sensory skills to teach concepts relating to size, measurement (pre-math), floating, sinking, hard, soft, and other scientific exploration will appeal to their curious nature as they open up to the exciting beginning of lifelong learning. Planned activities are described in the *Categorys* sections of Figures 7–7 through 7–10.

## TRANSITIONS ACTIVITIES: PREPARING TO CHANGE ACTIVITIES

Transitions are periods of time in a program that allow for passing from one activity to another. Transitions occur on a regular basis every day in a program. If deliberate transitions are not built into the day, changing activities can lead to confusion and chaos. Every early care educator understands that children are comforted when routines are built into their day. Establishing consistent transition routines will help them close an activity and move to another smoothly. Planned transitions built into the program day provide adequate time for children to participate in ending their activity, rather than the teacher

### Creating My Way:
### Tips for Creative Expression

Here are a variety of tips to use as general guidelines to set up and guide art and creative activities for the children. Refer to Figure 7–12 for recipes.

### Finger Painting

Prepare a dishpan of soapy water for quick clean-up at the end of the activity. Some children will have a hard time getting started. This is messy work and they may not like it, especially if parents have drilled them about maintaining clean hands. You might get them started with just one or two fingers until they're comfortable. Show the children different ways of using their hands: one or two fingers, palms, sides of hands in swirling motion, fingernails.

Finger paint with shaving cream on the table top. (Supervise the children to see that they don't get it in their eyes). You can sprinkle in a little water if the shaving cream gets too stiff. You can also add a bit of liquid tempera. You can make a print of a child's work by simply placing a piece of paper on his or her area and rubbing over it. You can finger paint in cookie trays.

Finger paint with pudding (use different flavors to provide new colors and tastes on different days).

You can also use yogurt or whipped cream.

Finger paint to music.

Let the children mix two colors of finger paint.

### Brush Painting Tips for Twos:

- You can start with plain water so they can understand the basic concept.
- Limit the number of children.
- Use smocks.
- Protect the floor, table, and walls.
- Use wide brushes and, if necessary, shorten the handles to approximately 6" (or buy ½" brushes with 6" handles at a hardware store and trim the brushes).
- Easels attached to walls provide permanent areas, cannot be tipped over, and should have a washable surface behind them. Or, attach paper directly to a washable surface and attach paint trays directly to wall. (For example, take a wide strip of thick vinyl, staple it to the wall, and place a contrasting strip of vinyl to provide a border.)
- Non-tip paint trays should be used—you can make wood or cardboard cup holders for the brushes. Baby food jars or cans can be used for the paint. Cut a hole in a sponge slightly smaller than the jar, but leave edges. The sponge will hold the jar and also catch drips.
- Start with just one or two colors, progress to more colors, and then mixing colors and adding white to experiment.

### Other painting implements

roll top deodorant bottles

small pieces of sponge held with a spring-type clothes pin

cotton tipped swabs

toothbrushes

feathers (wash with soap and water and a small amount of bleach)

### Suggested Surfaces to Explore

newsprint

newspaper—classifieds

shelf paper

butcher paper

grocery sacks

paper plates

**Figure 7-11**

Styrofoam trays (large) with paper glued inside

long strips of paper vs. rectangular

pellon

Prepare an area for drying the paintings (clothesline works fine)

## Other Painting Ideas

■ Use colored paper and only black and white paint.

■ Salt painting: the child can sprinkle salt on his painting before it is dry.

■ Sponge painting: cut sponges into various shapes (enough for a variety of colors) and dip them into a shallow paint substance, and imprint them on paper. Remind the child that there is no need to dip the sponge each time. If the child decides to smear the paint around with the sponge, that is how he or she has decided to use it!

## Crayons/Markers

Basic ideas for twos:

■ Use large crayons and take the paper off for ease of use.

■ Use large pieces of paper and tape them to a surface.

■ Place a few crayons or watercolor markers in a container for each child. *When each child has his or her own supplies, fighting occurs less often.*

■ Show children how to use crayons on their sides.

■ Band two crayons together for a different effect.

■ Preparing markers for use: Water soluble markers are wonderful fun because of their brilliancy. Children should be supervised, however, so they don't suck the ends or place the caps in their mouths. To prevent problems with caps, mix up plaster of paris and put it in an old container. **Dispose of any excess in the trash as it will harden in pipes.** Immerse the tops of the marking pen in the plaster of Paris and let the substance harden. Toddlers can then return the markers to the tops and one danger is removed!

## Collages

Provide a base, such as a piece of newspaper, construction paper, or cardboard for heavier items; a tray with a thin layer of glue (or use the paste recipe included in recipe section); and the things to glue, such as scraps of paper they have torn—include different thicknesses; fabric scraps; Styrofoam; old greeting cards; string, yarn, and ribbon; nylon netting; macaroni in various shapes and colors; cotton balls. Children can either dip the items in the glue, use cotton swabs to spread the glue, or dip their fingers in the paste and spread it. Children can create a mural in this same manner. Tape a long sheet of paper to the table or on the wall for better visualization.

## Sticker Designs

Place purchased stickers and bits of decorated contact paper on trays. Show the children how to peel the stickers and contact paper off and make a collage. Save your wildlife and other interesting stamps that come in the mail, and show the children how to wet these and use them for collages (place one wet sponge between two children).

## Chalk Drawing

Cover the children's work surface. Wet the paper and give them large, non-toxic chalks. (Recipe for chalk included in the recipe section of this chapter).

Use different shapes of paper for activities, just to add variety or to highlight a holiday.

## Beginning Carpentry

Let the children use Styrofoam (blocks, sheets, pieces) and golf tees (with points blunted with sandpaper) and a plastic hammer. They can also use a large lump of playdough in the same manner.

## Feely Art

Fill re-sealable freezer bags with one of the following: toothpaste (variety of colors), shaving cream, lotion, pudding, and the like. Feel the bags and talk about them; cool the bags and talk about them. After the children have experimented with the different bags, hang them on the wall and the children can continue to manipulate the materials while they are at the center.

**FIGURE 7–11** *(Continued)*

## Recipes

### Basic Finger Paint

Use purchased, washable, nontoxic finger paint, or make your own (much less expensive):

Combine 2 cups flour and ¼ cup of water (this mixture should be thick like glue).

Add a few drops of food coloring.

Each child needs only 2 or 3 tablespoons.

### Brush Paint

Basic recipe (less expensive than purchased paint)

1 cup bentonite mixed with 2 quarts hot water

Allow mixture to sit in a lidded container for 2–3 days, stirring each day (it will not be smooth initially).

When the bentonite becomes smooth, divide the mix into smaller jars.

Mix in 3 or more tablespoons of dry tempera in each jar and stir.

Add paint as needed for hue, and water to smooth it.

Store in covered jars.

### Play Dough

The children can help you make this!

### Mix:

¼ cup of vegetable oil

1½ cups of flour

½ cup of salt

Approx. ¼ cup of water

Color with a few drops of food coloring.

Knead (good exercise for little fingers) until you have a smooth mix and the color is even.

Add more flour or water as necessary.

Put in an airtight container (e.g., metal can with plastic top—be sure to check the can edges). Storing in a plastic bag is not advised as the dough will be too wet.

Change the texture of the dough by adding rice, salt, cornmeal, etc.

### Edible Play Dough

½ cup powdered milk

½ cup wheat germ

1 cup peanut butter

¼ cup honey

Stir all together, adding more powdered milk if mixture is too sticky.

### Bubble Mix

2 tablespoons dishwashing detergent

1 tablespoon glycerin

1 cup water

Change amounts as needed. Some detergents will work better than others. Add food coloring if you wish. Use plastic or pipe cleaner hoop blowers or fly swatters dipped in a tray of soap.

### Chunky Crayons

- Peel paper off old crayons and sort by color (let the children do this!). Or, mix colors and make confetti crayons.

- Away from the classroom (crayon wax is extremely flammable), melt the crayons in a throw-away pan surrounded by water. Pour the melted wax into small (hockey-puck size) non-flammable containers into which you've sprayed non-stick coating. A muffin tin with foil baking cups works well. Let cool and they will harden.

**FIGURE 7–12**

They are just right for little fists to grab before little fingers are dexterous. The saucepan is cleanable if you wipe it out while still warm.

**Paste Recipes**

**1.** White flour paste

**Mix:**

½ cup water

1 cup white flour

**2.** Wheat paste

**Mix:**

1½ cups of boiling water

½ teaspoon salt

2 teaspoons of wheat flour

Store in a covered jar.

Hint: To keep the lids of storage jars from sticking, rub petroleum jelly around the edges.

**Chalk**

**Mix:**

2 tablespoons powdered tempera paint

3 tablespoons of plaster of paris

½ cup of water

Let mixture harden in a small paper cup for approximately one hour.

Remove the cup for good, chunky chalk.

You can also make your own chalkboards—toddler size! Take a large piece of cardboard and spray it with several coats of chalkboard paint (from paint stores or hobby shops). Once it is dry, you can seal the edges with colored tape.

**FIGURE 7–12** *(Continued)*

autocratically demanding they abruptly end the activity without warning. Two-year-old children naturally find change difficult. Give them a warning a few minutes before a change in activities and they will be more responsive. Offering transition time will help them to change from one activity to the next with the least amount of protest.

Little children cannot be expected to sit and wait except for very short periods of time. Teach the children to sing or chant along with you as you are preparing their lunch table or preparing for outside play. Make it a simple song or chant, and use the same tune over and over. Choose words in your song or chant that will gain their attention and describe what you hope to accomplish. The fun rhythm of chant or song will provide a distraction and ease the transition. You may feel a little foolish at first, but teachers must be actors.

Some suggestions for transition activities for young children are:

**1.** Use a special puppet for giving directions—nothing else. Use different voices to interest the children. This method appeals to auditory and visual learners.

**2.** Give simple and fun directions, such as: Find your rug (each child has his or her own rug sample); sit down and wiggle your feet; or, wave your hands or point to body parts.

**3.** Invite helpers to assist you in setting set up for the next activity.

**4.** Hold up a picture of the next activity after ringing a bell, so that the children see what is next. They may even proceed more quietly to that activity.

5. Dismiss children one at a time for the next activity by describing something they are wearing (e.g., If you are wearing green, you may go to a center).

6. Make funny noises and faces and see if the children can mimic you.

7. Develop a broad repertoire of finger plays and songs including clapping, marching, and other movement. A good example of a singing game is "Can you do what I do, I do, I do? Can you do what I do, just like me?"

8. Imagine you are on a bus (or a plane, in a car, on a bicycle, a butterfly's wings) and have each child ride with you to the lunch table.

9. Offer books of all kinds to the children and let them sit wherever they want to.

10. Play special music for transition times—for nothing else. The children will begin to associate that particular tune with a sense that time is drawing near to end this activity.

Among the list of books in the reference section at the end of this chapter are some resource books that offer ideas for more transition activities. A variety of well-planned transition activities employed on a regular basis will promote safety and reduce stress for all parties involved.

## PERSONAL SUPPLY INVENTORY CHECKLIST

Two-year-olds require plenty of supplies! If your center depends on the children's families to provide supplies, use the personal supply inventory sheet to communicate when supplies need replenishing (see Figure 7–13 for an example). Form a habit of reporting the individual inventory once a week. Notify your clients when their child's supplies are low. Planning ahead will decrease the inconvenience caused by completely depleting needed supplies. Routinely inventory supplies on Thursday or Friday; this allows busy families to shop over the weekend.

## ENDING THE DAY WITH EACH CHILD: DEPARTURE

There are many details for you to remember upon a child's departure. Assist the parents or guardians to gather each child's personal belongings, such as soiled clothing, medications, ointments, and blankets to promote a pleasant transition. If time permits, briefly review the Twos Daily Observation Checklist with them and add any special observations you might have made that day. Provide the parent or guardian with a copy of this record so they, too, will have a record of their child's napping patterns, toileting patterns or diaper changes, eating patterns, and their overall mood and activity level. Or, if you do not use individual sheets, then make sure all pertinent reports are posted on the current events bulletin board for them to review. (Be sure to check your center's confidentiality requirements, to respect the privacy of families and children.) A couple of times per week help the parents gather and collect items in the cubbies (and mailboxes if you use them).

As you know, two-year-olds require a great deal of time and energy. The parents have often spent a long day fulfilling their career obligations. Although they are very pleased to see their children they often have an accumulation of stress from their day. Your pleasant attitude and helpful manner help them to make a smooth exit from the center that will be greatly appreciated, and will allow for the highest and best outcome for all involved. Prepare your room for the next day. Tidy up and finalize the tasks on the cleaning list.

As you bring your day to a close, take a few moments to appreciate yourself. You have touched many lives today by creating a safe and secure environment for children to play and learn. Your efforts have made it possible for parents and guardians to leave their

# PERSONAL SUPPLY INVENTORY CHECKLIST

**CHILD'S NAME:** _Tanya (Enter Last Name)_    **DATE:** _10-04_

| SUPPLY | FULL | HALF | NEED MORE |
|---|---|---|---|
| Diapers | | ✓ | |
| Disposable wipes | | | ✓ |
| Waterproof paper for diaper barrier (such as wax paper) | ✓ | | |
| Diaper ointment | | | ✓ |
| Pacifier | | | |
| Disposable trainers | | ✓ | |
| Plastic pants covers | ✓ | | |
| Underwear | ✓ | | |
| Shirts | ✓ | | |
| Long pants | ✓ | | |
| Short pants | | | |
| Socks | ✓ | | |
| Other: | | | |
| | | | |
| | | | |
| | | | |
| | | | |
| | | | |
| | | | |
| | | | |

**FIGURE 7–13** Personal Supply Inventory Checklist

children, with the confidence they are well cared for, so that they in turn can provide for their families. You are a vital link to the safekeeping of children in your community and your efforts have made a profound difference.

### REFERENCES

Ames, L. B., & Ilg, F. L. (1976). *Your two-year-old.* New York: Dell Publishing.

### RECOMMEND RESOURCES

Alchin, L. K. (n. d.). *Nursery rhymes lyrics and origins.* Retrieved October 23, 2004, from http://www.rhymes.org.uk

Allen, E. K., & Marotz, L. R. *Developmental profiles pre-birth through twelve* (4th ed.). Clifton Park, NY: Thomson Delmar Learning.

Broad, L. P., & Butterworth, N. T. (1974). *The playgroup handbook.* New York: St. Martin's Press.

Clark, A. (2003). *The ABC's of quality child care.* Clifton Park, NY: Thomson Delmar Learning.

Coletta, A. J., & Coletta, K. (1986). *Year' round activities for two-year-old children.* West Nyack, NY: The Center for Applied Research in Education.

Dibble, C. H., & Lee, K. H. (2000). *101 easy, wacky, crazy activities for young children.* Beltsville, MD: Gryphon House.

Feldman, J. (2000). *Rainy day activities.* Beltsville, MD: Gryphon House.

Fraiberg, S. H. (1987). *The magic years* (reissue ed.). New York: Fireside.

Harms, J. M., & Lettow, L. (1996). *Picture books to enhance the curriculum.* Bronx, NY: H.W. Wilson.

Herr, J. (1994). *Working with young children.* Tinley Park, IL: Goodheart-Willcox.

Kohl, M. F. (2000). *The big messy art book.* Beltsville, MD: Gryphon House.

Odean, K. (1998). *Great books for boys.* New York: Ballantine Books.

Odean, K. (1997). *Great books for girls.* New York: Ballantine Books.

Stephens, C. G. (2000). *Coretta Scott King award books.* Englewood, CO: Libraries Unlimited.

Wilmes, D., & Wilmes, L. (1983). *Everyday circle times.* Elgin, IL: Building Blocks.

### MORE RESOURCES

**Books Two-Year-Olds Enjoy**

Bailey, D. (1998). *My family.* Toronto: Annick Press.

Bourgeois, P., & Clark, B. (1995). *Franklin's blanket.* New York: Scholastic.

Bridwell, N. (1997). *Clifford the big red dog: Clifford's spring clean-up.* New York: Scholastic.

Brown, M. (1985). *Arthur's tooth.* Boston: Little, Brown

Cauley, L. B. (1992). *Clap your hands.* New York: Putman & Grosset Group.

Cole, B. (1980). *No more baths.* New York: Doubleday.

Day, A. (1993). *Carl goes to day-care.* New York: Farrar, Straus & Giroux.

Gikow, L. (1992). *Bye-bye, pacifier.* New York: Golden Books.

Lipkind, W., & Mordvinoff, N. (1979). *Finders keepers.* Orlando, FL: Harcourt Brace Jovanovich.

Murphy, M. (1999). *I make a cake.* Boston: Houghton Mifflin.

Oxenbury, H. (1982). *Shopping trip.* New York: Penguin Books.

Taback, S. (1999). *Joseph had a little overcoat.* New York: Penguin Group.

Watson, K. (2001). *Little Bill.* New York: Simon Spotlight.

### SUPPLY AND EQUIPMENT RESOURCES

United Art and Education, 1-800-322-3247, www.unitednow.com

To find your specific State's Licensing, Rules and Regulations go to:

http://nrc.uchsc.edu

# Educational Articles for Families and Staff

CHAPTER

8

This chapter offers short articles relevant for caring for and developing a better understanding of two-year-olds. Post these articles on the current event bulletin board, include them in program newsletters, or use them as a basis for parenting and staff education classes. Store copies of these articles and other informative articles you collect in the KIDEX class book for future reference. The articles include page 112, Mashed Fingers; page 113, Chicken Pox; page 114, Scabies; page 115, Submersion and Drowning Accidents; page 116, Tooth Injuries; page 117, Temper Tantrums; page 118, Toilet Training; page 119, Dental Care For Young Children.

Other books in the KIDEX series contain information on the following:

## KIDEX FOR INFANTS

Sudden Infant Death Syndrome
Colds
Respiratory Synctial Virus (RSV)
Strep Throat
Ear Infections
Diarrhea Illness
Diaper Rash
Convulsions/Seizures
Teething

## KIDEX FOR ONES

Impetigo
Pinworms
Ringworm
Provide Toddler Safety
Help Prevent Choking
Is Sharing Possible for Toddlers?
Biting Is A Toddler Affair

## KIDEX FOR THREES

Vision Screening
Learning from the Process, Not the Outcome
Conducting A Cooking Class for
    Three-Year-Olds
Whining Is a Form of Communication
Questions About Hearing for Young Children
When Does the Learning Start?
Pink Eye

## KIDEX FOR FOURS

Is My Child Ready for Kindergarten?
Healthy "Floor Posture"
Bedwetting
My Child Is Shy
Signs of Child Abuse
Styles of Learning
My Child Stutters!

## MASHED FINGERS

1. If the skin in broken, cleanse gently with soap and rinse thoroughly, but gently, with water.

2. Apply ice bag covered with cloth on the injured area for one half hour or until the swelling stops.

3. Any unusual appearance or deformity of the finger could signal a broken bone. Attempt to stabilize finger with no more than a little movement. Provide support with a splint, such as a piece of heavy cardboard or popsicle stick.

4. Rest the injured fingers.

5. Contact the parents and recommend medical examination to rule out bone breakage or tissue damage.

# CHICKEN POX

### What is it?

Chicken Pox is a contagious disease caused by the varicella virus.

### What does it look like?

Multiple red bumps surrounding a central fluid-filled blister as the disease progresses. They appear all over the body during a period of up to 4–5 days in crops, most prominently on the abdomen, chest and face. They can, however, erupt all over the body, including the mouth and the scalp. The blister becomes crusted and scabs. Several stages are usually present at the same time. The blisters usually do not scar if they do not become infected from bacteria often caused by scratching, since itching is common and can become quite intense. Fever varies from none to potentially very high prior to the outbreak on the skin. (*Avoid the use of aspirin if fever occurs to avoid potentially rare but fatal Reye's Syndrome.*)

### What is the incubation period?

The incubation period is 11–21 days.

### How long is it contagious?

It is contagious several days *before* the rash appears and until the blister pustules scab over, usually about 5–6 days after the first crop of blisters, or until the spots are all dried and crusted, whichever is longer.

### How does it spread?

The bacteria spread through droplets from the nose, mouth, or throat, usually from a cough or sneeze. The disease can spread from direct contact with shared personal items, such as drinks or toys that have been touched by contaminated saliva or blister fluid. Once scabs appear, the blisters are no longer contagious.

### What is a proper plan of action?

Isolate the infected person.
Notify parents.
Encourage the parents to seek medical supervision for treatment.
Check all other children for potential symptoms during the 21 days following the last eruption.
Wash all articles that could be contaminated with discharge from nose, throat, and blisters.

### Who should be notified?

The parents of the infected child.
Notify other parents and staff to watch for signs and symptoms.

### When can a child resume contact with other children?

Children can resume contact with others when the blister pustules scab over, usually about 5–6 days after the first crop of blisters, or until the spots are all dried and crusted, whichever is longer.

### Resources

American Academy of Pediatrics http://www.aap.org

# SCABIES

**What is it?**

Scabies is an infection of the skin caused by a tiny 8-legged insect called a *mite.*

**What does it look like?**

The mite is invisible to the eye. The female burrows under skin and lays a few eggs. When they grow and hatch, tiny blisters or pimples form. The blisters tend to form in areas, in adults such as elbows, wrists armpits and groins. In children, the infected areas are usually concentrated on the hands, feet, face, and genitalia. The larvae and waste products cause an outbreak of allergic reactions and severe itching.

**What is the incubation period?**

The incubation period is 10–30 days.

**How long is it contagious?**

It is very contagious until the mites and eggs are destroyed.

**How does it spread?**

The mites are usually present when conditions are crowded; if bathing is not regular, conditions become worse. They spread through contact with infected human skin, underwear, or bed linens. The mites cannot fly or jump. The eggs can only survive for 3 days off of the host body.

**What is a proper plan of action?**

Isolate the infected person.
Notify parents.
Insist that parents seek medical supervision for treatment and medication.
Check all other children for potential symptoms of infection.
Sanitize areas that could be infected. Send personal belongings home and place
    items that are difficult to wash in tightly secured plastic bags for at least 4 days before
    using again. Launder clothing and underwear used within the past 36 hours.

**Who should be notified?**

Notify the parents of the infected child.
Notify other parents and staff to watch for signs and symptoms.

**When can a child resume contact with other children?**

Children usually can resume contact with others after the first round of treatment and upon the doctor's approval. Scabies is so contagious that the doctor usually treats the whole family.

**Resources**

American Academy of Pediatrics http://www.aap.org

# SUBMERSION AND DROWNING ACCIDENTS

### Who is most at risk?

Nationwide statistics show that, on any given day in the year, a child under the age of 5 will be involved in a submersion or drowning incident. Toddler children are often the most vulnerable.

### Why are they most at risk?

Children are mobile, curious and capable of moving toward potentially dangerous areas. Toddlers have limited information about safety measures, and so they are at risk. An unsuspecting adult becomes preoccupied, drops their vigilant attention, and the accident occurs in five minutes or less.

### What is a submersion accident?

A submersion accident occurs when a child cannot breathe because water is covering the child's head and face. The child loses consciousness and stops breathing. Even if the child is revived, there is a danger of brain damage. Proper measures to restore breathing should be initiated the moment the child is retrieved. Seconds count when the brain is starved of oxygen due to the cessation of breathing.

### Where do most accidents occur?

Children are injured or drowned from unsupervised sources of water in a bathtubs, toilets, buckets of water, hot tubs, or water left on a pool cover that has not been drained of rainfall. A child can drown in as little time as it takes to answer a quick phone call.

### How can these accidents be prevented?

Provide protective barriers such as locked fences and gates around bodies of water such as pools, hot tubs, and ponds. Children always require supervision when swimming. Flotation devices should not be used in place of constant supervision. Even children who swim could drown silently due to a myriad of reasons. Install door alarms for the house and protective power safety pool covers. Instruct childcare providers in your home where potential harm exists. Make sure everyone who cares for your children knows proper rescue breathing and cardiopulmonary resuscitation (CPR).

# TOOTH INJURIES

## Knocked Out Tooth

1. Remain calm.
2. Reinsert the tooth back into the gum if it is a permanent tooth.
3. If the child will not cooperate, keep the tooth moist by placing it in milk or saline.
4. See your dentist immediately.

   Wash your hands and put on disposable waterproof gloves. Place a wet tissue on the child's gum to stop the bleeding. Apply very gentle pressure and do not apply ice or a cold object, such as a popsicle, to the area.

## Broken or Chipped Tooth

Call the parents if a child's tooth is broken or chipped, especially a permanent tooth. The child will need to see a dentist right away. Encourage the child to avoid touching the injured tooth until the dentist can examine and treat it.

## Impacted Tooth

When a child falls and drives a tooth deeper into her gums, the parents will need to seek dental consultation. An impacted tooth must be treated to avoid damage to the gums or underlying to permanent teeth.

## Discolored Tooth

An injury to a tooth can cause it to die. Sometimes the tooth will become discolored because of bleeding that occurs in the tooth following an accident. Seek the advice of a dentist to supervise its progress, and watch for potential signs of infection.

**Resources**
American Dental Association (ADA) http://www.ada.org

## TEMPER TANTRUMS

### What are temper tantrums?

Temper tantrums are intense emotions that are often a result of frustration, fear, and the child's inability to solve a problem. When life becomes too overwhelming for little children, they experience "mini emotional meltdowns."

### Why are young children noted for this kind of behavior?

It is natural for young children to pass through a period of oppositional behavior. This period is an intense time of rapid growth for very inexperienced little person who is just beginning to negotiate his or her way as an individual. Their behavior is often the result of a driving internal force to explore and understand how they influence others and the environment they inhabit. When they make decisions, they are building on their new-found independence with very primitive skills.

### Do toddlers throw temper tantrums intentionally?

At this age, toddlers are often surprised by the extreme emotional outburst driven by a very frustrating moment when they were unable to solve a challenge. At other times, the tantrum may be intentional. The child might choose to misbehave, or attempt to manipulate a situation to test a boundary or observe a reaction to their demand.

### What is the best response to a temper tantrum?

First, attempt to determine the cause of the outburst. Are they tired, hungry, or emotionally weary, and have they lost the ability to cope rationally? In that case, a good dose of love, and patience, and other measures can alleviate their stress. If possible, attempt to head off potential occurrences by distraction, redirecting their attention or removing the frustrating item or person. Help the little one find peace by rocking, holding, or feeding them as soon as possible. Sometimes the situation calls for creating a little distance. Refuse to give them the attention they are seeking, or control they are trying to gain, through this extreme behavior. If their temper tantrum at any time becomes violent or unsafe, with such actions as physical outbursts toward another person, pet, or damage to physical property, a measure of discipline is in order. Use discipline to teach them, by offering information with acceptable but firm boundaries. Lovingly but firmly stand your ground. It is okay to express strong emotions outwardly, as long as they do not hurt others in the ways just described. "*Tommy, it is okay that you say you are angry at Collin for taking your toy, but it is not okay to hit him.*" "*Hitting hurts.*" "*Or say, "It makes me unhappy when I can't go outside,"* not "*Mommy you are a stupid head.*" Children are capable of beginning to learn to control their impulses and follow simple rules.

### When will they learn to control their aggressive outbursts?

Young children will required continuous practice as they learn how their actions affect others. Abundant amounts of patience and gentle reminders are called for, from the adults who care for them, as they develop skills that lead to increased self-control. Self-control not something a two-year-old can accomplish consistently. Loving guidance will reassure them that you are in control and expect them to learn acceptable ways of expressing their disappointments in moments of anger and frustration. Learning and practicing, consistent socially acceptable behavior will continue to build over the next several years.

## TOILET TRAINING

### How will I know when to being toilet training my child?

When to begin toilet training is not always a clear cut decision. In the past, it was expected that parents would have their children trained before two years of age. Parents are often pressured by older family members to conform to these outdated ideas, and this often becomes the driving force behind initiating toilet training before the two-year-old is ready. By age two, many children have developed sphincter control for urine and bowel movement. You might notice that they are experiencing longer periods of dryness, or have expressed an interest in trying. Most early care, education professionals, and medical experts agree that many two-year-old children are beginning to show an interest in toileting, and by age 2½ most are ready to master the task of toilet training. Pay attention to the signs of readiness, and be prepared to encourage your child once they exhibit a desire to try. Sometimes it is best just to begin toilet training and see where it leads.

### What if my child cries and strongly resists, or appears to not understand?

It is worthwhile to note that some young two-year-olds might express a curiosity, but are not yet ready to make the commitment. In other words, their play time might be a bigger priority to them than preserving a clean and dry diaper. Be prepared, as well, to stop the training process at any time and begin at a later date, if the child changes their mind and exhibits signs they are not ready to accept responsibility yet. This is a common occurrence. If at any time the toilet training is met with resistance, it bears slowing the process or stopping completely until the two-year-old has time to mature.

### What if my child has "accidents"?

Once the process has begun, be prepared to take the time to share progress with the center staff, and at home, on a regular basis. Don't be disappointed if the child experiences more "accidents" at school. Children are often more involved in their activities and friends at school, and miss their cues. As long as they are showing positive acceptance of their new task and a willingness to proceed, continue the process. Expecting "accidents" as a natural part of the process will increase the probability of more positive toilet training experiences, and in the long run saves frustration caused by unrealistic expectations for the two-year-old. Using naptime and nighttime diapers are usually a good idea until a toddlers become more skilled with consistent toileting habits. Once they do give up that diaper, make sure to protect their mattress with a waterproof protective sheet for potential accidents that could occur for several years to come.

### What should we do before beginning the toilet training?

Toilet training is a collaborative effort that requires an open line of communication between home and the center. Before starting, bring several changes of clothing—socks, training plants, and plastic pant covers. Disposable training pants are now available and are constructed for the two-year-old to pull up and down with ease. Some programs and licensing agencies require the use of disposables to protect other children from harmful exposure brought on by an "accident." These disposables are well padded and will contain "accidents" during the course of training. Check with your center for a suggested clothing list. Disposable training pants are the most expensive option, but most parents already use disposable diapers and feel the added expense and laundry time makes them a reasonable choice. Sometimes the absorbent materials used in the disposable training pants mask the feeling of wetness and reduce the two-year-olds' ability to distinguish between wet and dry. Provide clothing that is easy for them to manage. Avoid zippers for boys and too many buttons or snaps. Young children are sometimes afraid of flush toilets; most prefer using the small chairs purchased at discount stores. If you have a big house, consider placing one in several bathrooms, especially if you have two floors.

The center staff will keep a detailed account of your child's progress each day. Review this sheet and feel free to discuss any questions you might have on a regular basis. Over the course of the next few weeks, your child's progress will be monitored closely to determine if they are demonstrating a continued interest with the program. The staff is very interested in the home progress as well, so feel free to share as often as possible. This is a very exciting time for you and your little one. The center staff is very willing to offer support, and looks forward to assisting you and your child attain this next big milestone!

# DENTAL CARE FOR YOUNG CHILDREN

### When will my child have a full set of teeth?

Usually, the first set of primary teeth (baby teeth) will have fully erupted between 6–36 months of age.

### When will my child begin to replace baby teeth with permanent teeth?

The process of losing the first set of teeth will begin to occur around age 5 or 6.

### When should we begin brushing their teeth?

As soon as the first tooth erupts, begin brushing it with water and a soft toothbrush. Children will not need toothpaste until around age 2. Consult your dentist for advice. By age two, begin to use a pea-size amount of toothpaste with fluoride, but encourage the child not to swallow it. Rinse with water after spitting out the toothpaste.

### How often should they brush?

Assist your child with tooth brushing at least twice per day, usually in the morning and in the evening.

### Do they need to floss?

Once teeth begin to touch, they will require flossing to remove tooth-decaying plaque, especially in places the toothbrush does not reach.

### When should my child first see a dentist?

The American Dental Association recommends that a child see a dentist as soon as her first tooth erupts, but at least no later than the first birthday.

### How can my child avoid cavities?

Avoid sugary snacks and candy that can stick to the teeth and promote decay or cavities, brush and floss according to recommendations, and talk to your dentist about sealants that can protect teeth from cavities, when permanent teeth erupt.

**Resources**

American Dental Association (ADA) http://www.ada.org

## Recommended Resources

Ames, L. B., & Ilg, F. L. (1976). *Your Two-Year-Old.* New York: Dell Publishing.

Ames, L. B., Ilg, F. L., & Haber, C. C. (1982). *Your One-Year-Old.* New York: Dell.

Conner, B. (2000). *Everyday Opportunities for Extraordinary Parenting* (Revised). Naperville, IL: Sourcebooks Inc.

Kinnell, G. (2002). *No Biting.* St. Paul, MN: Redleaf Press.

Polly, J. A. (2001). *The Internet Kids & Family Yellow Pages.* Berkely, CA: McGraw-Hill.

Rimm, S. (1996). *Dr. Sylvia Rimm's Smart Parenting.* New York: Crown Publishers, Inc.

VanGorp, L. (2001). *1001 Best Websites for Parents.* Westminister, CA: Teacher Created Materials Inc.

# Index

To find your specific
State's Licensing, Rules
and Regulations go to:

http://nrc.uchsc.edu

# Forms and Templates

APPENDIX

A

Organized by chapter this appendix contains the following forms and templates for your convenience.

## Cleaning Schedule

**For the Week of _____**

**Classroom _____**

| | Daily Cleaning Projects | Mon | Tue | Wed | Thr | Fri |
|---|---|---|---|---|---|---|
| 1. | Mop floors | | | | | |
| 2. | Clean all sinks (use cleanser) | | | | | |
| 3. | Wipe down walls (around sinks) | | | | | |
| 4. | Clean & disinfect toilets (with brush in & out) | | | | | |
| 5. | Clean water fountains/wipe with disinfectant | | | | | |
| 6. | Clean inside of windows and seals | | | | | |
| 7. | Clean inside & outside glass on doors | | | | | |
| 8. | Clean & disinfect changing table & under the pad | | | | | |
| 9. | Run vacuum (carpet & rugs) | | | | | |
| 10. | Dispose of trash (replace bag in receptacle) | | | | | |
| 11. | Wipe outside of all cans & lids with disinfectant | | | | | |
| 12. | Repeat 10 & 11 for diaper pails | | | | | |
| 13. | Clean & disinfect high chairs/tables/chairs | | | | | |
| 14. | Clean & disinfect baby beds/cots | | | | | |
| 15. | Reduce clutter! (Organize!) | | | | | |
| 16. | (infant & toddler groups) Wipe/sanitize toys after each individual use | | | | | |
| 17. | Change crib sheets as directed | | | | | |
| 18. | | | | | | |

| Once A Week Projects | Initial | Date |
|---|---|---|
| Scrub brush & mop (corners) | | |
| Wipe down all bathroom walls | | |
| Scrub step stools | | |
| Use toothbrush on fountain (mouth piece) | | |
| Clean windows | | |
| Wipe off door handles | | |
| Organize shelves | | |
| Move furniture and sweep | | |
| Wipe underneath tables & legs | | |
| Wipe chair backs and legs | | |
| Wipe off cubbies/shelves | | |
| **Immediate Project** | | |
| Disinfect any surface area contaminated with body fluids such as blood, stool, mucus, vomit, or urine | | |
| **Carpet Cleaning-Quarterly** | | |
| Clean carpets | | |

Lead Teacher: _____          C – Complete   N/A – Not Applicable

# DAILY TWOS SCHEDULE OUTLINE

| | |
|---|---|
| Early Morning | |
| Mid Morning | |
| Late Morning | |
| Mid Day | |
| Early Afternoon | |
| Mid Afternoon | |
| Late Afternoon | |
| Early Evening | |

## DAILY TWOS SCHEDULE DETAILS

| | |
|---|---|
| Early Morning | |
| Mid Morning | |
| Late Morning | |
| Mid Day | |
| Early Afternoon | |
| Mid Afternoon | |
| Late Afternoon | |
| Early Evening | |

# KIDEX *for TWOS*
# Class Book

_____
**GROUP NAME**

# Introduce Us to Your Two-Year-Old
## (25–36 Months)

Date _____

Last Name: _____ First Name: _____ Middle: _____

Name your child is called at home: _____

Siblings: Names & Ages: _____

Favorite Play Materials: _____

Special Interests: _____

Pets: _____

What opportunities does your child have to play with others the same age? _____

_____

Eating Patterns:

    Are there any dietary concerns? _____

    Does your child use a bottle/breast feed at home?  Yes _____  No _____

    If yes, when? _____

    Does your child feed him/herself? _____

    Are there any food dislikes? _____

    Are there any food allergies? _____

    When eating, uses:  fingers ____ spoon ____ fork _____ cup ____

                       needs assistance _____

Sleeping Patterns:

    What time is bedtime at home?  _____ Arise at? _____

    What time is nap time? _____ How long? _____

    Does your child have a special toy/blanket to nap with? _____

    How is your child prepared for rest (e.g., story time, quiet play, snack)

    _____

Eliminating Patterns:

    Toilet trained yet?     Yes _____  No _____

    If not, when do you anticipate introducing toilet training? _____

    Would you like more information? _____

    In training? _____ If trained, how long? _____

    Is independent—doesn't require help. _____

    Does your child need to be reminded? _____

    If yes, at what time intervals do you suggest? _____

Does your child have certain words to indicate a need to eliminate? _____

_____

Child wears:

    Nap time diaper _____       Disposable training pants _____

    Cloth underwear _____      Plastic pants over cloth underwear _____

Stress/Coping Patterns:

    Does your child use a pacifier at home?  Yes _____  No _____

    If yes when _____       Brand _____

Does your child have any fears: _____  Storms _____  Separation anxiety _____

        Dark _____    Animals _____    Stranger anxiety _____

        Being alone _____    Other _____

    How do you soothe him or her?_____

Personality Traits:        shy/reserved  outgoing/curious     sensitive/frightens easily
(Circle all that apply)    very verbal    active           restless
                            cuddly        demonstrative    cautious
                            warms slowly to new people or situations

Health Patterns:

    List other allergy alerts: _____

    List any medications, intervals, and route (mouth, ears, eyes, etc):

    _____

    List any health issues or special needs: _____

    _____

    How often a day do you assist your child with brushing his or her teeth? _____

Activity Patterns:

    When did your child begin:  Creeping _____  Crawling _____  Walking _____

Is there any other information we should know in order to help us know your child better?

_____

_____

_____

                                _____
                                  Parent / Guardian completing form

```
OFFICE USE ONLY
Start Date: _____ Full Time: _____ Part Time: S M T W T F S ½ a.m. p.m.
Group Assigned: a.m. _____ p.m. _____
Teacher(s): _____
Please keep an adjustment record yes _____ no _____ for _____ weeks.
Assign a cubby space: _____ Assign a diaper space: _____
```

# KIDEX for Twos
## Individual Monthly Profile

Month: _____  Teacher: _____

Child's Name: _____  Group: _____

Age: _____  Birth Date: _____  Allergy Alerts: _____

Parent/Guardian's Names: _____ Start Date: _____

When eating uses:  fingers ____  spoon ____  fork ____  cup ____  needs assistance _____

Weaned: Yes _____  No _____  Uses bottle/breast feeds at home: Yes _____No _____

Food dislikes: _____

Diapers: _____  Nap Time Diaper Only: _____  Toilet Trained: _____

Independent: _____  Needs reminding/assistance: _____Toilet training: _____

Special Diapering Instructions (special ointments, etc): _____

Personality Traits:        shy/reserved     outgoing/curious       sensitive/frightens easily
(Circle all that apply)   very verbal       active                restless
                          cuddly            demonstrative         cautious
                          warms slowly to new people or situations

Health Concerns: _____

Daily Medications:        yes _____          no _____        (see med sheet for details)

Special Needs Instructions: _____

Stress/Coping Pattern:  fears _____    storms _____   loudness _____  strangers _____
          dark _____   animals _____   separation anxiety _____   others _____

Uses pacifier at home  Yes _____  No _____  Pacifier Type: _____

Special Blanket/Toy: _____  Name: _____

Average Nap Length:  _____to_____

Special Nap Instructions: _____

_____

Favorite Activities This month: _____

Days Attending:      Sun.   Mon.   Tues.   Wed.   Thurs.  Fri.    Sat.   1/2 days  Full days

Approximate Arrival Time _____  Approximate Departure Time _____

Those authorized to pick up: _____

_____

***Warning: If name is not listed, consult with office and obtain permission to release child.  If you are not familiar with this person, always request I.D.***

# PROGRAM ENROLLING APPLICATION

Child's Full Name: _____ Nickname: _____

Date of Birth: _____ Sex: _____ Home Phone: _____

Address: _____ City: _____ Zip Code: _____

Legal Guardian: _____

Mother's Name: _____Home Phone: _____

Cell Phone: _____ E-Mail: _____

Address: _____ City: _____ Zip Code: _____

Employer: _____ Work Phone: _____

Address: _____ City: _____ Zip Code: _____

Father's Name: _____Home Phone: _____

Cell Phone: _____ E-Mail: _____

Address: _____ City: _____ Zip Code: _____

Employer: _____ Work Phone: _____

IN THE EVENT YOU CANNOT BE REACHED IN AN EMERGENCY, CALL:

Name: _____ Relationship: _____ Phone: _____

Address: _____ City: _____ Zip Code: _____

Name: _____ Relationship: _____ Phone: _____

Address: _____ City: _____ Zip Code: _____

OTHER PEOPLE RESIDING WITH CHILD

Name: _____ Relationship: _____ Age: _____

Name: _____ Relationship: _____ Age: _____

Name: _____ Relationship: _____ Age: _____

## PEOPLE AUTHORIZED TO REMOVE CHILD FROM THE CENTER:

Your child will not be allowed to go with anyone unless their name appears on this application, or you provide them with an "authorization Card," or you make other arrangements with the management. Positive I.D. will be required.

Name: _____ Relationship: _____

Name: _____ Relationship: _____

Name: _____ Relationship: _____

Child Will Attend:     Mon - Tues - Wed - Thur - Fri - Sat - Sun

Child Will Be:         Full Time or Part Time

Time Child Will Be Dropped Off (Normally): _____

Time Child Will Be Picked Up   (Normally): _____

## MEDICAL INFORMATION/AUTHORIZATION

Physician's Name: _____ Phone: _____

Address: _____ City: _____ Zip Code: _____

Dentist's Name: _____ Phone: _____

Address: _____ City: _____ Zip Code: _____

Allergies: _____

I agree and give consent that, in case of accident, injury, or illness of a serious nature, my child will be given medical attention/emergency care. I understand I will be contacted immediately, or as soon as possible if I am away from the numbers listed on this form.

## PERMISSION TO LEAVE PREMISES

I hereby give the school/center _____ permission to take my child
                                                  (name)

on neighborhood walks using a _____ (state equipment, e.g. a

child buggy that seats six children & has safety straps). YES _____    (INITIAL)

NO, I do not give permission at this time: _____ (INITIAL)

Parent/Guardian's Signature: _____

Parent/Guardian's Signature: _____

Date: _____

AUTHORIZED
PERSON
CARD

AUTHORIZED
PERSON
CARD

AUTHORIZED
PERSON
CARD

AUTHORIZED
PERSON
CARD

AUTHORIZED
PERSON
CARD

AUTHORIZED
PERSON
CARD

AUTHORIZED
PERSON
CARD

AUTHORIZED
PERSON
CARD

AUTHORIZED
PERSON
CARD

AUTHORIZED
PERSON
CARD

**USE HEAVY CARD STOCK (FRONT OF CARD)**

Name of Authorized Person

May pick up my child _____

on my behalf.

_____  _____
Parent/Guardian Signature       Date

Name of Authorized Person

May pick up my child _____

on my behalf.

_____  _____
Parent/Guardian Signature       Date

Name of Authorized Person

May pick up my child _____

on my behalf.

_____  _____
Parent/Guardian Signature       Date

Name of Authorized Person

May pick up my child _____

on my behalf.

_____  _____
Parent/Guardian Signature       Date

Name of Authorized Person

May pick up my child _____

on my behalf.

_____  _____
Parent/Guardian Signature       Date

Name of Authorized Person

May pick up my child _____

on my behalf.

_____  _____
Parent/Guardian Signature       Date

Name of Authorized Person

May pick up my child _____

on my behalf.

_____  _____
Parent/Guardian Signature       Date

Name of Authorized Person

May pick up my child _____

on my behalf.

_____  _____
Parent/Guardian Signature       Date

Name of Authorized Person

May pick up my child _____

on my behalf.

_____  _____
Parent/Guardian Signature       Date

Name of Authorized Person

May pick up my child _____

on my behalf.

_____  _____
Parent/Guardian Signature       Date

**USE HEAVY CARD STOCK (BACK OF CARD)**

# Twos Daily Observation Checklist

Child's name: _____     Date: _____

Arrival: _____     Departure: _____

|  | Ate Partial | Ate Complete | Water Juice Oz |
|---|---|---|---|
| Breakfast |  |  |  |
| Snack |  |  |  |
| Lunch |  |  |  |
| Snack |  |  |  |
| Dinner |  |  |  |
| Evening Snack |  |  |  |
|  |  |  |  |

|  | Medications * | Treatments * |
|---|---|---|
| Time |  |  |
| Time |  |  |
| Time |  |  |

\* see daily medication sheets for details

| Diaper Changes | | | | |
|---|---|---|---|---|
| Time | Wet | BM | Dry | Initials |
|  |  |  |  |  |
|  |  |  |  |  |
|  |  |  |  |  |

Nap Times: _____   _____   Other: _____

| Toilet Training Progress | | | | | |
|---|---|---|---|---|---|
| Time | Wet | Dry | Bowel Movement | Accident Clothing Change | Seemed confused upset/resisted/refused re-evaluate readiness |
|  |  |  |  |  |  |
|  |  |  |  |  |  |
|  |  |  |  |  |  |
|  |  |  |  |  |  |
|  |  |  |  |  |  |
|  |  |  |  |  |  |

**Moods / Activity Level:**
*Circle all that apply*
Busy • Curious •
Adventurous •
Active • Cheerful •
Quiet • Content •
Cuddly • Drowsy •
Bubbly • Verbal •
Assertive •
Focused •
Frustrates Easily

Today's Play Center Choices: _____   _____

Comments: _____     Lead Teacher: _____
_____     Shift Time: _____
_____     Teacher: _____
                                       Shift Time: _____
_____     Teacher: _____
                                       Shift Time: _____
_____     Teacher: _____
                                       Shift Time: _____
_____     Teacher: _____
                                       Shift Time: _____

# OUR DAY

DATE _____     Day of Week _____

**Early morning activities/centers:   (Beginning the day during morning arrival)**

_____
_____
_____

***KIDEX: Fun with Language and Telling Tales*: Activities to build our vocabulary were:**

_____

**Finger plays & songs we sang today were:**

_____

**Our morning outdoors activity was:**

_____
_____

***KIDEX: My Body is Wonderful*: Activities to exercise our fine and large muscles were:**

_____

**Our morning project was:**

_____
_____

**AFTERNOON**
***KIDEX Exploring My World/Creating My Way*: Our creative/sensory activities were:**

_____
_____

**The story we read was:**

_____

**Our afternoon outdoor activity was:**

_____
_____

**Late afternoon activities/centers:  (Ending the day during departures)**

_____
_____
_____

**Extra activities today were:**

_____

# EATING PATTERNS

| Classroom: | Week of: | | | | |
|---|---|---|---|---|---|
| Child's Name | Mon | Tues | Wed | Thur | Fri |
| | | | | | |
| | | | | | |
| | | | | | |
| | | | | | |
| | | | | | |
| | | | | | |
| | | | | | |
| | | | | | |
| | | | | | |
| | | | | | |
| | | | | | |
| | | | | | |
| | | | | | |
| | | | | | |
| | | | | | |
| | | | | | |
| P = Ate Partial | | | | | |
| C = Complete | | | | | |

# Nap Time

**Classroom**                                    **Week of:**

| Name | Monday | | Tuesday | | Wednesday | | Thursday | | Friday | |
|------|--------|--------|---------|--------|-----------|--------|----------|--------|--------|--------|
| | Asleep | Awake | Asleep | Awake | Asleep | Awake | Asleep | Awake | Asleep | Awake |
| | | | | | | | | | | |
| | | | | | | | | | | |
| | | | | | | | | | | |
| | | | | | | | | | | |
| | | | | | | | | | | |
| | | | | | | | | | | |
| | | | | | | | | | | |
| | | | | | | | | | | |
| | | | | | | | | | | |
| | | | | | | | | | | |
| | | | | | | | | | | |
| | | | | | | | | | | |
| | | | | | | | | | | |
| | | | | | | | | | | |
| | | | | | | | | | | |
| | | | | | | | | | | |
| | | | | | | | | | | |
| | | | | | | | | | | |

# Diaper Changing Schedule

**Day:** _____

**Date:** _____

| Child's Name | 8:00 am–9:00 am | | | 11:00 am–12:00 pm | | | After Nap | | | 5:00 pm–6:00 pm | | | Bedtime | | | Wake up | | |
|---|---|---|---|---|---|---|---|---|---|---|---|---|---|---|---|---|---|---|
| | BM | WET | DRY | BM | WET | DRY | BM | WET | DRY | BM | WET | DRY | BM | WET | DRY | BM | WET | DRY |
| 1. | | | | | | | | | | | | | | | | | | |
| 2. | | | | | | | | | | | | | | | | | | |
| 3. | | | | | | | | | | | | | | | | | | |
| 4. | | | | | | | | | | | | | | | | | | |
| 5. | | | | | | | | | | | | | | | | | | |
| 6. | | | | | | | | | | | | | | | | | | |
| 7. | | | | | | | | | | | | | | | | | | |
| 8. | | | | | | | | | | | | | | | | | | |
| 9. | | | | | | | | | | | | | | | | | | |
| 10. | | | | | | | | | | | | | | | | | | |
| 11. | | | | | | | | | | | | | | | | | | |
| 12. | | | | | | | | | | | | | | | | | | |

**Initial the appropriate box when diapering is completed.**

# Child Transitioning Report

Name _____ Teacher _____

Date of Report _____ Teacher _____

Day 1 2 3 4 5 6 7 8 9 10 11 12 13 14 15

|  | SOME | A LOT | NOT YET |
|---|---|---|---|
| Played with toys | _____ | _____ | _____ |
| Participated in activities | _____ | _____ | _____ |
| Played with the children | _____ | _____ | _____ |

| **Appetite** | COMPLETE | PARTIAL |
|---|---|---|
| Breakfast appetite | _____ | _____ |
| AM snack appetite | _____ | _____ |
| Lunch appetite | _____ | _____ |
| PM snack appetite | _____ | _____ |
| Dinner appetite | _____ | _____ |

**Naptime**

Indicate time          From _____ To _____

**Bowel & bladder pattern** (See diaper changing sheet if applicable)

**Overall day**

Great! _____ *Seemed comfortable with new environment*

Fair _____ *Adjustments to the new group and environment will improve as your child grows accustomed to the new environment*

Staff Comments:_____

Parent's Comments or Questions (If any): _____

- Use for 1-3 weeks until the new child feels comfortable with the group.

# OUR MENU TODAY

Date_____

Breakfast _____

_____

_____

Lunch _____

_____

_____

Snack _____

_____

_____

Mini Snack

_____

_____

# CENTER CALENDAR

**MONTH:**

| Sunday | Monday | Tuesday | Wednesday | Thursday | Friday | Saturday |
|--------|--------|---------|-----------|----------|--------|----------|
| Theme: | | | | | | |
| Theme: | | | | | | |
| Theme: | | | | | | |
| Theme: | | | | | | |
| Theme: | | | | | | |

## Diaper Changing Procedures for Disposable Diapers

**Supplies:** Disposable nonabsorbent gloves, nonabsorbent paper liner disposable wipes removed from container, child's personally labeled ointments (under medical direction) diapers, cotton balls, plastic bags, tissues, physician-prescribed lotions, lidded hands-free plastic-lined trash container, soap, disinfectant, and paper towels.

Use a nonabsorbent changing surface. Avoid dangerous falls: keep a hand on baby at all times and never leave alone. In emergency, put child on floor or take with you.

| | Steps for Changing Disposable Diapers | | | | |
|---|---|---|---|---|---|
| 1 | Wash hands with soap and water. | 2 | Gather supplies. | 3 | Put on disposable waterproof gloves (if used). |
| 4 | Cover diapering surface with nonabsorbent paper liner. | 5 | Place baby on prepared diapering area (minimize contact: hold baby away from your body if extremely wet or soiled). | 6 | Put soiled clothes in a plastic bag. |
| 7 | Unfasten diaper. Leave soiled diaper under the child. | 8 | Gently wash baby's bottom. Remove stool and urine from front to back, and use a fresh wipe each time. Dispose directly in designated receptacle. | 9 | Fold soiled diaper inward and place in designated receptacle followed by the disposable gloves (if used). |
| 10 | Use disposable wipe to clean surface of caregiver's hands and another to clean the childís. | 11 | Check for spills on paper. If present, fold over so fresh part is under buttocks. | 12 | Place clean diaper under baby. |
| 13 | Using a cotton ball or tissue, apply skin ointment to clean, dry area if indicated/ordered. | 14 | Fasten diaper and dress with fresh clothing. | 15 | Wash baby's hands with soap and water between 60°F and 120°F for 15–20 sec. and dry. Turn faucet off with a paper towel, then place baby in a safe location. |
| 16 | Clean and disinfect diapering area, leaving bleach solution in contact at least 2 minutes. Allow table to air dry, or wipe it after 2 minutes. | 17 | Wash your hands with soap and water for at least 15–20 seconds. Turn off faucet with paper towel. | 18 | Chart diaper change and any observations. |

## Diaper Changing Procedures for Cloth Diapers

**Supplies:** Disposable nonabsorbent gloves, non absorbent paper liner, disposable wipes removed from container, child's personally labeled ointments (under medical direction), diapers, cotton balls, plastic bags, tissues, physician-prescribed lotions, lidded hands-free plastic-lined trash container, soap, disinfectant, and paper towels.

**Soiled Diapers:** *Contain in a labeled and washable plastic-lined receptacle that is tightly lidded and hands-free only. Don't require separate bags. However, any soiled diapers sent home are to be secured in a plastic bag, separately bagged from soiled clothing. Clean and disinfect receptacle daily and dispose of waste water in toilet or floor drain only.*

Use a nonabsorbent changing surface. Avoid dangerous falls: keep a hand on baby at all times and never leave alone. In emergency, put child on floor or take with you.

| | Steps for Changing Cloth Diapers | | | | |
|---|---|---|---|---|---|
| 1 | Wash hands with liquid soap and water. | 2 | Gather supplies. | 3 | Put on disposable waterproof gloves (if used). |
| 4 | Cover diapering surface with nonabsorbent paper liner. | 5 | Place baby on prepared diapering area (minimize contact: hold baby away from your body if extremely wet or soiled). | 6 | Put soiled clothes in a plastic bag. |
| 7 | Unfasten diaper. Leave soiled diaper under the child. Close each safety pin immediately out of child's reach. Never hold pins in mouth. | 8 | Gently wash baby's bottom. Remove stool and urine from front to back, and use a fresh wipe each time. Dispose directly in designated receptacle. | 9 | Fold soiled diaper inward and place in designated receptacle followed by the disposable gloves (if used). |
| 10 | Use disposable wipe to clean surface of caregiver's hands and another to clean the child's. | 11 | Check for spills on paper. If present, fold over so fresh part is under buttocks. | 12 | Place clean diaper under baby. |
| 13 | Using a cotton ball or tissue, apply skin ointment to clean, dry area if indicated/ordered. | 14 | Fasten diaper with pins, placing your hand between the child and the diaper on insertion, and dress with fresh clothing. | 15 | Wash baby's hands with soap and water between 60°F and 120°F for 15–20 sec. and dry. Turn faucet off with a paper towel, then place baby in a safe location. |
| 16 | Clean and disinfect diapering area, leaving bleach solution in contact at least 2 minutes. Allow table to air dry, or wipe it after 2 minutes. | 17 | Wash your hands with soap and water for at least 15–20 seconds. Turn off faucet with paper towel. | 18 | Chart diaper change and any observations. |

Standard 3.014 Diaper changing procedure. Caring for our children, National health and safety performance standards, (2nd ed.). Used with permission, American Academy of Pediatrics.
Permission to photocopy is granted by Thomson Delmar Learning.

# Return Practice Demonstration for Disposable Diapering Procedures

Name: _____     Date: _____

Observer: _____

*Procedure:*

_____   Wash hands with liquid soap and water.

_____   Gather supplies.

_____   Put on disposable waterproof gloves (if used).

_____   Cover diapering surface with nonabsorbent paper liner.

_____   Place baby on prepared diapering area (minimize contact: hold baby away from your body if extremely wet or soiled).

_____   Put soiled clothes in a plastic bag.

_____   Unfasten diaper. Leave soiled diaper under the child.

_____   Gently wash baby's bottom. Remove stool and urine from front to back, and use a fresh wipe each time. Dispose directly in designated receptacle.

_____   Fold soiled diaper inward and place in designated receptacle followed by the disposable gloves (if used).

_____   Use disposable wipe to clean surface of caregiver's hands and another to clean the child's.

_____   Check for spills on paper. If present, fold over so fresh part is under buttocks.

_____   Place clean diaper under baby.

_____   Using a cotton ball or tissue, apply skin ointment to clean, dry area if indicated/ordered.

_____   Fasten diaper and dress with fresh clothing.

_____   Wash baby's hands with soap and water between 60°F and 120°F for 15–20 seconds and dry. Turn faucet off with a paper towel, then place baby in a safe location.

_____   Clean and disinfect diapering area, leaving bleach solution in contact at least 2 minutes. Allow table to air dry, or wipe it after 2 minutes.

_____   Wash your hands with soap and water for at least 15–20 seconds. Turn off faucet with paper towel.

_____   Chart diaper change and any observations.

# Return Practice Demonstration for Cloth Diapering Procedures

Name: _____     Date: _____

Observer: _____

*Procedure:*

_____     Wash hands with liquid soap and water.

_____     Gather supplies.

_____     Put on disposable waterproof gloves (if used).

_____     Cover diapering surface with nonabsorbent paper liner.

_____     Place baby on prepared diapering area (minimize contact: hold baby away from your body if extremely wet or soiled).

_____     Put soiled clothes in a plastic bag.

_____     Unfasten diaper. Leave soiled diaper under the child. Close each safety pin immediately out of child's reach. Never hold pins in mouth.

_____     Gently wash baby's bottom. Remove stool and urine from front to back, and use a fresh wipe each time. Dispose directly in designated receptacle.

_____     Fold soiled diaper inward and place in designated receptacle followed by the disposable gloves (if used).

_____     Use disposable wipe to clean surface of caregiver's hands and another to clean the child's.

_____     Check for spills on paper. If present, fold over so fresh part is under buttocks.

_____     Place clean diaper under baby.

_____     Using a cotton ball or tissue, apply skin ointment to clean, dry area if indicated/ ordered.

_____     Fasten diaper with pins, placing your hand between the child and the diaper on insertion, and dress with fresh clothing.

_____     Wash baby's hands with soap and water between 60°F and 120°F for 15–20 seconds and dry. Turn faucet off with a paper towel, then place baby in a safe location.

_____     Clean and disinfect diapering area, leaving bleach solution in contact at least 2 minutes. Allow table to air dry, or wipe it after 2 minutes.

_____     Wash your hands with soap and water for at least 15–20 seconds. Turn off faucet with paper towel.

_____     Chart diaper change and any observations.

# TOILET TRAINING

## Child's Name: _____
## Lead Teacher: _____ Date: _____

| Time | Wet | B.M. | Dry | Refused | Seemed Confused | Comments |
|---|---|---|---|---|---|---|
| 6:00 – 6:30 | | | | | | |
| 6:30 – 7:00 | | | | | | |
| 7:00 – 7:30 | | | | | | |
| 7:30 – 8:00 | | | | | | |
| 8:00 – 8:30 | | | | | | |
| 8:30 – 9:00 | | | | | | |
| 9:00 – 9:30 | | | | | | |
| 9:30 – 10:00 | | | | | | |
| 10:00 – 10:30 | | | | | | |
| 10:30 – 11:00 | | | | | | |
| 11:00 – 11:30 | | | | | | |
| 11:30 – 12:00 | | | | | | |
| 12:00 – 12:30 | | | | | | |
| 12:30 – 1:00 | | | | | | |
| 1:00 – 1:30 | | | | | | |
| 1:30 – 2:00 | | | | | | |
| 2:00 – 2:30 | | | | | | |
| 2:30 – 3:00 | | | | | | |
| 3:00 – 3:30 | | | | | | |
| 3:30 – 4:00 | | | | | | |
| 4:00 – 4:30 | | | | | | |
| 4:30 – 5:00 | | | | | | |
| 5:00 – 5:30 | | | | | | |
| 5:30 – 6:00 | | | | | | |
| 6:00 – 6:30 | | | | | | |
| 6:30 – 7:00 | | | | | | |
| 7:00 – 7:30 | | | | | | |
| 7:30 – 8:00 | | | | | | |

## Posted Hand Washing Procedures

| 1 | Turn on warm water and adjust to comfortable temperature. | 2 | Wet hands and apply soap. | 3 | Wash vigorously for approximately 15–20 seconds. |
|---|---|---|---|---|---|
| 4 | Dry hands with paper towel. | 5 | Turn off faucet with paper towel. | 6 | Dispose of paper towel in a lidded trash receptacle with a plastic liner. |

Use hand washing procedures for staff and children

- before and after preparing bottles or serving food.
- before and after diapering or toileting.
- before and after administering first aid.
- before and after giving medication.
- before working with the children and at the end of the day.
- before leaving the classroom for a break.
- after wiping nose discharge, coughing, or sneezing.
- before and after playing in the sand and water table.
- after playing with pets.
- after playing outdoors.

## Medical Authorization
## for Nonprescription Medication*

Name of Child: _____  Date: _____

The staff is authorized to dispense the following medications as ordered by your physician and directed by the parents/guardian.

**Please indicate specific medication, route it is to be given, dosage, and frequency.**

| Type | Medication | Route | Dosage | Frequency |
|---|---|---|---|---|
| Nonaspirin Preparation | | | | |
| Aspirin Preparation | | | | |
| Cough Preparation | | | | |
| Decongestant | | | | |
| Skin Ointment | | | | |
| Diaper Wipes | | | | |
| Sunscreen | | | | |
| | | | | |
| | | | | |

_____  _____  _____
Print Name of Physician        Signature of Physician          Phone Number

_____
Parent/Guardian Signature

* Complete this form on admission and update annually.  Store medical authorizations in an index box and place in or near locked cabinet for quick referencing.

## Daily Medication Sheet

| Child's Name | RX Number & Type of Medication | Amount & Route Administered | Date | Time | Given By: First Name | Last Name |
|---|---|---|---|---|---|---|
| | | | | | | |
| | | | | | | |
| | | | | | | |
| | | | | | | |
| | | | | | | |
| | | | | | | |
| | | | | | | |
| | | | | | | |
| | | | | | | |
| | | | | | | |

# SUGGESTED ILLNESS

Child's name: _____    Date: _____

SYMPTOMS ARE:

_____    Body Temperature (under arm, add 1 degree)

_____    Vomiting

_____    Diarrhea

_____    Exhibiting signs of a communicable illness

_____    Skin condition requiring further treatment

Other: _____

Report initiated by: _____

Were parents notified? Yes _____ No _____ By whom? _____

Time parents notified:    1st Attempt _____    _____
                                                    Which Parent Notified

                          2nd Attempt _____    _____
                                                    Which Parent Notified

                          3rd Attempt _____    _____
                                                    Which Parent Notified

Time child departed:        _____

Director's signature: _____

Children exhibiting a temperature that exceeds 100°F, symptoms of vomiting (1–3 forceful rushes), diarrhea (defined as watery, mucous, foul-smelling bowel movement), or an unrecognized rash shall not return to group care for a minimum of 24 hours after treatment or before symptoms subside.

1. Office Copy      2. Parent/Guardian Copy

## Illness Tracking Report

| Name of Child | Time | Type of Illness | Person Reporting Illness | Director Notified | Report Filed | Parent Notified | Time Called |
|---|---|---|---|---|---|---|---|
| | | | | | | | |
| | | | | | | | |
| | | | | | | | |
| | | | | | | | |
| | | | | | | | |
| | | | | | | | |
| | | | | | | | |
| | | | | | | | |
| | | | | | | | |
| | | | | | | | |
| | | | | | | | |
| | | | | | | | |
| | | | | | | | |

# Head Lice Checklist

Group Name: _____

| Name | Sunday | Monday | Tuesday | Wednesday | Thursday | Friday | Saturday |
|------|--------|--------|---------|-----------|----------|--------|----------|
|      |        |        |         |           |          |        |          |
|      |        |        |         |           |          |        |          |
|      |        |        |         |           |          |        |          |
|      |        |        |         |           |          |        |          |
|      |        |        |         |           |          |        |          |
|      |        |        |         |           |          |        |          |
|      |        |        |         |           |          |        |          |
|      |        |        |         |           |          |        |          |
|      |        |        |         |           |          |        |          |
|      |        |        |         |           |          |        |          |
|      |        |        |         |           |          |        |          |
|      |        |        |         |           |          |        |          |
|      |        |        |         |           |          |        |          |
|      |        |        |         |           |          |        |          |
|      |        |        |         |           |          |        |          |
|      |        |        |         |           |          |        |          |
|      |        |        |         |           |          |        |          |
|      |        |        |         |           |          |        |          |
|      |        |        |         |           |          |        |          |
|      |        |        |         |           |          |        |          |
|      |        |        |         |           |          |        |          |
|      |        |        |         |           |          |        |          |
|      |        |        |         |           |          |        |          |

**C = Clear**          **A = Absent**          **P = Possible**

(**Reminder**:  *Please check weekly on different days of the week*.)

# SUGGESTED FIRST AID DIRECTIVES

## CHOKING

*(Conscious)* - Stand or kneel behind child with your arms around his waist and make a fist. Place thumb side of fist in the middle of abdomen just above the navel. With moderate pressure, use your other hand to press fist into child's abdomen with a quick, upward thrust. Keep your elbows out and away from child. Repeat thrusts until obstruction is cleared or child begins to cough or becomes unconscious.

*(Unconscious)* - Position child on his back. Just above navel, place heel of one hand on the midline of abdomen with the other hand placed on top of the first. Using moderate pressure, press into abdomen with a quick, upward thrust. Open airway by tilting head back and lifting chin. **If you can see the object**, do a finger sweep. Slide finger down inside of cheek to base of tongue, sweep object out but be careful not to push the object deeper into the throat. Repeat above until obstruction is removed or child begins coughing. If child does not resume breathing, proceed with artificial respiration (see below).

**Infants** - Support infant's head and neck. Turn infant face down on your forearm. Lower your forearm onto your thigh. Give four (4) back blows forcefully between infant's shoulder blades with heel of hand. Turn infant onto back. Place middle and index fingers on breastbone between nipple line and end of breastbone. Quickly compress breastbone one-half to one inch with each thrust. Repeat backblows and chest thrusts until object is coughed up, infant starts to cry, cough, and breathe, or medical personnel arrives and takes over.

## POISONING

Call Poison Control Center (1-800-382-9097) immediately! Have the poison container handy for reference when talking to the center. Do not induce vomiting unless instructed to do so by a health professional. Check the child's airway, breathing, and circulation.

## HEMORRHAGING

Use a protective barrier between you and the child (gloves). Then, with a clean pad, apply firm continuous pressure to the bleeding site for five minutes. Do not move/change pads, but you may place additional pads on top of the original one. If bleeding persists, call the doctor or ambulance Open wounds may require a tetanus shot.

## SEIZURE

Clear the area around the child of hard or sharp objects. Loosen tight clothing around the neck. Do not restrain the child. Do not force fingers or objects into the child's mouth. After the seizure is over and if the child is not experiencing breathing difficulties, lay him/her on his/her side until he/she regains consciousness or until he/she can be seen by emergency medical personnel. After the seizure, allow the child to rest. Notify parents immediately. If child is experiencing breathing difficulty, or if seizure is lasting longer than 15 minutes, call an ambulance at once.

## ARTIFICIAL RESPIRATION *(Rescue Breathing)*

Position child on the back; if not breathing, open airway by gently tilting the head back and lifting chin. Look, listen, and feel for breathing. If still not breathing, keep head tilted back and pinch nose shut. Give two full breaths and then one regular breath every 4 seconds thereafter. Continue for one minute; then look, listen, and feel for the return of breathing. Continue rescue breathing until medical help arrives or breathing resumes.

If using one-way pulmonary resuscitation device, be sure your mouth and child's mouth are sealed around the device.

(Modification for infants only)     Proceed as above, but place your mouth over nose and mouth of the infant. Give light puffs every 3 seconds.

## SHOCK

If skin is cold and clammy, as well as face pale or child has nausea or vomiting, or shallow breathing, call for emergency help. Keep the child lying down. Elevate the feet. If there are head/chest injuries, raise the head and shoulders only.

# Accident/Incident

Child's Name: _____

Date of accident/injury: _____ Time: _____

Brief description of accident/injury: _____

_____

_____

Was first aid given? _____ If so, describe: _____

_____

Was blood present in accident? _____ How much? _____

Were Universal Precautions employed? _____

Was medical intervention required?* _____ If yes, describe: _____

_____

Person initiating this report: _____ Witness: _____

Name of parent contacted: _____ Time contacted: _____

Director's signature: _____

* *In some states it is required to file a copy of this report with the child care licensing department if medical intervention is required.*

# Accident/Incident Tracking Reports

| Name of Child | Date | Time | Type of Accident | Person Reporting Accident | Director Notified | Report Filed | Parent Notified | Time Called |
|---|---|---|---|---|---|---|---|---|
|  |  |  |  |  |  |  |  |  |
|  |  |  |  |  |  |  |  |  |
|  |  |  |  |  |  |  |  |  |
|  |  |  |  |  |  |  |  |  |
|  |  |  |  |  |  |  |  |  |
|  |  |  |  |  |  |  |  |  |
|  |  |  |  |  |  |  |  |  |
|  |  |  |  |  |  |  |  |  |
|  |  |  |  |  |  |  |  |  |
|  |  |  |  |  |  |  |  |  |

# Emergency Contacts: *Post Near Every Telephone*

Your Facility Address: _____

_____

Nearest Main Intersection: _____

Your Facility Phone Number: _____

| **Contact** | **Phone Number** |
|---|---|
| Operator | |
| Emergency | |
| Fire | |
| Police | |
| Consulting Dentist | |
| Poison Control | |
| Local Hospital Emergency Dept | |
| Other | |
| Other | |

## Emergency Evacuation Plan

Draw First Choice Escape Route, Draw Second Choice Escape Route

In Case of Fire Call: _____

In Case of Bomb Threat Call: _____

In Case of Gas Leak Call: _____

Fire Extinguisher expires Date: _____

Emergency Bag and Blanket are located: _____

For two-year-olds – Stretch the evacuation rope out on the floor. Have each child grab a knot and hold tight. Account for all children in attendance. If the door is cool, open door slowly, make sure fire or smoke isn't blocking your escape route. If your escape is blocked, close the door and use an alternative escape route. Smoke and heat rise. Be prepared to crawl where the air is clearer and cooler near the floor. Move as far from the building as possible. In case of a real fire, do not reenter the building until it is cleared by the proper authorities.

How to create an emergency evacuation rope:
    Create an emergency evacuation rope by using a rope long enough for 5-7 children. Tie a knot every 12" for them to hold onto and guide them to a safe area.

**When the rope is not in use, place it on a hook out of reach to avoid a potential strangulation accident.**

12"        12"        12"        12"        12"        12"        12"

## Hurricane Emergency Instructions

**Hurricane/Tropical Storm Watch:** indicates conditions are possible in the specified area within 36 hours.

**Hurricane/Tropical Storm Warning:** conditions are expected within 24 hours.

Send the children home.
Learn your specific evacuation route.
Secure your facility.
Close storm shutters.
Turn utilities off at main valves if instructed by authorities.
Take emergency phone numbers with you.

Your Evacuation Route:  _____

_____

_____

## Tornado Emergency Instructions

Your county or region is: _____

**Tornado Watch**:  A tornado is possible. Remain alert for approaching storms. Tune your portable (battery-operated) radio to a local weather station.

**Tornado Warning**: A tornado has been sighted. Activate your emergency shelter plan immediately.

Grab your emergency bag and blanket. They are located:  _____

_____

For two-year-olds – Stretch the evacuation rope out on the floor.  Evacuation rope is located: _____
Have each child grab a knot and hold on tight. Account for all children in attendance. Move children calmly and quickly to an interior room or hallway.
Your best location is:  _____

_____

_____

_____

_____

_____

Cover the children with heavy blankets or cushions, if available, in case of flying glass or debris. Avoid windows, doors, outside walls, and corners of rooms.

## Earthquake Emergency Instructions

Prior to an earthquake:
- Brace high and top-heavy objects.
- Fasten cubbies, lockers, toy shelves to the wall.
- Anchor overhead lighting fixtures.
- Install flexible pipe fitting to avoid gas or water leaks.
- Know when and how to shut off electricity, gas, and water at main switches and valves.
- Locate safe spots in the room to protect yourself from dropping debris such as under a sturdy table or crib.

Your safest location is:    _____

The shutoff for gas is located:    _____

The water main is located:    _____

Your emergency bag is located:    _____

During an earthquake:

- Stay inside until shaking stops and it is safe to go outside.
- Move the children to your safe location (inside a crib on an inside wall).
- Describe where:_____

_____

_____

_____

- Place a heavy blanket or lightweight mattress over the crib.
- If you are on the playground, move away from the building.

When the shaking stops be prepared for aftershocks.  Check for injuries and administer first aid as indicated.  Use flashlights if electricity is out.  DO NOT light candles or matches in case of gas leakage.

## Tornado / Earthquake Drill Log

| Date | Time of Drill | Time Needed to Seek Cover | Comments | Full Name of Person in Charge |
|---|---|---|---|---|
| | | | | |
| | | | | |
| | | | | |
| | | | | |
| | | | | |
| | | | | |
| | | | | |
| | | | | |
| | | | | |
| | | | | |

# Building Evacuation Log

| Date | Time of Drill | Evacuation Time | Comments | Full Name of Person in Charge |
|------|---------------|-----------------|----------|-------------------------------|
|      |               |                 |          |                               |
|      |               |                 |          |                               |
|      |               |                 |          |                               |
|      |               |                 |          |                               |
|      |               |                 |          |                               |
|      |               |                 |          |                               |
|      |               |                 |          |                               |
|      |               |                 |          |                               |
|      |               |                 |          |                               |
|      |               |                 |          |                               |
|      |               |                 |          |                               |
|      |               |                 |          |                               |
|      |               |                 |          |                               |
|      |               |                 |          |                               |

# Beginning Our Day    Date: _____

## Welcome

| Child's Name | Time Awoke | Last Meal/Snack | Last Diaper Change or Toilet Break | Comments, if any |
|---|---|---|---|---|
| | | | | |
| | | | | |
| | | | | |
| | | | | |
| | | | | |
| | | | | |
| | | | | |
| | | | | |
| | | | | |
| | | | | |
| | | | | |
| | | | | |
| | | | | |
| | | | | |
| | | | | |
| | | | | |
| | | | | |
| | | | | |
| | | | | |
| | | | | |
| | | | | |

# Twos Weekly Lesson Plans

**Stage of Play Development:**
Parallel (dominant) (emerging) Cooperative

Group Name: _____
Theme: _____
Lead Teacher: _____

**Week of:** _____

| Activities | Sun | Mon | Tues | Wed | Thurs | Fri | Sat |
|---|---|---|---|---|---|---|---|
| Concept | | | | | | | |
| Sharing Time | | | | | | | |
| Language Skills | | | | | | | |
| KIDEX *Fun with Language & Telling Tales Activities* | | | | | | | |
| Songs/Finger Plays | | | | | | | |
| Reading/Stories (Flannel Board/ Vocabulary/ Puppets) | | | | | | | |
| KIDEX: *Exploring Our World* Activities | | | | | | | |
| Cognitive / Sensory / Pre-Math / Science | | | | | | | |
| KIDEX: *Creating My Way* Activities | | | | | | | |
| Arts Exploration/ Crafts | | | | | | | |
| KIDEX: *My Body Is Wonderful* Activities – Large Muscle Practice | | | | | | | |
| Small Muscle Practice | | | | | | | |
| Indoor/Outdoor Activities | | | | | | | |

| Daily Play Centers | Housekeeping / Dramatic Play / Toys Center | Active Play / Music Movement / Toys |
|---|---|---|
| | Fine Motor / Art / Eating / Water Table | Library / Music / Quiet Play / Block Center / Computer |

| **Self-Help Skills/Social Skills** 25–36 Months—Integrate and encourage the development of skills during this 12-month span | Managing Clothing with help Wash & dry hands Feed self/use of fork & spoon & cup Toilet training practice (18 months & older only) | Help with clean up Practice please & thank you Learning basic self-control skills Verbal skills-building | Refining body movements Body/Self awareness Safety awareness Follow basic instructions Building imagination |

# 25-27 Months

## DEVELOPMENTAL MILESTONES

### TWOS CAN:

_____ DEVELOP A VOCABULARY OF 50 OR MORE WORDS

_____ BEGIN UNDERSTANDING MORE ABSTRACT CONCEPTS
(e.g. BIG/LITTLE; COLD/HOT; UP/DOWN)

_____ BEGIN TO COMBINE WORDS & ANSWER SIMPLE QUESTIONS

_____ DEVELOP AN INTEREST IN NAMING PICTURES IN BOOKS

_____ UNDERSTAND & FOLLOW SIMPLE DIRECTIONS

_____ BEGIN SELF-HELP SKILLS, SUCH AS WASHING HANDS &
BRUSHING TEETH WITH ASSISTANCE

_____ ABLE TO USE CUP & EATING UTENSILS

_____ CAN IMITATE BUILDING A STACK OF CUBES

_____ BUILD WITH NESTING BLOCKS

_____ USE SIMPLE STACKING TOYS

_____ PLAY SIMPLE MUSICAL INSTRUMENTS

_____ JUMP UP & STEP UP TO HIGHER SURFACE

_____ BEGIN TO ROLL AND THROW LARGE BALLS

_____ IMITATE SOUNDS

_____ PARTICIPATE IN MUSIC

> *Important Note: Children will develop at similar rates but each in a unique pattern. If you find a child is not exhibiting the majority of characteristics listed, there could be many plausible reasons ranging from premature birth to a more reserved and cautious personality. This list is a broad overview and not all-inclusive of developmental milestones two year olds experience.*

| Y = YES | S = SOMETIMES | N = NOT YET |
|---------|---------------|-------------|

Child's Name: _____  Teacher: _____

Date Initiated: _____  Date Completed: _____

# 28-30 Months

## DEVELOPMENTAL MILSTONES

**TWOS CAN:**

_____ BEGIN TO SOLVE PROBLEMS MENTALLY

_____ MATCH FAMILIAR ITEMS TO SOUNDS OR PICTURES

_____ SING ALONG WITH FAMILIAR SONGS AND FINGER PLAYS

_____ LISTEN TO A FIVE-MINUTE PICTURE BOOK AND IDENTIFY 3–4 PICTURES BY NAME

_____ PARTICIPATE IN PRETEND PLAY

_____ BEGIN TO USE PLEASE AND THANK YOU

_____ MORE AWARE OF OTHERS' FEELINGS

_____ PARTICIPATE IN SAND AND WATER PLAY

_____ BEGIN TO UNDERSTAND SAFETY RULES

_____ DEVELOP AN AWARENESS OF SELF (INCLUDING BODY PARTS) AND OTHERS

_____ BEGIN TO TAKE SHOES AND SOCKS (OR OTHER ARTICLE OF CLOTHING) ON AND OFF

_____ WASH AND DRY HANDS

_____ HELP WITH CLEAN UP TIME

_____ JUMP DOWN OFF A SURFACE, LAND ON TWO FEET

_____ WALK ON TIP-TOE

_____ BALANCE ON ONE FOOT

_____ USE SMALL MUSCLE SKILLS (e.g. STRING LARGE BEADS/COMPLETE PUZZLES OF 3–4 PIECES/DRAW SCRIBBLES ON PAPER)

_____ REFER TO SELF BY NAME

> *Important Note: Children will develop at similar rates but each in a unique pattern. If you find a child is not exhibiting the majority of characteristics listed, there could be many plausible reasons ranging from premature birth to a more reserved and cautious personality. This list is a broad overview and not all-inclusive of developmental milestones two-year-olds will experience.*

| Y = YES | S = SOMETIMES | N = NOT YET |
|---------|---------------|-------------|

Child's Name: _____ Teacher: _____

Date Initiated: _____ Date Completed: _____

# 31-33 Months
## DEVELOPMENTAL MILESTONES

### TWOS CAN:

_____ MAKE CHOICES AND DECISIONS

_____ UNDERSTAND USE OF FAMILIAR OBJECTS

_____ NAME FAMILIAR ITEMS AND PICTURES

_____ UNDERSTAND CONCEPTS OF SAME/DIFFERENT;
ONE/MANY; SOFT/HARD

_____ IDENTIFY SIX BODY PARTS

_____ DESCRIBE THEIR ACTIVITIES

_____ MANAGE SIMPLE CHORES

_____ PARTICIPATE IN PARALLEL PLAY

_____ IDENTIFY SOME FRIENDS BY NAME

_____ CLEAR EATING IMPLEMENTS FROM THE TABLE

_____ COMPLETE 4–5 PIECE PUZZLES

_____ SORT SIMPLE COLORS AND SHAPES

_____ MATCH OBJECTS BY COLOR/SHAPE/SIZE

_____ PEDAL A RIDING TOY

_____ BALANCE RIGHT, LEFT FOOT

_____ BUTTON AND ZIP OWN CLOTHING

_____ ENJOY SMALL GROUP ACTIVITIES

_____ IDENTIFY SELF WITH CHILDREN OF SAME GENDER

_____ SHOW INTEREST IN TOILET TRAINING

_____ SHARE SOMETIMES

> _Important Note: Children will develop at similar rates but each in a unique pattern. If you find a child is not exhibiting the majority of characteristics listed, there could be many plausible reasons ranging from premature birth to a more reserved and cautious personality. This list is a broad overview and not all-inclusive of developmental milestones two-year-olds experience._

| Y = YES | S = SOMETIMES | N = NOT YET |
|---------|---------------|-------------|

Child's Name: _____   Teacher: _____

Date Initiated: _____   Date Completed: _____

# 34-36 Months

## DEVELOPMENTAL MILESTONES

**TWOS CAN:**

_____ HELP TELL A STORY

_____ DEVELOP A VOCABULARY OF 300 TO 1000 WORDS

_____ USE DESCRIPTIVE WORDS

_____ USE 2 OR 3 SENTENCES IN CONVERSATION

_____ BECOME MORE ATTENTIVE TO ART ACTIVITIES AND STORIES

_____ USE PREPOSITIONS (e.g., IN, BY, FOR, WITH, TO)

_____ FOLLOW A TWO-OR THREE-PART COMMAND

_____ NAME BASIC COLORS

_____ BEGIN TO UNDERSTAND NUMBER CONCEPTS (SHOW 2 FINGERS)

_____ DRAW A SIMPLE DESIGN AND COPY HORIZONTAL/VERTICAL LINE AND CIRCLES

_____ RUN SMOOTHLY, CAN STOP AND START

_____ GALLOP AND TROT

_____ BEND OVER WITHOUT FALLING

_____ PEDAL AND STEER RIDING TOY

_____ WALK BACKWARDS

_____ BEGIN TO MASTER SNAPS, LARGE BUTTONS AND ZIPPERS

_____ USE PEG BOARDS

_____ FIT LIDS ON JARS

_____ THROW A BALL OVERHAND

_____ BEGIN TO DRESS HIMSELF OR HERSELF

_____ INCLUDE OTHER CHILDREN DURING PLAY

_____ BEGIN USING SCISSORS

_____ USE TOILET WITH HELP

> _Important Note: children will develop at similar rates but each in a unique pattern. If you find a child is not exhibiting the majority of characteristics listed, there could be many plausible reasons ranging from premature birth to a more reserved and cautious personality. This list is a broad overview and not all-inclusive of developmental milestones two-year-olds experience._

| Y = YES | S = SOMETIMES | N = NOT YET |
|---------|---------------|-------------|

Child's Name: _____ Teacher: _____

Date Initiated: _____ Date Completed: _____

# 25-27 Months

## ACTIVITIES

| | |
|---|---|
| **Category**<br><br>**1** | **Telling Tales – Simple Picture Books – Language Activities**<br>• Using small sandwich bags, insert one picture in each bag, punch two holes, and connect with yarn; then name the pictures.<br>• Provide commercially purchased <u>cardboard</u> or <u>plastic</u> books w/ simple pictures to name.<br>• Ask parents to bring in "family photo albums"—these can be made from single pictures in plastic bags, and can include grandmother and grandfather, family pets, pictures of the house, the child's favorite toy, etc.<br>• Use a book with simple pictures of animals. Look at each picture, name the animal, and see if the child can imitate the sound the animal makes.<br>• Make a book of the child's favorite toys, pets, foods, etc. Review the book with him or her and other children.<br>• Make a book of pictures of simple things a child uses, and ask him or her to find a picture by identifying its use: e.g., *We eat with this; We brush our teeth with this; We use this when we play outside.*<br>• Look at a picture book and collect matching real objects to pull out of a box as you name the pictures in the book. |
| **Category**<br><br>**2** | **Fun With Language Activities**<br>• Match picture cards of toys and the actual toy.<br>• Play chanting or singing games whenever possible, when starting an activity or finishing one.<br>  a. *We are sitting in our chairs one by one... We are washing both our hands to eat our lunch... (To the tune of "If you're happy and you know it")*<br>  b. *We are eating with our spoons and drinking with our cups and pretty soon we'll have eaten everything up.*<br>• Use puppets to tell simple stories and as a gimmick to help a child talk. A child will sometimes talk to a puppet or other inanimate object before talking to the teacher.<br>• Talk or sing or chant quietly to children when things have become a little too chaotic and use their attention to redirect their behavior or progress to the next activity.<br>• Help the children learn to use words to express emotions and get along with others. Show pictures of people displaying various emotions and discuss familiar situations where the children would have positive and negative feelings. Give examples of ways to handle different emotions and ask the children for suggestions. Try to avoid telling them they are wrong if they suggest hitting, for example, ask what might happen if they did that and if they have another way to manage the situation. Use the book for reminders occasionally, and direct the children to the book in conflict situations to see if you can get them to talk about acceptable behavior. |

Child's Name: _____ Teacher: _____

Date Initiated: _____ Date Completed: _____

# Continued 25–27 Months Activities

| | |
|---|---|
| **Category**<br><br>**3** | **My Body Is Wonderful — Large & Small Muscle Activities**<br>• Children at this age enjoy wheeled riding toys which they can push with their feet.  This is an important stage for progressing to toys that require peddling.  You can make up a course with tape or obstacles to contain "the little drivers" and control the number of crashes!  Wagons are also great fun for *pulling* and *pushing, loading* and *unloading.*  Pushing boxes around is great fun, too.<br>• Big, soft balls (6"–10") can be rolled back and forth.  Teach children to push the ball to guide it in the right direction.  Retrieval also provides muscle exercise and release of energy.<br>• Children this age like to move in various ways around a large object.  Talk about & model the different ways of moving around, stressing the word around.  Use other words for spatial relations and movement – *under, over....*<br>• Make climbing and obstacle games.  Bean-bag chairs and pillows can be arranged or piled to create inside climbing areas.  A blanket draped over chairs provides a tunnel; big foam blocks can make steps for practice in stepping up and down.<br>• Children love to chase bubbles.  Change the height of the bubbles so children can stretch and reach, or bend over to pop them *(Bubble recipe included in table  7-18).*<br>• Talk about different types of walking and use them to move to specific areas.  *Tiptoe* to the cots for nap time; *march* to the playground; *walk with hands behind you* with big steps to the lunch table; *hop* to the centers; *hands on waist* to the bathroom.<br>• Use a 6" or 8"-wide board flat on the carpet to give children practice for the balance beam.  It does not need to be long, and can be covered with fabric to prevent ankle injury. |
| **Category**<br><br>**4** | **Creating My Way — Creative Exploration**<br>• Model building towers with blocks; create shapes, trains, a structure for small cars, etc.<br>• Play dough provides many experiences for fine muscle control.  Edible play dough can be used for those who just can't resist tasting (recipe included in table 7-18).<br>• Finger paint with pudding.  Use different colors of pudding to add to the experience.<br>• Take tubs of water outside and let the children "paint" the sidewalk or the outside of the building.<br>• Color and draw on dark construction paper with large pieces of chalk.<br>• Part one — Glue pictures about your weekly theme, e.g., animals, to paper plates, talk about each one, and then hang to dry.<br>• Part two — Cut paper plates into 2–3 pieces — use as a puzzle. |
| **Category**<br><br>**5** | **Exploring Our World — Activities to Explore Cognitive, Pre-Math, Sensory and Science**<br>• Put some small sturdy toys like beads or Legos in a bowl or plastic bin.  Give the children several plastic bottles with tops of varying circumferences.  As they find a fit and put all the toys in bottles, they can dump them out and start again.<br>• Create your own small water table with a plastic bin or baby tub.  Use pouring cups and pitchers and basting tools, and talk about pouring, the feel of the water, etc. Use sponges (can cut to different shapes and sizes) and show children how to squeeze the water out.<br>• Tissue boxes make great hiding and sorting boxes—paint or cover them with printed sticky shelf paper.<br>• Use a large spoon to transfer cubes from one container to another.<br>• Explore objects that float and sink in water table or dishpans.<br>• Separate and sort different–shaped large beads in muffin tins and bowls according to the color.<br>• Sort a box of gloves or socks and match up pairs or colors.<br>• Cover toilet paper rolls or cut paper towel cardboard tubes in half. Cover with peanut butter, roll in seed, and then hang on tree outside. Watch the birds enjoy them from the window. |

Child's Name: _____   Teacher: _____

Date Initiated:   _____   Date Completed: _____

# 28-30 Months

## ACTIVITIES

<table>
<tr>
<td rowspan="2">Category<br><br>1</td>
<td>

**Telling Tales — Simple Picture Books — Language Activities**
- Box book — Tape simple pictures to the outside of an oatmeal box and cover with sticky shelf paper. Let the child roll it and name the pictures. You can create several with themes, and also make up simple stories together about the pictures.
- Glue several pictures to pages of your book to make "peek-a-boo" books. Alternate picture pages with pages cut into three strips. Let the child turn one strip at a time to discover the picture. Discuss what he or she is seeing while turning each strip.
- As you are reading a short story, change your voice to mimic that which might be appropriate (e.g., child's high voice; Daddy's low voice; animal sounds). Or, use a simple picture book and tell a story. Ask the children to imitate the voices.
- Show the children how to handle books and how they are replaced on shelves.
- Practice turning pages and even finding a quiet place to enjoy a book.
- Use a puppet to tell a simple story. Tell it again and see if the children can help with words or simple details.
- Introduce short finger plays and simple songs. Make a book to illustrate a song/finger play and the children can look at it by themselves and perhaps remember the chant or song.
</td>
</tr>
</table>

<table>
<tr>
<td>Category<br><br>2</td>
<td>

**Fun With Language Activities**
- Discuss the routine activities with the children before they happen. (e.g., *We are going to have a cracker now. Let's go over to the sink and wash our hands. Now let's sit on the mat and when you are sitting, I will get a cracker for you; or, We are going to sit on a cushion and look at a book. Can you find a cushion and sit down?*)
- Think of things that the children can find on their own and give them directions to get them for you. Discuss what they did.
- Take a small group of children on a walk through the center. Listen for sounds and talk about the sounds you are hearing.
- Gather a few items from places the children can identify. Place them in a box so they can't be seen. Remove one item at a time and hold it up for all to see. Make a game of returning it to its correct location (e.g., pretend you don't know where it goes and ask for help, or put it in the wrong place and let the children correct you). This can be done with different routines during the day (e.g. cups set at each place at the table or art supplies, so that children can help set up activities and help with routine tasks.
- Try to spend a few minutes talking individually with each child shortly before she or he leaves. Talk about progress that child is making, especially if you are working hard on a specific activity or improvement of a social interaction skill.
- Show the children pictures of people "in action." Talk about and imitate the action (e.g., *clapping, walking, sitting with legs crossed, waving, sleeping.*
- Collect objects that demonstrate big and little (2 plastic glasses, for example), sort them, and tell whether big or little.
</td>
</tr>
</table>

Child's Name: _____     Teacher: _____

Date Initiated: _____     Date Completed: _____

## Continued 28–30 Months Activities

| | |
|---|---|
| **Category** **3** | **My Body Is Wonderful — Large & Small Muscle Activities**<br>• Move like the animals: *flap wings; crawl and squirm; tiptoe; stand on one leg.* Use a quiet animal last to calm down the children. Tell a story about the animal to get the children to move in different ways (e.g., *I see a little turtle; he's sleeping on a rock; now he's going to slide into the water and swim around; brrr, it is cold and he wants to sun himself on the rock again, so he slips back up on the rock and stretches in the sun and falls asleep again.*)<br>• Follow the leader games are good for attention; following verbal directions; moving from one place to another with no noise when requested (*"we will have to stop if I hear noise"*); as well as exercise of muscles. Falling and getting up is one of the favorite exercises for children.<br>• Create a throwing corner: use soft toys like crochet balls, nerf balls, beanbags, and yarn balls.<br>• Jumping activities are great fun. If a child is having difficulty, hold hands and jump with him to help him learn. Jump on leaves or targets made with tape on the floor.<br>• A large inner tube provides good experience for climbing in and out, bouncing up and down while straddling it, etc.<br>• Use carpet squares for a game like musical chairs. Start and stop the music and tell the children to find a square. Do not remove squares—simply play until children are tired of it.<br>• Show the children how to "scoot" around the floor on their carpet squares—using their heels to propel themselves or lie on their stomachs and pull themselves with their arms.<br>• Practice balancing on one foot, initially holding on to something. |
| **Category** **4** | **Creating My Way — Creative Exploration**<br>• Shape boxes are good for picking up and turning shapes to place in the correct hole. You can make one with any round container with a plastic lid into which shape holes are cut.<br>• Fun with cotton balls. Use a plastic bin filled with cotton balls and discusses their color and softness. Give the children cups to fill with cotton balls and later toast tongs to enhance the difficulty. These could also be stuck to a mural for snow or buds on trees. You should control the glue and watch that children do not taste the cotton balls! Painting with cotton balls and cotton swabs is also great fun.<br>• Trace each child's hand let them "color" it with a crayon.<br>• Cut and glue differently shaped macaroni or cereal pieces, such as Toasty O's, to paper.<br>• Use chalk to draw on sidewalks outdoors.<br>• Roll and pound play dough.<br>• Spread and explore shaving cream on the table. Have damp paper towels ready to wipe little faces.<br>• Place an object under paper, e.g., a large leaf, ribbons or yarn, construction squares. Tape paper over it and allow children to scribble new textures. |
| **Category** **5** | **Exploring Our World — Activities to Explore Cognitive,**<br>**Pre-Math, Sensory and Science**<br>• Collect sets of pictures that show big and little. Make a picture book with these pictures to discuss (add other concepts you are teaching e.g., *up and down*).<br>• Put several inches of rice in a sturdy dishpan. Provide cups, spoons, other containers. You may want to put an old shower curtain or a piece of vinyl under the rice container. Hide small cars or other small items to find.<br>• Find a variety of squeezable items and place in a bin. Try to use different types of items to offer a variety of experiences. Some may be easier to squeeze than others (examples: sponge block, infant squeeze toy, nerf balls, large scraps of cloth; a softball, crumpled paper). Discuss how soft the items are and verbalize what the children are doing: one hand, two hands; soft.<br>• Provide squeeze bottles (old dish detergent containers). Let the children "clean" the tables or mats or make interesting spray patterns on the sidewalks.<br>• Make a "track" on the wall with colored masking tape. Let the children run a small wheeled car or their finger on the track — be sure to use curves, V's and even circles.<br>• Hang a shoe bag on the wall or door. Let children put things in and take things out of the pockets. You can tape pictures to the outside of the pockets to add a sorting activity (put all the red things in the red row; all the animal pictures in the zoo row).<br>• Show the children how to use one finger (vs. fist or palm) to push the levers or buttons on a push toy. |

Child's Name: _____ Teacher: _____

Date Initiated: _____ Date Completed: _____

# 31-33 Months

## ACTIVITIES

| | |
|---|---|
| **Category 1** | **Telling Tales — Simple Picture Books — Language Activities**<br>• Read short books to small groups of children. All children may not be ready for a story. Find pictures in the story when you are finished. (Do you remember that the boy was looking for something? Can you show me or tell me what it was? Or what happened next?)<br>• Make picture books of opposites to elicit the words (e.g., same/different, one/many, tall/short).<br>• Make a class photo album of children doing different things inside and outside. Discuss what is going on in the picture, and perhaps what could happen next, or what happened before.<br>• Find pictures of places children might go (e.g., grocery store, movie theatre, park). Ask what they might do there; if it would be fun; if they would they sleep or eat there.<br>• Play the find it game with books: Find the airplane or the thing that is flying. Find two boys in this picture.<br>• Make your own (large) book about an activity the children completed. Remember simple steps and create simple drawings to illustrate the activity. Use this later to discuss the activity again. |
| **Category 2** | **Fun With Language Activities**<br>• Talk about the clothes they're wearing; names of items; colors; clothes specific for weather conditions; types of shoes; long socks/short socks, etc.<br>• Hide something small in a place all the children can reach. Ask one child to help you find it, giving one direction at a time (e.g., Chris, can you help me find the bear puppet? Look over by the blocks. Good. Now find a blue bucket. Look in the bucket. You found it! As the children progress, your directions can become more complex).<br>• Make a habit of talking to children about what they are doing and about what other children are doing. This is a good activity to orient a new child or while cuddling one who is having a hard day. The child just might become interested in one of the activities as you are discussing it.<br>• Talk about what just happened, what is to happen next, or the preparation needed for a specific activity. We sure have been playing hard outdoors. I'll bet you feel hot and I think it would be nice to have a nice cool drink of ____. Before we go outdoors, we need to do something. What is it? Before we eat our snack, we need to... What did we just do? Right, we ate our snack. Now we need to put our napkins and cups in the trash basket.<br>• Some children will respond well to a puppet. Let the puppet "tell a story" about something familiar to the children and they can fill in specific words. Let the puppet "give directions" of things to do. Let the puppet "orient" the shy child and "talk" about feelings.<br>• For a good mouth and tongue exercise, make silly sounds and ask the children to imitate you. Make faces and use your tongue and mouth to form sounds in isolation. (Exaggerate the sound and mouth movements.) |

Child's Name: _____  Teacher: _____

Date Initiated: _____  Date Completed: _____

# Continued 31–33 Months Activities

| | |
|---|---|
| **Category**<br><br>**3** | **My Body Is Wonderful — Large & Small Muscle Activities**<br>• Set up a target area for kicking balls (8" – 10"). You can use a long piece of vinyl (long, to provide a wide target area) and hang it low on the playground fence. Let the children try to kick the balls into the target.<br>• Music generally elicits movement. Children will often bounce up and down or move side to side, changing weight from one foot to the other. Creative movement to music is fun and beneficial and you can teach children many ways to move their bodies and to stop when the music stops (or fall down, which is much more fun).<br>• Batting beach balls around is great fun and provides movement, eye-hand coordination, jumping up— and may also cause crashes, so you will want to limit the number of balls and children.<br>• Make walkways for the children with chalk outside, or tape on the floor inside. Tell the children to walk between the lines, trying not to step on either one. Limit the length of the walkway or they will want to run!<br>• Create a bowling area with plastic bowling pins, plastic bottles or plastic milk bottles. Each child should stand about 3' away from the pins and roll a large ball at them. Show the children how to re-set the pins! (You can fill the bottles with sand to make it easier to "re-set" them.)<br>• On the playground, watch how things around them move. Imitate the leaves blowing; the wheels on the cars going around; the flag flapping; birds flying.<br>• Running and jumping into a pile of pillows is great fun. Watch carefully that there is no open floor space between pillows and that the children go one at a time.<br>• Cut some footprints out of colored contact paper and make a path to the bathroom or places to stand when lining up to go outside. Make sure to space footprints closely together for short legs, but provide enough space between each set to prevent conflict. |
| **Category**<br><br>**4** | **Creating My Way — Creative Exploration**<br>• Peg boards with large pegs (or smaller if the child is ready) provide good fine muscle exercise, and you can direct a child to colors, simple patterns and shapes, etc. Use these when you can supervise. It is very tempting to check out how the pegs taste!<br>• Let the children practice tearing all kinds of paper. You will need to show them how to grasp the edges with their fingers and pull in opposite directions. Use different thicknesses of paper and show them how to put the torn bits into a plastic bin. This can be used for collages later on or for falling confetti (limited amounts) which they can try to catch and then pick up and give to you to toss again. Picking up the paper will be tedious (though good for small muscles), so use the larger, thicker pieces and limit the number for this game.<br>• Play different types of music during creative activities.<br>• Spread a small amount of paint on construction paper, have children explore making paint tracks on their paper with toy car wheels.<br>• Play with oatmeal instead of water in the table. Talk about full and empty.<br>• Have children spread non-toxic glue or homemade paste (flour and water) on a piece of construction paper. Sprinkle sand on it, pieces of yarn, pieces of scrap paper to create a collage of textures.<br>• Hang several feet of Contact paper on wall at their height. Have children stick different colors and sizes of construction squares to it. |
| **Category**<br><br>**5** | **Exploring Our World — Activities to Explore Cognitive,<br>Pre-Math, Sensory and Science**<br>• Go on a hunt for soft and hard objects in the room. Talk about how you can squeeze a soft object, but not a hard one.<br>• Finger plays offer lots of good practice and chanting and repetition are good for memory development and rhythm. Open hands and close in a fist; wave with one hand up and down, sideways; wave with one finger; feather fingers; put fingertips together; point with one finger.<br>• Create garages for toy cars and trucks. Cover a shoe box with contact paper and cut out a door or two. Use an equal number of cars and boxes and introduce the child to one-to-one correspondence.<br>• Play a quiet game with large stickers or pieces of colored contact paper. Have them imitate where you put the sticker—hand, nose, chin, leg, and forehead.<br>• Part I: Glue rough pieces to paper (burlap, sand paper, pieces of course netting) and talk about textures.<br>• Part II: Glue smooth pieces to paper (velvet squares, aluminum foil, wax paper) and talk about smooth textures.<br>• Part III: Glue soft pieces to paper (cotton balls, tissues, feathers) and discuss soft textures.<br>• Part IV: Glue hard pieces to paper (popsicle sticks, small blocks) and talk about hard textures.<br>• Part V: Stack all pictures together, punch a hole and tie together loosely, creating a texture book for each child. |

Child's Name: _____ Teacher: _____

# 34-36 Months

## ACTIVITIES

| | |
|---|---|
| **Category**<br><br>**1** | **Telling Tales — Simple Picture Books**<br>• Make a story book for your room. Take pictures of children involved in different activities. Ask the children to help write the story, telling about what is happening in each picture. Use this book to remind the children silently that it is time to get ready for lunch, nap, center time, etc.; to show new parents that their children are happily involved in activities; to orient a new child (be sure to take a picture soon after he or she starts!); to help someone "tour" the room, etc.<br>• Make felt books with 5–6 felt pages. Glue simple pictures (e.g., sun, pond, house, etc.) on each page and put a figure or an animal in a pocket on the front. Let the child remove the felt figure and go through the book telling a story as she goes. Other felt shapes and pictures can be added from a boxed collection to increase the complexity of the activity.<br>• Make a book with simple pictures and outlines of two pictures on the opposite page. Ask the child which page shows the outline or shadow of the picture, and why. Use metal binder rings and change the pictures around and add/delete for new challenges.<br>• Find books to use in the classroom that provide a purpose other than a story (e.g., a book about a specific concept, which can be read several times until the children can say and use the concept. Find a book that shows spatial relations and ask questions about what is on, under, beside, between, after you have talked about these concepts with real objects.)<br>• Once you have read a story to the children a few times: read it and leave out key words for them to fill in; stop and ask them what happens next; choose a different ending; remember the characters' names; use puppets or act out the story with assistance; make a set of flannel board characters so they can "tell" the story on their own. Let them change and add to the story, as this is natural at this age. |
| **Category**<br><br>**2** | **Fun With Language Activities**<br>• Show pictures of things that make sounds and practice the sounds (tea kettle, race car, train, squeaky door).<br>• Talk about the recent past and future. Ask children if they can remember the art project or snack they had this morning and/or tell them what might be happening in the afternoon or tomorrow.<br>• Make simple language mistakes in ways that a child can correct; e.g. *Here is a book for you to read, when handing the child something else*. Let the child correct you. This can also be a gimmick for directing a child to something he or she doesn't want to do — *"let's go wash our hands in the toy box."* The silly nature of the request may be the catalyst to urge the child in the right direction.<br>• Make some matching cards with simple pictures. Gather 2 or 3 children and ask who has the picture of the ball. Give that child your picture of the ball and when all are matched, trade cards and start again.<br>• Sing hello, hello _____ (child's name) how are you today?<br>• Look at animal pictures and match their sounds. |

Child's Name: _____     Teacher: _____

Date Initiated: _____     Date Completed: _____

# Continued 34–36 Months Activities

| | |
|---|---|
| **Category**<br><br>**3** | ## My Body Is Wonderful — Large & Small Muscle Activities<br>• Use instrumental music to create rhythmic movement; show children how to march; tiptoe walking to quiet music; swaying from side to side; bending up and down; moving head in various ways; patting parts of the body as well as clapping; shoulders up and down, etc.<br>• Make a safe balance beam by covering a smooth board with heavy fabric or vinyl. Show the children how to move forward and back, sideways, one foot close to the other, tiptoe, etc.<br>• Make plastic bag balls. Stuff one plastic bag with several others. Tie the outer bag in tight knots and you have a ball you can throw as hard as you want without hurting anyone.<br>• Make a hanging target for the children to jump up and touch. This could be a large ball in a cloth bag. You can also hang the target lower and use foam batting forms.<br>• Create a walking path to follow with chalk on the sidewalk, or tape on the floor inside. Make zig-zags and curves and shapes and show the children different ways to move on the path (e.g., forward, backward, side-stepping, hopping, on tiptoe, swimming, rocking, bending, swaying, swinging arms and marching; one foot close in front of the other, scooting, skating, galloping, etc.)<br>• Create a stepping stone path or obstacle course with carpet squares—spaced so the children have to stretch to reach the next one. They can move in various ways on the path or course—walking, crawling, jumping with one leg out, etc.(You may need to use double-sided sticky tape to secure "stepping stones.")<br>• Move like the animals—show pictures of various animals and discuss how they move—then imitate the movements and add variations—fast and slow/stop when music stops/high and low/big and small (for baby or momma animals).<br>• Show children how to roll across a mat or a row of pillows set in a line. |
| **Category**<br><br>**4** | ## Creating My Way — Creative Exploration<br>• Make your own lacing cards by gluing appealing pictures (or in relation to your weekly theme) to cardboard and covering with contact paper. Punch holes for the child to use in threading a shoelace. The pattern the child follows is not important.<br>• Plastic bottles and jars with screw tops can provide the same experiences as noted in letter A.<br>• Let the children cut their snacks into bite-sized portions before eating or preparing for a cooking activity.<br>• Play dough: cut different sizes of plastic straws and let children explore sticking the straw pieces in the dough.<br>• Paint with feathers and Q-tips.<br>• Make circle pictures: cut out round fruit—lemon, oranges—to dip in paint and stamp on paper.<br>• Practice spreading icing on a cookie and decorate it for a special snack.<br>• Wash dishes today in the water table. |
| **Category**<br><br>**5** | ## Exploring Our World — Activities to Explore Cognitive, Pre-Math, Sensory and Science<br>• Make a simple roadway on a piece of vinyl. Show the child how to "trace" the roadway with one finger, or a toy vehicle. You can add obstacles to go around, under, over.<br>• Show the children how to pretend that their hands are insects, with the fingers "crawling" up their arms or down their legs; up the sides of their faces to the top of their heads (a good activity for "waiting" time).<br>• Surprise bags—Put small familiar objects (e.g., toy car, block, Lego, sponge, etc) in a fabric bag with a drawstring top. Let the child put a hand in and touch and describe the object. The child can then guess what it is, or ask the other children if they can guess from his or her "clues".<br>• A variety of boxes and other containers with lids offers many good experiences: matching size and developing dexterity and small muscles; matching patterns on the outside of containers; the delight of finding something inside (e.g., a picture glued to the bottom; a small toy to move around inside the box on the track; a small soft ball to toss back into the box).<br>• Toilet paper, paper towel, and wrapping paper tubes make great tunnels for cars. Paint or cover with printed sticky paper. The children can run the cars through them; create an obstacle course; combine two or more to make longer tunnels; run the cars over the top.<br>• Large metal clips (the type used for hanging clothes) make for good muscle exercise. Show the children how to squeeze them and attach to a cup or other container. You can also sort colors and introduce the concept of one-to-one correspondence with one clip per cup.<br>• Use a muffin tin to sort several different kinds of color cubes by color, by shape, etc.<br>• A variation on peg boards: Use a plastic bowl (like one for whipped topping) with a lid, etc. and punch holes around the lid with a paper punch. File the points off golf tees, and the children can put the tees into the holes in the lid. The container is used for storing, and another dimension can be added by using different colored tees and identifying the container with a colored paper tee held onto the top with contact paper.<br>• Explore water in different forms make ice cubes — watch them melt. What happens when ice cubes float in warm water? |

Child's Name: _____   Teacher: _____

Date Initiated: _____   Date Completed: _____

# PERSONAL SUPPLY INVENTORY CHECKLIST

**CHILD'S NAME:** _____  **DATE:** _____

| SUPPLY | FULL | HALF | NEED MORE |
|---|---|---|---|
| Diapers | | | |
| Disposable wipes | | | |
| Waterproof paper for diaper barrier (such as wax paper) | | | |
| Diaper ointment | | | |
| Pacifier | | | |
| Disposable trainers | | | |
| Plastic pants covers | | | |
| Underwear | | | |
| Shirts | | | |
| Long pants | | | |
| Short pants | | | |
| Socks | | | |
| Other: | | | |
| | | | |
| | | | |
| | | | |
| | | | |
| | | | |
| | | | |
| | | | |

To find your specific
State's Licensing, Rules
and Regulations go to:

http://nrc.uchsc.edu

# Gloving

APPENDIX

B

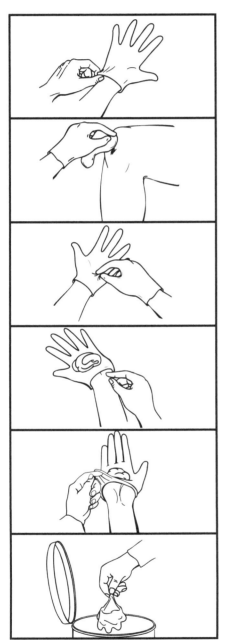

Put on a clean pair of gloves.

Provide the appropriate care.

Remove each glove carefully. Grab the first glove at the palm and strip the glove off. Touch dirty surfaces only to dirty surfaces.

Ball-up the dirty glove in the palm of the other gloved hand.

With the clean hand strip the glove off from underneath at the wrist, turning the glove inside out. Touch dirty surfaces only to dirty surfaces.

Discard the dirty gloves immediately in a step can. Wash your hands.

Reference: California Department of Education. *Keeping Kids Healthy: Preventing and Managing Communicable Disease in Child Care.* Sacramento, CA: California Department of Education, 1995.

To find your specific
State's Licensing, Rules
and Regulations go to:

http://nrc.uchsc.edu

# Washing Hands

1) Wet hands.

2) Add soap.

3) Rub hands together.

4) Rinse hands with fingers down.

5) Dry your hands with a towel.

6) Turn off water with paper towel.

7) Toss the paper towel in the trash.

Good Job!

Reprinted with permission from the National Association of Child Care Professionals, http://www.naccp.org.